CRISIS PROOFING:

HOW TO SAVE YOUR COMPANY FROM DISASTER

Dedicated to the memory of my father
Pat Jaques, 1903–1980

TONY JAQUES

CRISIS PROOFING:
HOW TO SAVE YOUR COMPANY FROM DISASTER

OXFORD
UNIVERSITY PRESS
AUSTRALIA & NEW ZEALAND

UNIVERSITY PRESS

Oxford University Press is a department of the University of Oxford. It furthers the University's objective of excellence in research, scholarship, and education by publishing worldwide. Oxford is a registered trademark of Oxford University Press in the UK and in certain other countries.

Published in Australia by Oxford University Press
253 Normanby Road, South Melbourne, Victoria 3205, Australia

© Issue Outcomes 2016

The moral rights of the author have been asserted.

First published 2016

All rights reserved. No part of this publication may be reproduced, stored in a retrieval system, or transmitted, in any form or by any means, without the prior permission in writing of Oxford University Press, or as expressly permitted by law, by licence, or under terms agreed with the appropriate reprographics rights organisation. Enquiries concerning reproduction outside the scope of the above should be sent to the Rights Department, Oxford University Press, at the address above.

You must not circulate this work in any other form and you must impose this same condition on any acquirer.

National Library of Australia Cataloguing-in-Publication entry

Creator: Jaques, Tony, author.
Title: Crisis proofing : how to save your company from disaster / Tony Jaques.
ISBN: 9780190303365 (paperback)
Notes: Includes index.
Subjects: Crisis management. Strategic management. Issue management. Leadership.

Dewey Number: 658.4056

Reproduction and communication for educational purposes
The Australian *Copyright Act 1968* (the Act) allows a maximum of one chapter or 10% of the pages of this work, whichever is the greater, to be reproduced and/or communicated by any educational institution for its educational purposes provided that the educational institution (or the body that administers it) has given a remuneration notice to Copyright Agency Limited (CAL) under the Act.

For details of the CAL licence for educational institutions contact:

Copyright Agency Limited
Level 15, 233 Castlereagh Street
Sydney NSW 2000
Telephone: (02) 9394 7600
Facsimile: (02) 9394 7601
Email: info@copyright.com.au

Edited by Pete Cruttenden
Typeset by Newgen KnowledgeWorks (P) Ltd, Chennai, India
Indexed by Karen Gillen
Printed by Sheck Wah Tong Printing Press Ltd

Links to third party websites are provided by Oxford in good faith and for information only. Oxford disclaims any responsibility for the materials contained in any third party website referenced in this work.

CONTENTS

List of Tables and Figures ix
Preface: Crisis Is an Equal-Opportunity Risk xi
About the Author xv
Acknowledgments xvi

CHAPTER 1: WHY CRISIS PROOFING IS IMPORTANT 1
Crisis proofing as a goal 2
Is crisis proofing really possible? 4
Is my watch waterproof or water-resistant? 6

CHAPTER 2: OPPORTUNITY AND THE PENALTY FOR BAD BEHAVIOUR 8
Is a crisis really an opportunity? 9
Self-inflicted crises 10
The tsunami effect 12

CHAPTER 3: THE HIGH COST OF NOT CRISIS PROOFING 14
Effect on market value 17
Effect on reputation 18
Planning must be a priority 19

CHAPTER 4: HOW TO KNOW A CRISIS IS COMING 23
Crisis as inevitability 24
Crisis as predictability 25
Red flags and warnings 28

CHAPTER 5: GETTING THE LANGUAGE RIGHT 33
The importance of terminology 34
Some definitions 35
Issue management 38
Crisis management 43
Language and positioning 46

CHAPTER 6: FITTING IT ALL TOGETHER ... 49
Crisis preparedness ... 50
Crisis prevention ... 53
Crisis incident management ... 55
Post-crisis management ... 58

CHAPTER 7: ACTIONS YOU CAN TAKE TO PREVENT A CRISIS HAPPENING IN THE FIRST PLACE ... 61
Issue sources ... 64
Linking issues and risk ... 66
Risk versus resources ... 68
Developing priorities ... 70

CHAPTER 8: TAKING A STRATEGIC APPROACH ... 75
Introducing an issue management model ... 77
Step one: definition ... 79
Step two: objective ... 81
Step three: intended outcomes ... 83
Step four: tactics ... 84
Evaluation ... 85
Strategic planning ... 87

CHAPTER 9: THINGS YOU CAN DO TO PREPARE FOR THE OBVIOUS CRISES 90
A case study of what went wrong ... 91
Undervaluing the impact of a crisis ... 93
'Natural' crises ... 95

CHAPTER 10: PUTTING THE CRISIS PLAN TOGETHER ... 98
Designated Crisis Management Team ... 99
Activating the team ... 101
Crisis management location ... 102
Clear roles and responsibilities ... 103
Contact lists ... 104
Pre-approved information ... 104
Crisis training ... 105

CHAPTER 11: HOW TO MINIMISE DAMAGE WHEN A CRISIS STRIKES ... 110
The impact of bad communication ... 112
The role of spokesperson ... 113

Should the CEO be crisis spokesperson?..115
Should the CEO go to the scene to take charge?...116
So, what to say?...118

CHAPTER 12: WHAT TO DO AFTER THE CRISIS SEEMS TO BE OVER 122
Recovery/business resumption..124
Post-crisis issue impacts...125
Responding to post-crisis issues..129
Evaluation and modification..131
How to review and learn...133

CHAPTER 13: NO, IT'S NOT JUST ABOUT FACTS AND DATA......................136
Piling on the data..138
What's a fact anyway?..140
Truth doesn't always prevail..143
What's the solution?...145

CHAPTER 14: NO, IT'S NOT JUST ABOUT THE LAW EITHER.......................147
Strategy development..149
When legal advice goes feral...151
Legal versus ethical..154
The flow of information..155
Listening to lawyers..157
Silence is not golden..158

CHAPTER 15: WHY LAWYERS DON'T LIKE YOU TO APOLOGISE 161
When apologising reduces liability..162
The challenge of a good apology..163
Apologising and reputation...167

CHAPTER 16: SOCIAL MEDIA: BOTH A STRENGTH AND A THREAT 170
Social media and the CEO..171
The roles of social media in crisis management.......................................173
Monitoring and responding...177

CHAPTER 17: SOCIAL MEDIA: DO IT FAST AND DO IT RIGHT 182
When things go wrong...183
Control and the dark website..185
Role of the CEO...187

CHAPTER 18: MANAGING CRISES ACROSS BORDERS 196
Crises spanning multiple nation states 197
Multinational organisational crises 198
Organisational crises across borders 199
The nature of multinationals 201

CHAPTER 19: RECOGNISING AND RESPONDING TO CROSS-BORDER CRISES 206
When things go wrong 207
Recognising cross-border crisis impact 209
Recognising cultural differences 211

CHAPTER 20: IT'S ALL ABOUT LEADERSHIP 215
Crisis and leadership 216
Barriers to executive learning 218
Leadership crisis roles 220
Crises and personal cost 225
Response versus responsibility 226
Introducing the crisis-proof organisation 227

References 229
Index 250

LIST OF TABLES AND FIGURES

Tables
5.1 Definitions of key terms 36
7.1 Approaches to identifying emerging issues 63

Figures
6.1 Effective crisis management: a relational model 50
8.1 The Do-it Plan 78

PREFACE:
CRISIS IS AN EQUAL-OPPORTUNITY RISK

This book is for executives who care about their organisation.

There are a few executives who *say* they care, but are actually more focused on the trappings of office: rubbing shoulders with politicians and celebrities; getting their face into special editions of stamps; getting people to nominate them for awards; and getting free tickets to elite sporting events. Legend has it that on the day Enron collapsed, CEO Ken Lay was selecting the upholstery for his corporate jet.

If you are one of that small band, then put this book down right now. It's not for you. It's for the responsible majority—people who want what's best for their organisation and not just for themselves. It's for executives who understand the threat which is generated by crises and who are prepared to do the work necessary to protect their organisation from the terrible impacts a crisis can bring.

Crisis proofing requires leadership from the top, and this book is devoted to that central idea—to help senior executives understand what you can do to reduce the chances of a crisis, and how to minimise the damage from any crisis which does occur.

The book is also devoted to another central idea—crises don't discriminate between organisations. The threat and impact of crises applies equally to corporations, governments, charities and not-for-profits, as well as institutions such as hospitals and schools. No type of organisation is immune, and headlines around the world reveal a sorry parade of organisations of every type which have suffered crises, because crisis truly is an equal-opportunity risk.

One day in a workshop I was running, two sincere women from a high-profile children's organisation were obviously taking it all in. But when we took a break for coffee they told me, 'We are enjoying this, but it doesn't really apply to us.' Naturally I asked why not, and they said, 'Because we are a charity, so we don't have issues that might turn into crises'.

When I suggested a couple of fairly basic crisis scenarios which might affect them—the accountant absconding with donated funds, or the CEO arrested for having child porn on his computer—they were not only in denial but also seemed genuinely offended at the idea that their long-serving colleagues might behave in such a way.

A few months later the organisation was on the front page of all the local newspapers because they had knowingly allowed street kids to take drugs on their premises. The predictable outcry was a serious blow to their reputation and funding. Now, I didn't give them a call and say, 'I told you so'. But it was a reminder that no one is immune, no matter how pure their intentions.

The reality is that all organisations, regardless of size, structure or the nature of their business, are vulnerable to a crisis, and one of the greatest vulnerabilities is the unwarranted belief that 'it won't happen to us'.

What genuinely separates organisations in terms of vulnerability is the difference between being crisis prepared and not crisis prepared. Crisis preparedness is built around two closely related objectives—resistance and resilience.

Resistance is about reducing the risks of a crisis occurring; that is, making your organisation less vulnerable to a potential crisis. *Resilience* is about minimising the amount of damage from any crisis which occurs; that is, increasing your organisation's capacity to survive. Crisis proofing will show you how to achieve both resistance and resilience, and help to reduce the chances of a disaster.

This book is not a 'how to' crisis management manual—though it covers some basic requirements. Nor is it just a collection of crisis anecdotes—though it contains many examples and case studies to illustrate key points. Its purpose is to emphasise why crisis management is important, how you can take practical steps to help prevent crises from happening in the first place, how to manage any unavoidable crisis, and why crisis prevention is a senior executive responsibility.

Bloggers and commentators around the world commonly talk about the CEO as Chief Communication Officer, or as Chief Environmental Officer, or occasionally even as Chief Reputation Officer. What is needed now is the CEO or other senior executive as Chief Crisis Management Officer. That is a harder sell along the mahogany-lined halls of the executive suite, but it has to be done if organisations are to be protected.

There's a whole library of books that purport to be about crisis *management*, but are really just about crisis *response*—what to do when it all goes wrong, how to handle the media, how to explain what happened and, hopefully, what's being done about it. Although those steps are important, they are mainly about damage limitation after the event—in other words, mopping up after the flood rather than preventing the water level rising.

By contrast, the main focus of this book is practical actions you can implement *now* to help avoid damage before the crisis strikes. Naturally it contains detail on what to do when a crisis occurs, and the role of top management, but what makes this book different is placing crisis management in a proactive executive context.

The American practitioner Mark Schannon coined a very stylish distinction between what he called *operational preparedness*—plans to contain the problem and quickly get back to normal—versus *organisational preparedness*, which he described as primarily about the creation of a 'crisis mindset' among those in charge.[1] Crisis proofing is very much about the latter—helping to create a crisis mindset at the top of the organisation.

What to expect

This book sets out in practical language and realistic steps—with relevant examples—what senior executives can do to crisis proof their company.

It starts in Chapters 1–4 with a description of the benefits and limits of crisis proofing and the terrible cost of failing to prepare the organisation for a crisis, with many examples of the dire consequences for organisations and for individual executives. It then discusses crisis warning signs and why they are sometimes ignored.

Chapters 5–12 focus on the importance of using the right language when communicating different activities within the organisation, and introduces an innovative model to show how the interrelated crisis proofing roles fit together into an integrated continuum of executive responsibility. These chapters introduce issue management as a proven executive tool for identifying and prioritising crisis risks and implementing plans to prevent crises before they happen; how to develop a crisis plan; the critical importance of communication in a crisis and the role of the spokesperson; and how to survive the post-crisis period when risk to the organisation can be at its greatest.

Chapters 13–19 focus on some of the challenges and techniques for effective crisis proofing, including the delicate balance between fact and perception; how to navigate the legal minefield; mastering social media as a crisis tool; and extending crisis proofing to potential crisis risks in another country.

The final chapter focuses on the specific role of leadership and stresses that crisis proofing is a top management responsibility which cannot be deferred, delayed or delegated.

Master each of these relatively straightforward phases and you can save your company from disaster.

Tony Jaques

ABOUT THE AUTHOR

Dr Tony Jaques is an internationally recognised consultant and authority on issue and crisis management, who has spoken at conferences and seminars around the world and has written for some of the leading publications in the field.

He worked for more than 20 years as Asia–Pacific Issue Manager for a major US multinational, before establishing his own company which provides issue and crisis counsel to companies and not-for-profits, specialising in analytical reviews of organisational systems and processes.

He is a former Director of the Issue Management Council in Leesburg, Virginia, which presented him with the Howard Chase Award to recognise his contribution to the industry and his leadership in developing the benchmark Issue Management Best Practice Indicators.

Dr Jaques is the author of the 2014 book *Issues and Crisis Management: Exploring Issues, Crises, Risk and Reputation*, and his work with managers and organisations around the world led to development of the concept of crisis proofing as a practical tool for CEOs and senior executives. He writes the specialist online issue and crisis publication Managing Outcomes (www.issueoutcomes.com.au).

ACKNOWLEDGMENTS

Thanks to the many individuals whose support and encouragement made this book possible and to the many writers and thinkers whose ideas have expanded our understanding of issue and crisis management. Thanks in particular for input and review of different chapters to Peter Sandman and Larry Smith in New York, Richard Levick in Washington DC, Chris Galloway in New Zealand and Jane Jordan-Meier in Sydney.

Some parts of this book draw on previous publications by the author, in particular *Issue and Crisis Management: Exploring Issues, Crises, Risk and Reputation* (Oxford University Press 2014). Specific citations from the author's other work is referenced in the normal way.

Thanks to Wayne Burns, CEO of the Australasian Centre for Corporate Public Affairs, for permission to adapt material for the figure in Chapter 7; Anthony Concil, Director of Communications at IATA, for permission to reprint the social media guidelines in Chapter 16; Dominic Cockram, Managing Director of Steelhenge Consulting UK, for permission to use the leadership principles in Chapter 20; Charlie Pownall of Hong Kong for his reputation roles of social media in Chapter 12; and Adam Treiger for the quotation in Chapter 14.

The author and the publisher also wish to thank the following copyright holders for reproduction of their material.

Cover: Getty/Jonathan Kitchen

Dominic Cockram for 'Requirements of crisis leadership'; **Elsevier** for 'Crisis Management: Four Lessons learned' by Ross J from *Encyclopedia of Security Management*, John Fay (ed), Copyright Elsevier, 2007; **IATA** for 'Dealing with the news media after an aviation accident: Best practices in the age of social media' www.iata.org; **Sage Publications** for 'Do (Some) Organizations Cause Their Own Crisis? The Cultural Profiles of Crisis-Prone vs Crisis-Prepared Organizations' Ian I Mitroff et al, Organization and Environment, 1989.

Every effort has been made to trace the original source of copyright material contained in this book. The publisher will be pleased to hear from copyright holders to rectify any errors or omissions.

CHAPTER 1

WHY CRISIS PROOFING IS IMPORTANT

Crisis proofing is a low-cost investment which has a real bottom-line return. Nothing destroys reputation faster or deeper than an issue or crisis mismanaged. Just ask Volkswagen, BP or FIFA. This book features many such examples of the high probability of a crisis occurring and the terrible cost of not being prepared.

There's also the high risk of a crisis turning into a terminal disaster, and I will show worrying data that any organisation struck by a crisis has at least a one in four chance it won't survive. Think no further than Enron, WorldCom, Arthur Andersen, Lehman Brothers or Ansett Airlines.

So, crisis proofing should not be a priority because it's a new management fashion, or because it will help executives avoid being embarrassed at the golf club. It should be a priority because taking steps to recognise emerging issues and to effectively manage crises protects people and the environment, protects strategic objectives and protects reputation, which in turn protects the entire enterprise. This interconnection is no theoretical assertion. It's a reality of the modern organisation, and the single most important factor in effective crisis proofing is leadership.

A few years ago the veteran British commentator Bill Sweetman wrote:

> Since White Star Line President Bruce Ismay hopped into Titanic's Collapsible Boat C and left 1,502 of his employees and customers to drown or freeze to death, companies have been looking for better ways to respond to a disaster.[1]

While Sweetman's conclusion was maybe just a little overstated, no one could dispute the sentiment. It's also a reminder about the role of senior executives, and of a central theme throughout this book; specifically, that crisis proofing and crisis management are not just about response—what to do when the crisis strikes, or when the ship hits an iceberg—but about all the steps that need to be taken in advance.

It's this integration of ongoing management processes where executive leadership is essential—to lead from the top by example (unlike Mr Ismay of the White Star Line); to identify issues and crisis threats early; to assign sufficient resources to make a difference; to break down cross-functional barriers and promote integration of processes and systems; and to drive crisis proofing as an organisational priority.

In fact, everything in this book leads to one overriding conclusion—responsibility for managing issues and crises resides absolutely at the top of the organisation and cannot properly be delegated downwards.

CRISIS PROOFING AS A GOAL

What is the goal of crisis proofing and what does a crisis-proof organisation look like? To optimise protection, your organisation requires four interlocking steps, outlined below. In a later chapter I introduce a relational model to graphically illustrate how they fit together.

THE FOUR KEY PHASES OF CRISIS PROOFING

1. Crisis preparedness—getting ready in case a crisis strikes
2. Crisis prevention—proactive steps to help prevent the crisis from occurring in the first place
3. Crisis incident response—activating proper plans to respond to the crisis and minimise ensuing damage
4. Post-crisis management—dealing with the risks, particularly financial and reputational, which frequently occur after the crisis event itself is over.

A crisis-proof organisation has all four major elements in place—with direct support and involvement from top management—in order to achieve two strategic outcomes: (a) reduce the likelihood of a crisis occurring and (b) minimise damage if a crisis does occur. In other words, resistance *and* resilience (as defined in the Preface).

While the key phases of crisis proofing will be expanded and explored in due course, right now I would like to introduce one other very important concept—the distinction between crisis preparedness and crisis prevention.

This is one of the least understood areas of crisis management and it lies at the heart of our objective—namely, strategic, integrated crisis *management* as opposed to tactical crisis *response*. This in turn is central to crisis proofing the organisation.

A helpful way to think about this distinction is to consider home security. Let's assume you are a responsible homeowner. You will most likely take out insurance to provide financial assistance in the event that your house suffers fire, flood or burglary. But the insurance policy itself does nothing to prevent the fire or flood or to deter the burglar. Although it's very important, it comes into play only *after* the event. Thus it can be seen as the equivalent of crisis *preparedness*—it's only useful when the event has already occurred.

However, as a responsible homeowner you don't just take out insurance (crisis preparedness). You also install burglar alarms, smoke detectors and security locks on doors and windows; that is, you take protective action before the event to reduce the risk of fire and burglary. These actions might be called the equivalent of crisis *prevention*.

Most importantly, as a responsible homeowner you would never do just one task and think the job was done. Effective home security requires both advanced planning to provide protection if it all goes wrong (crisis preparedness) and proactive actions to keep your home safe (crisis prevention). In exactly the same way, organisations need both crisis preparedness and crisis prevention.

Sadly, companies sometimes develop a crisis manual (which sits on a shelf gathering dust) and undertake an occasional crisis simulation or team training exercise and think they are done. It's only when a crisis strikes that they discover how wrong they are.

IS CRISIS PROOFING REALLY POSSIBLE?

Let's get this clear right away. It simply is not possible to make any organisation *totally immune to every conceivable crisis*. If a guarantee is what you want, then you'd do better to look for all that paperwork which came with your latest home appliance (and you likely didn't bother to read at the time).

But it *is* possible to protect your organisation from the risk and impact of crises, and that's what crisis proofing is all about. However, the reality is that absolute crisis proofing can't be done, any more than you can produce a watch which is waterproof under all conceivable conditions; or erect a building which is earthquake-proof in the face of the greatest-magnitude quakes capable of levelling entire cities; or weatherproof your home against a tornado which could blow the entire building away. As Madame Butterfly sings in my favourite opera: 'A storm can uproot the strongest oak.'

But that's no reason not to try to design everyday watches which are *more* resistant to water; or create buildings which will stand up to *most* tremors and minimise casualties when an earthquake strikes; or to make homes which are *more* stormproof.

Exactly the same applies to striving to make organisations *more* crisis proof and less vulnerable to disastrous consequences. It's no guarantee, but it's certainly worth the effort. Just think about the devastating impact a major crisis could have on your organisation. I mean *really* think about what's the worst thing that could possibly happen, no matter how unlikely. And how badly would it affect you? Got that clear in your mind? Now, the only real question is what steps are you taking to protect your organisation from such a crisis?

The idea of proofing goods against adverse outcomes is a common one—from waterproof jackets to leak-proof pens and fireproof safes. And don't even get me started on creative labels such as smudge-proof mascara and kiss-proof lipstick!

Apart from obviously cosmetic claims, society has come to accept such language, even though we know that many waterproof jackets are showerproof at best; that leak-proof pens won't survive rough handling; and that fireproof safes will preserve paper documents from fire but are useless at protecting heat-sensitive electronic media such as CDs, DVDs, flash drives and computer discs. In addition, experts tell us that fireproof safes are typically less resistant to being forced open by determined thieves.

Similarly, we know that childproof locks can be a challenge rather than a barrier to adventurous kids. Indeed, the effectiveness of locks caused a major crisis for the Kryptonite company when young people on social media showed how to open Kryptonite bicycle locks in seconds with nothing more complicated than a ballpoint pen and some online instructions. YouTube videos racked up over a million views and, with the story spreading to the mainstream media, the embarrassed company was forced to change some locking mechanisms and exchange 380,000 locks worldwide.[2] One expert claimed the problem cost the company US$10 million, which was almost half its annual revenue at the time.[3]

So, in a world full of nervous lawyers and mealy-mouthed phrases like 'an excess of caution', companies and regulators have come up with an entire vocabulary designed to modify perceived consumer expectation and to reduce legal liability.

CRISIS PROOFING DEMANDS LEADERSHIP, NOT JUST TOOLS

The ill-fated US energy trading company Enron was once a media darling and regarded as a great corporate citizen. It was listed as the most admired global company in the year 2000; for six years it was ranked the United States' most innovative company; and it enjoyed three years rated as one of the best companies to work for. But in early 2001 it collapsed into financial disaster, with its senior executives sent to prison for dishonesty.

In terms of crisis preparedness, communications expert Robert Heath says Enron developed a mammoth database monitoring and response system that could track threats and opportunities, calculate impact on business plans and operations, and suggest coordinated responses. He said this was the 'essence of an excellent issues management program'. But it had at least one fatal flaw—namely, no commitment to corporate responsibility that truly reflected the reality of sound business practices, rather than what he called 'sheer opportunism'.[4]

IS MY WATCH WATERPROOF OR WATER-RESISTANT?

The watch industry gives us a good example of the importance of language. The International Organization for Standardization (ISO 22810) forbids the use of the term 'waterproof' in relation to watches. It contains specific requirements for how to grade 'water resistance' from the humblest wristwatch, through 'sports watches', to the most sophisticated timepieces designed for deep-sea divers. A common description is 'water-resistant to 30 metres' (3 ATM). However, officially that actually means: 'Suitable for everyday use. Splash and rain resistant. Not suitable for showering, bathing, swimming, snorkelling, water-related work and fishing.'

In other words, despite the label, it is not expected to continue to work at 30 metres underwater. In fact, some watches labelled 'water-resistant' are not even recommended to be worn while washing your hands.

Other industries have also tried to address the uncertainty of 'proofing' their goods. Take the pharmaceutical industry, which had to face up to this problem in the wake of the notorious Tylenol crisis in 1982. When unknown persons spiked headache capsules with cyanide, killing seven people in the Chicago area, new types of protective packaging were rushed into production.[5] Today, most countries have official standards which mandate the language and level of protection to be used in relation to drug packaging, and include legal definitions such as child-resistant and tamper-proof or, more commonly, 'tamper-evident'.

The term 'tamper-resistant' (rather than 'tamper-proof') is even used to describe sealed nuclear reactors (SSTAR) designed for developing countries to prevent them from using reactor material to make nuclear weapons.[6] Tamper-*resistant* nuclear plants? That's hardly reassuring.

If we can readily accept the idea of making consumer goods proof against adverse consequences, it's hardly a stretch to apply the same concept to organisations. But we have to accept that it's not possible to make any organisation totally proof against every conceivable crisis. Unlike, for example, the official standard for drug packaging, crisis management is not governed by enforceable regulations. Therefore, crisis proofing is not a guarantee or an absolute condition. It is, in fact, more of a leadership goal.

And for any executive accustomed to the strategic territory of vision, mission, goals and objectives, the concept of crisis proofing the corporation as a stretch goal should be entirely familiar.

CHAPTER KEY TAKEAWAY

It's not possible to totally crisis proof any organisation. But there are proven practical steps any leader can take both to reduce the chance of a crisis happening and to reduce the impact and duration of any crisis which does occur.

CHAPTER 2

OPPORTUNITY AND THE PENALTY FOR BAD BEHAVIOUR

A crisis is never a good thing. Contrary to the theorists and academics who suggest that crises provide positive opportunities, it just isn't so.

Pay no heed to the endless flow of books, articles, speeches and PowerPoint presentations on crisis management which start off with the seemingly profound statement that the Chinese character for crisis combines both threat and opportunity. The description of the Chinese character may or may not be true, but either way it's not very helpful.

To claim that a crisis is an opportunity is like saying that a divorce is a great opportunity to get rid of unwanted furniture. Or that Hurricane Katrina was a great opportunity to provide improved flood protection for New Orleans. Or that being convicted of bank robbery is a great opportunity to go straight. Or that a business bankruptcy is a great opportunity to resolve financial challenges and 'clear the books'.

However, even if not an opportunity in the conventional sense, a crisis can sometimes result in inquiries and investigations which eventually produce improvement. And it's true that a crisis may lead an organisation to do things differently and better in future. But the reality is that such long-term benefits are most often vastly outweighed by the short- and medium-term damage and pain caused by the crisis event.

This idea was nicely captured by the American practitioner John Budd, who concluded: 'Crisis management is a costly catharsis. Its victories are more often pyrrhic than positive.'[1] In case you've forgotten, the pyrrhic victory is named for Pyrrhus, the Greek king of Epirus, who won two great battles against the Romans, but suffered such terrible, irreplaceable casualties that it was tantamount to defeat. He is reported to have said: 'If we are victorious in one more battle with the Romans, we shall be utterly ruined.'

The same applies to the supposed opportunities claimed to lie within crises, which are much more likely to leave the organisation ruined. As Budd observed, there is nothing really positive about a crisis. Organisational planning should not be built on slogans like 'every crisis is an opportunity'. That's about as valuable as those supposedly motivational or inspirational posters which can still be found in the corridors of some organisations, usually featuring a picture of an awesome sunset or soaring eagle.

CRISIS AS OPPORTUNITY—A CONTRARIAN VIEW

The only people who believe that a crisis is an opportunity are people who either have never been through one or have had the good fortune to survive. Crises seriously damage individuals and organisations. Some never recover. The survivors get to write history accompanied by self-serving reflections that attribute success to the leadership of those in charge.

Eric Dezenhall, Washington-based consultant[2]

IS A CRISIS REALLY AN OPPORTUNITY?

The supposed promise of opportunity in adversity is reinforced by a much-quoted statement from Andy Grove, CEO and co-founder of Intel, and a man who has had more crisis experience than most: 'Bad companies are destroyed by crisis, good companies survive them and great companies are improved by them.'[3]

It's a comforting thought, but let there be no mistake—crises are a terrible risk to reputation and survival for all companies, no matter how bad, good or even great they are. The effort here should not be in trying to discover some opportunity in disaster but rather taking steps to avoid the crisis happening in the first place.

A crisis is not just an inconvenience or an embarrassment. In a real crisis, the survival of the organisation itself truly is at risk and it's an illusion to think we'll get through it okay because we're a good company or even a great company. The road to business success is littered with the bleeding corpses of companies which thought they were too good, too strong or too important for it to happen to them.

The record reinforces the reality. For example, a study of crises in Australia over a 10-year period showed that one in four of the organisations affected did not survive.[4] And American academic John Penrose cites early research which shows that while large companies with ample prestige, goodwill and financial resources may survive even the worst disasters, smaller, lesser-known organisations must heed the fact that 80 per cent of companies without a well-conceived and tested crisis plan go out of business within two years of suffering a major disaster.[5]

There have been other similar studies, and the detailed numbers vary. But the bottom line remains invariably consistent—that a serious crisis is a massive risk to organisational survival.

SELF-INFLICTED CRISES

The demise or near-death of organisations in the aftermath of a crisis can be divided into three main areas. The first is what I call self-inflicted crises— where hubris, greed or dishonesty, or all three, have destroyed organisations. There is, sadly, an extensive rogue's gallery of such organisational disasters.

Think of WorldCom, where CEO Bernie Ebbers was jailed for an US$11 billion accounting fraud which cost 30,000 jobs and a claimed US$180 billion loss to investors. The company went bankrupt and changed its name to MCI.

Think of Tyco, where CEO Dennis Kozlowski and CFO Mark Swartz were jailed for stealing more than US$170 million from the company and fraudulently selling over US$400 million in stock options. The company survived but was broken up and large parts were sold off.

Think of mega-fraudster Bernie Madoff, the former Nasdaq Chairman whose investment scam sent him to jail for life after a collapse which cost investors perhaps US$50 billion.

Think of Anglo-Canadian newspaper mogul Conrad Black who defrauded millions from his company, Hollinger Inc. The company, once the third-largest media empire in the world, went bankrupt and Black went to prison.

Think of the Indian outsourcing giant Satyam, where founder and CEO Ramalinga Raju, his brother and others were eventually sentenced to jail for more than US$1 billion in accounting fraud. Satyam shares fell over 90 per cent, causing massive losses to investors, before the company was sold and rebranded.[6]

Satyam was known as the 'Indian Enron', which brings us to the infamous Enron debacle, which saw the spectacular collapse of one of America's most admired energy companies and the jailing of its dishonest executives. Enron was the largest bankruptcy in US history (before being surpassed by WorldCom the next year), and resulted in 4000 lost jobs. It also led to the effective demise of its auditor Arthur Andersen, which at the time was one of the world's five largest accounting firms.

However, my personal favourite self-inflicted crisis is Gerald Ratner, CEO of a British group of High Street jewellery shops, who gave a speech in which he described his own products as 'total crap' and said his company's earrings were 'cheaper than a prawn sandwich and probably wouldn't last as long'. It may have been an honest statement … but it wasn't smart. The result was virtual destruction of the business, which lost £500 million in shareholder value and led to the closure of 330 outlets and the loss of 2500 jobs, including that of the CEO himself. He has even given his name to this form of failure—'doing a Ratner'.[7]

In all of these cases—and many more like them—it wasn't just senior executives who suffered but also creditors and investors who lost massive amounts of money, and thousands of innocent employees who lost their jobs, their investments and sometimes their pensions as well.

Remaining within the category of self-inflicted crises is a sub-set of individual crises where organisations survived but foolhardy top executives didn't. In recent times we discover Chip Wilson, the gaffe-prone founder and CEO of clothing company Lululemon, who stepped down after making a statement which was angrily interpreted by the company's female customers as being critical of their bodies.[8] Then there's Dov Charney, founder and CEO of edgy clothing brand American Apparel, who was ousted after alleged sexual harassment of employees.[9] Or Brendan Eich, CEO of software company Mozilla, whose board asked him to resign after widespread public protest over his stated opposition to gay marriage.[10] Or Patrick Couderc, UK Managing Director of the French fashion house Herve Leger, who was fired after telling a newspaper reporter that their clothes were not suitable for lesbians, flat-chested women or 'voluptuous' ladies.[11]

Let me add that the cost in terms of market value and organisational reputation can be very heavy. When Hewlett Packard CEO Mark Hurd resigned after misusing his expenses to support a relationship with a female contractor, the company's share value fell by US$10 billion in a day and more than US$14 billion over four days.[12] It's little wonder this was followed by announcement of a massive class action by disgruntled shareholders.

Of course Mr Hurd is just one of the high-profile executives forced out after inappropriate relationships with female employees, and joined the club with Boeing CEO Harry Stonecipher (2005), Starwood Hotels CEO Steven Heyer (2007) and travel site Priceline CEO Darren Huston (2016).[13]

Maybe these hapless executives don't really belong in a serious discussion of how to crisis proof an organisation. But they do serve as an important reminder that crises can start at the very top with a demonstrated lack of judgement (and doubtless they all thought, 'It won't happen to me').

THE COST OF BAD BEHAVIOUR

One study of 219 cases of arrests, lies or extramarital affairs by CEOs and other top executives showed an average shareholder loss of US$226 million in the three days after the announcement of the executive indiscretion, and a fall in the stock price of between 11 per cent and 14 per cent over the next 12 months.[14] Worryingly, the study also found that 65 per cent of the accused executives kept their jobs—even those known to be repeat offenders.

THE TSUNAMI EFFECT

The second area of crises which destroy organisations is those which strike as part of a larger event, which is either wholly or partly beyond the organisation's control. I call this the *tsunami effect*—where organisations are simply swept away by overwhelming forces. A prime example would be the Global Financial Crisis (GFC) of 2007–08 (sometimes called the Great Recession), which halved the total global market value of publicly traded companies and affected millions of jobs.

The share value drop of about US$35 trillion between October 2007 and March 2008 was more than the (then) GDP of the United States, European Union and Japan combined, and crippled thousands of companies. In the finance sector alone, 50 banks, savings and loans associations, building societies and insurance companies around the world were acquired, nationalised or bankrupted during the GFC firestorm. In most cases no amount of crisis proofing would likely have saved them.

But it's important not to draw the wrong lessons. Organisations go out of business every day of the week for a wide variety of reasons, financial or otherwise. And it's not always crisis-related.

When an organisation closes down and people lose their jobs it may seem like a crisis for the people or the community concerned. In such cases, the crisis tends to be the *result* of the organisational demise not the *cause* of it. However, crises can be the direct *cause* of organisational demise and that's the focus of the next chapter.

CHAPTER KEY TAKEAWAY

Crisis protection sometimes depends on character and morals as much as on systems and processes.

CHAPTER 3

THE HIGH COST OF NOT CRISIS PROOFING

We come now to the third main area of crisis impact—where crisis proofing can have its greatest value—and that's when specific crisis events lead directly or indirectly to organisational disaster and demise. In some cases, mismanagement or bad decisions are contributing factors. In truth, such crises have brought down some very famous brands.

The organisational risk of a conventional crisis is illustrated by some high-profile examples of companies which failed to survive intact through the longer-term effects of a crisis event.

Pan American Airways (Pan Am), once the Western world's largest airline, was already facing a number of financial challenges, but the final straw was the Lockerbie disaster when a terrorist bomb brought down a plane over Scotland. Many other airlines have survived fatal accidents, but Pan Am's poor management of the crisis hastened its demise. The same applied to American low-cost airline ValuJet, which tried to blame others for a fatal crash into the Florida Everglades. In their case the company lived on under another name, but the brand was destroyed.

Perrier, the producer of luxury bottled water, was rocked by a contamination crisis, which led to a worldwide recall of its one and only product. They never fully recovered from a five-month suspension of production and were bought out by Swiss rival Nestlé.

The Australian Wheat Board faced an international crisis when it was revealed they had breached the UN's Oil-for-Food program by paying illegal kickbacks to Saddam Hussein's regime in Iraq. The company survived, but was stripped of its crucial monopoly licence to sell Australian wheat. With profits crashing, the AWB was forced to sell out to a Canadian competitor.

Then there was the crisis which engulfed the Chinese dairy giant Sanlu when it was found to have used melamine-contaminated milk in its baby formula. Six babies died of kidney failure and perhaps 300,000 became sick. Not only was Sanlu bankrupted, along with hundreds of associated suppliers and other companies, but the CEO and several senior managers were imprisoned and two supply contractors were executed.

In all of these cases, it wasn't just the event itself but the subsequent perceived mismanagement of the crisis which spelled the end.

While there are many lesser-known examples of companies destroyed, or nearly destroyed, by crises, it's self-evident that organisational crises are not always fatal. In fact, critics and self-appointed experts are sometimes far too quick to call down the curtain.

A good example is the Toyota vehicle recall of 2010 which resulted from what was politely called 'unintended acceleration'. Car recalls are nothing new. They happen all the time, and the Toyota share price took quite a beating. What's important about this case is the response of the mainly American commentariat. Many so-called experts declared that this was the end for Toyota. Some claimed the company would never survive the crisis, and others claimed that, at the very least, the Toyota brand was irreparably damaged and they would have to change the company name.

There was also a chorus of condemnation about the way Toyota had handled public relations around the crisis. Critics, including a congressional committee, claimed that the CEO had 'gone into hiding' because he didn't instantly respond to US media inquiries. Now it's true that he was slow to respond to the media, but what Toyota actually did was much more powerful. They shut down their US car plants and said they would not reopen and would not make another single car until the problem had been fixed. How about that for a crisis response? How about that for a response to the pundits?

And what about all those predictions of doom? The following year Toyota regained its position as the top carmaker in the world.

The vocal vultures were out in force again in 2014 after Malaysia Airlines lost two aircraft in the space of a few months—MH370 which disappeared somewhere over the Indian Ocean and MH17, shot down over war-torn Ukraine. There was a relentless chorus from around the world that the airline could never survive the twin crises, or that it had no choice but to rebrand. But it did survive (though financially restructured), and passenger loadings slowly recovered.

More recent is the Volkswagen recall crisis after revelations in late 2015 of deliberate deceit over diesel emission performance. The share price fell 30 per cent in less than a week and the company recorded its first quarterly loss in 15 years. Investment bank Credit Suisse estimated a worst-case eventual loss could total seven times the previous year's net earnings.[1] Here again the pundits were quick to predict the demise of the brand.

Toyota, Malaysia Airlines and Volkswagen all highlight that crises can bring with them two other major impacts—on market value and on reputation. The link between market value and a crisis—or a perceived crisis—can be rapid and brutal, and it doesn't even have to be based on fact.

FALSE REPORTS WHICH HAD VERY REAL IMPACTS

- Hackers took control of the Associated Press Twitter account in 2013 and sent hoax reports that the US President had been injured in two explosions at the White House. The US stock market briefly plunged, wiping US$136.5 billion off the S&P share index before quickly recovering.[2]
- A false rumour spread in 2008 that (then) Apple CEO Steve Jobs had suffered a major heart attack, and company shares fell almost 10 per cent in 10 minutes. The shares quickly recovered, but when it was announced a few months later that Mr Jobs was taking a leave of absence from the company to take care of his health, the shares fell 7 per cent in a day and almost 12 per cent over the next two weeks.[3]

- Australian anti-coal activist Jonathan Moylan issued a fake news release in the name of a major bank saying it had withdrawn funding for a planned massive new open-cut coal mine in New South Wales. More than A$300 million was briefly wiped off the value of miner Whitehaven Coal as shares fell 9 per cent before the elaborate hoax was exposed and the share price largely recovered.[4]
- In July 2015, Twitter's shares jumped more than 8 per cent after a fake online story said the company had received a US$31 billion takeover offer. The false story was designed to mimic a genuine Bloomberg announcement and even carried the name of a well-known Bloomberg writer. But within minutes the hoax was revealed and the share price quickly returned to its normal level.[5]

EFFECT ON MARKET VALUE

None of these 'false report' cases were 'genuine' crises—except, of course, to the long-suffering investors who lost money—yet such incidents can have just as much impact on market value as a real crisis. A frequently cited rule of thumb, used in research by the financial communications consultancy FD, is that a company can typically lose in excess of 30 per cent of its share value as a result of a highly publicised crisis. And the researchers Charles Fombrun and Cees van Riel have calculated that the losses associated with crises, on average, amount to 8–15 per cent of the market value of affected companies.[6]

Most importantly, these financial losses can be long-lasting and depend to some extent on how well the company was crisis proofed. This longer-term bottom-line importance of being properly crisis prepared was demonstrated in ground-breaking research at Oxford University by Rory Knight and Deborah Pretty.[7] This respected study showed that companies with effective crisis plans in place suffered on average an initial 5 per cent fall in share value, but that after 12 months their share value on average had recovered to 7 per cent above the pre-crisis level.

By contrast, companies with no effective crisis plan in place saw their shares initially fall by an average of 10 per cent, and after 12 months their shares were 15 per cent below the pre-crisis level. In other words, the study showed that for companies without effective planning in place, the share price initially fell twice as far, and a year later there was a difference of 22 per cent of the organisation's market value compared with the well-prepared companies. A 22 per cent impact on long-term market value is surely a powerful reason to put effort into crisis proofing.

Averages are, of course, just that. And some companies find themselves well outside the norm. Take, for example, BP and the notorious *Deepwater Horizon* rig fire and oil spill in the Gulf of Mexico in 2010. In the wake of that environmental and management disaster, the company's share price fell by 50 per cent. It was still down by one-third five years later, at the time when it was announced that the British-based company would pay a record fine of US$18.7 billion, taking the total pre-tax cost to about US$53.8 billion.[8]

EFFECT ON REPUTATION

The BP case also shows that the other long-term impact is on reputation. Reputation is not as easy to quantify as market value, but it is no less real when it comes to reasons why you need to crisis proof your company. Moreover, it's an important asset not only for corporations and individuals, but also for governments, NGOs, not-for-profits and other organisations.

In theory, the value of reputation is calculated by taking the market value of the organisation and subtracting the tangible assets. That leaves a net figure for intangibles, of which reputation is an important part. Hundreds of experts around the world have tried to calculate these values and have come up with just about as many different numbers. For example, the Institute of Practitioners in Advertising reported that intangible assets such as ideas, knowledge, expertise, talent, identity, customer service and reputation comprise up to 70 per cent of the market value of companies listed on the Fortune 500 and FTSE 500. Moreover, they said this proportion had tripled over the past 30 years.[9]

This increase in potential risk is reflected in the work of Geoff Colvin in *Fortune* magazine, who has calculated the intangible asset value of the S&P 500 over the last 40 years. According to the annual Study of Intangible Asset Market Value, in 1975 the S&P 500 was valued at 83 per cent tangible assets and only 17 per cent intangible. By 2015, that had been reversed to 16 per cent tangible assets and 84 per cent intangible.[10]

Regarding the reputation element of intangible assets, such hard data is strongly reinforced by executive perception. One international reputation survey found that global business influencers attributed 63 per cent of a company's value to reputation.[11] Other studies produce slightly different percentage results, but broadly there is a consistent belief that reputation alone can account for well over half of an organisation's value.

When it comes to a crisis, that's a massive exposure. And here again the potential impact is certainly long lasting. A survey of 685 business leaders from Fortune 1000 firms found they believe it would take more than four years to recover from a crisis which damaged an organisation's reputation, and three years for a crisis to fade from the memory of most stakeholders.[12]

HOW AN UNEXPECTED CRISIS DESTROYED A COMPANY

Shirt maker Andrew Fowler built a good business selling print-on-demand T-shirts. Then he developed a computer program to randomly select words based on the British World War II propaganda slogan 'Keep Calm and Carry On'. It seemed like a clever idea until Amazon banned his products in the face of designs such as 'Keep Calm and Knife Her', 'Keep Calm and Rape Them' and 'Keep Calm and Choke Her'. Fowler explained that he had no idea offensive messages had been created, and blamed a 'computer error' for the 'unintended outcome'. He was genuinely sorry, but his typical orders dropped from 800 to just three, and the company was doomed.[13] As celebrity blogger Perez Hilton commented: 'Well, we're certainly glad no one actually intended to make shirts that condone rape. But honestly, how could anyone be careless enough not to notice?'

PLANNING MUST BE A PRIORITY

So given these risks to market value and reputation, you'd think that crisis proofing would be a no-brainer. And it *should* be. But data and experience from around the world reinforces over and again that organisations fail to put proper crisis planning in place.

The terrorist attacks on New York and Washington on 11 September 2001 predictably triggered a close interest in crisis preparedness. A survey of members and customers by the American Management Association immediately afterwards found that only 49 per cent had a crisis management plan, and only 39 per cent had ever carried out a drill or simulation. A follow-up survey a year later showed that in the wake of the attacks the number of companies with a crisis plan had increased to 64 per cent, but it soon started to fall back again.[14]

More recently, a 2013 study found 49 per cent of companies did not have a crisis plan in place, yet 50 per cent of them expected to experience a crisis in the next 12 months.[15] And a survey of companies in Europe showed that although 60 per cent of the business decision-makers polled had experienced a crisis—more than half within the past year—only 53 per cent currently had a crisis plan in place.[16] Furthermore, there is no reason to believe the situation is improving. A global survey, published in 2016,[17] found that three-quarters of board members questioned were confident that their organisations could deal with a crisis situation, yet fewer than half believed they were adequately prepared. The same survey also found that only 49 per cent of the non-executive directors said their company monitored or had the capacity to detect trouble; only 49 per cent said their company had a playbook for likely crisis scenarios; and even fewer (32 per cent) said their company engaged in crisis simulations or training.

The purpose here is not to scare you into action—after all, you've already started to read this book. The purpose is to reinforce why you should take action, and to help counter the inevitable doubters, cynics and penny-pinchers in your company who 'don't think it's important right now'. Presumably they think it's okay for your company to 'take its chances'.

No self-respecting CEO would ever say, 'We don't bother with strategic planning' or 'I'm too busy to worry about safety'. But well-regarded CEOs have told me directly: 'I know our crisis management system is not up to scratch, but it's not a priority at the moment.' And that response is sometimes followed by, 'Right now we are focused on our end of year results' or 'integrating our latest acquisition' or 'launching our new product' or whatever.

Now that might be a polite way of saying: 'We don't want to hire an expensive crisis management specialist at present.' Yet the basic steps of crisis proofing are not expensive, are not complicated, and don't necessarily take up a lot of executive time. The primary requirement is a commitment to improve.

So why don't organisations put proper planning in place? One of the most detailed studies to address this question was reported by Ian Mitroff and Thierry Pauchant based on over 350 interviews with top executives in more than 120 companies. They analysed the explanations for why companies fail to be properly crisis prepared, which were first published in the delightfully titled book *We're So Big and Powerful Nothing Bad Can Happen to Us*.[18]

Mitroff and Pauchant identified more than 30 different rationalisations managers gave for *not* putting crisis planning in place. It would be too depressing to record all 30 here, but these are just a sample:

- Well-managed companies just don't have crises.
- It's good enough to react once a crisis has already happened.
- Most crises resolve themselves. Therefore time is our best ally.
- In a crisis, just refer to the procedures laid out in the manual.
- We are a team that will function well in a crisis.
- Every crisis is so different it is not possible to prepare for them.
- We know how to manipulate the news media.
- The most important thing in a crisis is to protect our image through clever public relations and advertising

Really? These are adequate reasons to put your organisation at risk?

In my own research interviewing CEOs in the chemical and energy sector, this lack of commitment to crisis planning seems to be not so much linked to wilful blindness as to a lack of willingness or experience to prioritise resources.[19] One CEO told me:

> People prioritise based on day-to-day issues and pressures. And, hopefully, on more than 99 per cent of days, crisis management is not an issue or priority. Consequently, I think there is a tendency for people to put it off. When it's time to do the crisis management stuff, there is always something else which is more important in the short term. It's a matter of planning and priority setting and leadership.

His comment was frankly disheartening. By way of response, this book has been written not only to show why crisis proofing *should* be a priority, but also to demonstrate that it *really* isn't too hard.

CHAPTER KEY TAKEAWAY
Crises do more to define an organisation—and do it more quickly—than any other single event.

CHAPTER 4

HOW TO KNOW A CRISIS IS COMING

Some crisis commentators like to say: 'It's not a question of *if* you will have a crisis, only a question of *when*.' That sounds like a clever maxim, but it doesn't take a lot of thought to realise that this alarming statement is not really very smart—unless you are a crisis consultant selling expensive workshops and advice.

The statement *might* be true, but equally it might not. Major crises are in fact relatively rare, which is one reason why they still create such headlines when they occur. Many crisis consultants have never personally managed a genuine crisis, and some of those who have done so then spend the next few years on the conference speaking circuit talking about their experience.

Similarly, many organisations operate for decades and never face a genuine crisis. Needless to say, that doesn't mean they won't face a crisis tomorrow. If you flip a coin 99 times and it comes up heads every time, what are the odds it will come up heads again on flip number 100? The answer, as any high school maths student should know, is that the odds are 50:50, the same as on flip number one.

CRISIS AS INEVITABILITY

It's a reminder that the past is not a reliable guide to the future. If no serious problem has arisen recently, we tend to downgrade the likelihood of a future one. In management terms that leads to the dangerous fallacy of, 'We've never had a crisis so why worry about it now?' which is one of the barriers to crisis proofing.

So to propose that 'every organisation will have a crisis one day' is not really very helpful. What sort of crisis? Will it affect the whole organisation or just one division? And over what time period? The current strategic planning cycle? The life of the organisation? The tenure of the incumbent CEO?

Although 'every organisation will have a crisis one day' is a common statement which might jolt you into action, it may also have the opposite effect: 'If a crisis is inevitable at some vague time in the distant future there's not much I can do about it, so I'll focus on the here and now.' I propose that it's better to say: 'Every organisation *could* have a crisis any day', which is much more accurate and realistic, and is more likely to lead to practical action.

Think of the familiar statement: 'We will all die one day.' This is an undeniable fact, although very few of us know what day that will be. For most of us it's not something we worry about all the time, and it's not generally a statement intended to jolt us into immediate action. Instead, it's something we are constantly aware of and which guides some of our priorities. For example, you might take out life insurance to help your family when it happens. You might make a will to ensure orderly disposal of your estate. And you might even take exercise, eat healthily and avoid risky behaviour to delay the inevitable.

At an organisational level you might take out key executive insurance to help the company through any unexpected transition. Think of the crisis which confronted the Australian mining company Sundance Resources when it lost its board and CEO in a plane crash in West Africa in June 2010. Sundance said the following day that it was 'fully insured for the tragedy', although experts said allowing the management group to fly on the same charter plane from a non-approved airline was in breach of both industry protocols and the company's own travel policy.[1]

The Sundance tragedy illustrates a critical aspect of crisis proofing. Namely, that effective crisis management needs formal actions both to prevent the crisis from happening in the first place (policies and compliance) as well as steps to prepare the organisation in case a crisis strikes (insurance). In other words, as I have already described, crisis proofing is built around two closely related objectives—*resistance* (reducing the risks of a crisis occurring) and *resilience* (minimising damage and improving survival).

IS CYBER SECURITY THE EXCEPTION?

There is one specific category of crisis which just might genuinely justify the label of inevitable, and that's the risk of a cyber-security breach. In fact, cyber-security professionals say there are only two kinds of online businesses—those that have been hacked, and those that don't yet know they have been hacked.

Of course, not every data breach triggers a crisis, and it most often evolves into a headline crisis only if it is a high-profile organisation or if it is badly managed. But many security experts now argue that data breaches truly are inevitable, and the numbers are frightening. Google and McAfee say there are thousands of cyber attacks *every day* around the world, costing the global economy about US$460 billion a year.[2]

While opinions about inevitability may still be divided, Cisco's Chief Security Officer John Stewart is in no doubt that a data breach is not a unique experience: 'You're eventually going to be hit. It's not worth the effort of thinking you won't be hit. It's no longer a relevant conversation.'[3]

CRISIS AS PREDICTABILITY

More useful than the idea of crises in general being *inevitable* is the notion of crises as *predictable*. The former can breed inertia and hopelessness. The latter helps to create a clear path for action. If crises can be predicted, then there ought to be clear steps that leaders can take towards prevention.

This has led to two main ideas which provide clear and actionable directions for senior managers: (a) the concept of 'predictable surprises'; and (b) realisation that most crises are preceded by red flags, or warning signs.

The concept of predictable surprises is championed by Harvard Professors Max Bazerman and Michael Watkins, who claim that many surprises, in all types of organisations, are predictable and avoidable. Their argument is that predictable surprises are a failure of leadership, and happen when leaders have all the data and information they need to recognise the potential, or even inevitability, of major problems, but fail to respond with effective preventative action. These are what they call 'the disasters you should have seen coming'.[4] And who would want to be remembered in organisational folklore as a failed leader?

Bazerman and Watkins readily admit that many surprises—or for our purposes many crises—are unpredictable and genuinely strike out of the blue. In such cases leaders can't legitimately be blamed for lack of foresight. Similarly, leaders should not be blamed if they have taken all reasonable preventive measures against an impending crisis. The problem, say Bazerman and Watkins, is when the event *was* foreseeable and preventable, and no action was taken.

One of their best-known examples is the terrorist assault on the United States on 11 September 2001, which they argue was a genuine predictable surprise. I sometimes ask participants in my crisis workshops to imagine that they were sitting in a boardroom in the World Trade Center on 10 September 2001, doing an executive group exercise to identify worst-case scenarios and to prioritise potential risks to the business. It seems like a safe bet that no one sitting at the board table would have said: 'I think our greatest risk is a hijacked jetliner crashing in through the window.'

For their part, Bazerman and Watkins don't suggest that the US government, or anyone else for that matter, should have known that four aircraft would be used to attack New York and Washington on that day and that the World Trade Center twin towers would fall. But they do argue that the US government's lack of preparedness for a terrorist attack using passenger aircraft rendered the nation dangerously, and avoidably, vulnerable.

And they demonstrate in painful detail that government agencies and officials had all the data they needed to know of dangerous deficiencies in airline security that could be exploited in a variety of ways, and that required urgent attention. Sadly, the report of the official government commission into this disaster reached the same conclusion: 'The 9/11 attacks were a shock, but they should not have come as a surprise.'[5]

The great Danish physicist Niels Bohr once famously quipped: 'Prediction is very difficult, especially about the future.' While Bazerman and Watkins argue that the idea of predictable surprises is about identifying trends and developments rather than specific crises, the important point here is that from a management perspective, prediction is of no value if it isn't linked to action.

One memorable example of this took place in early 2001, when the Federal Emergency Management Agency (FEMA) commissioned a study to identify the three most probable catastrophes facing the United States. Top of their list were a terrorist attack in New York City; a catastrophic earthquake in San Francisco; and a hurricane and levee break in New Orleans.[6] The first of these happened just four months later on 11 September 2001, and Hurricane Katrina devastated New Orleans in August 2005. At this stage the nervous citizens of San Francisco are still waiting for 'the big one'.

While Bazerman and Watkins argue that the 11 September attack on the World Trade Center was very much a 'predictable surprise', Hurricane Katrina is perhaps more instructive for our purposes.

In July 2004, just one year before Katrina came ashore and destroyed much of New Orleans, FEMA staged a massive five-day emergency exercise which involved more than 300 participants from all 13 New Orleans parishes, more than 20 Louisiana state agencies, and 15 federal agencies. The disaster simulation was built around a fictional Hurricane Pam which was imagined to have struck New Orleans with sustained winds of 120 mph, dumping up to 20 inches of rain and creating a storm surge which topped the levees and flooded much of the city.

At the end of the exercise some critics argued that the simulated event was far too expensive and was unrealistic! But just over a year later (August 2005) Hurricane Katrina struck in an almost identical fashion, breaching the levees and flooding much of the city. The impact of the real hurricane was eerily similar to the simulation scenario, including details such as the depth of flooding in the city; the number of homes destroyed; the number of people who lost electricity; the number of people in public shelters prior to landfall; the number of residents displaced; and the predicted collapse of a major bridge. The key differences were that the simulated loss of life was overstated and the financial cost of the disaster was understated.[7] (In fact Katrina proved to be the most costly natural disaster in American history.)

However, despite the extraordinary similarities, after the real Hurricane Katrina struck, US Homeland Security Secretary Michael Chertoff argued that it was 'particularly unpredictable' and 'exceeded the foresight of planners, and maybe anybody's foresight'.[8]

Some people suggest that the systemic challenge for management in such cases is not a lack of good information but rather: (a) lack of imagination; (b) faulty or inadequate analysis; (c) failure to see the big picture; and, most critically here, (d) failure to link information to action.[9]

This deficiency was well captured by the final report of the 2006 US House of Representatives Select Bipartisan Committee that was set up to investigate the preparation for and response to Hurricane Katrina. The committee's 520-page report was tellingly titled *A Failure of Initiative*, and the committee concluded:

> While there was no failure to predict the inevitability and consequences of a monster hurricane—Katrina in this case—there was a failure of initiative to get beyond design and organisational compromises to improve the level of protection afforded.[10]

By any measure it was a deliberate and damning conclusion.

RED FLAGS AND WARNINGS

In his best-selling book *The Black Swan*, Nassim Nicholas Taleb introduced the idea of Black Swan events—which are 'highly improbable' but can produce enormous shocks. Taleb wasn't writing specifically about crises, though he could have been. A Black Swan event, he says, has three key attributes:

- It is an outlier, outside the realm of reasonable expectations, because nothing in the past can convincingly point to its possibility.
- It carries an extreme impact.
- In spite of its outlier status, human nature makes us concoct explanations for its occurrence after the fact, making it explainable and predictable.

Most importantly for our purposes, he says that although Black Swan events have a huge impact, they're nearly always impossible to predict. Taleb's advice: 'Invest in preparedness, not prediction.'

As I've mentioned before, preparedness and prevention are the two foundation actions for crisis proofing and we'll come to discuss them later in more detail. For the present however, in the context of the tension between inevitability and predictability, a key element is red flags—the warning signs that a potential crisis is looming—and how senior executives identify and then choose to either act on or ignore those warnings.

In this book you'll meet a sad catalogue of warnings ignored and the sometimes devastating consequences for organisations and even governments. In the previous chapter I listed some of the rather worrying 'reasons' organisations and their senior executives give for ignoring warnings and not being properly prepared for crises.

Unfortunately, warning alarms are sometimes literally switched off. Following the disastrous explosion and fire on the ill-fated *Deepwater Horizon* oil rig in the Gulf of Mexico in 2010, evidence was given that vital warning systems had been deliberately disabled to spare workers being awoken by false alarms.[11] I wonder how they explained *that* to the families of the 11 men who were killed.

This may be an extreme example, but even if crises are not strictly predictable in the common meaning of the word, there is no doubt that most crises are preceded by a trail of red flags and warning signs that something is wrong.

NO SURPRISE?

As any adult knows, a magician cannot produce a rabbit unless it is already in (or very near) his hat. In the same way, surprises in the business environment almost never emerge without a warning.[12]

French oil executive Pierre Wack

On the subject of crises, the prolific crisis expert Ian Mitroff went so far as to boldly claim that in every crisis he had ever studied, there were *always* a few key people on the inside of an organisation, or on its edge, who saw the early warning signs and tried to warn their superiors. 'In every case,' he concluded, 'the signals were either ignored or blocked from getting to the top or having any effect.'[13]

Now it's possible Mitroff was overstating his case to make the point, but there is good research data to support his argument. The Institute for Crisis Management in Denver, Colorado, has been tracking crises in the media for well over 20 years and its conclusion from analysing tens of thousands of crises is that about two-thirds are not sudden unexpected events at all. They are what the ICM categorises as 'smouldering crises'—in other words events which should have and could have prompted prior intervention.

I like the way this idea is expressed by the French writer Christophe Roux-Dufort who refers to what he calls the *genealogy* of crises. He says the existence of such a genealogy suggests crises may be potentially tracked long before the acute phase, and that crises are the ultimate moment of a continuous cumulative process of organisational failures.[14]

While everyone knows that hindsight always has 20:20 vision, it has to be conceded that warning signs are generally easier to see *after* a crisis. Aside from natural events such as Hurricane Katrina, business crises often reveal a litany of warnings which were ignored, and resulted in disaster.

A classic example of failure to link information to action is the calamity which befell the venerable Baring's Bank, a British financial institution in business for more than 200 years. While the bank was destroyed by the activities of a single rogue trader, it was evident very early on that the bank's internal control systems failed to catch signals such as increased trading activity, the extensive use of leverage and escalating volume of trades.[15]

You might think it was a clear warning sign to banks everywhere about the need to monitor suspicious trading—but no. Just a few years later the French bank Société Générale lost €4.9 billion (US$7 billion) through the activities of a rogue trader. Unlike the hapless British bank, the giant French institution was big enough to survive, but an independent panel found the company failed to act on 75 red flags or early warnings over a period of 18 months.[16]

Shortly afterwards in the United States, in the wake of the US$65 billion Madoff investment scandal, Securities and Exchange Commission

Inspector General David Kotz admitted that the agency missed 'numerous red flags' from 1992 until fraudster Bernie Madoff was arrested in December 2008. Inspector General Kotz conceded that five separate investigations into the affair had been bungled.[17]

More recently, consider the 'London Whale' trading scandal which JP Morgan Chase CEO Jamie Dimon initially dismissed in 2012 as 'a tempest in a teapot'. However, it cost his bank a US$6.2 billion loss and its market value fell US$40 billion in a matter of weeks. Most importantly, a US Senate Panel reported that bank management had 'disregarded multiple warnings', including the fact that internal risk limits were breached more than 300 times. The panel concluded: 'The breaches did not, however, spark an in-depth review … or require immediate remedial action to lower risk. Instead the breaches were largely ignored or ended by raising the relevant risk limit.'[18]

JP Morgan eventually paid over US$1 billion in fines to regulators in the United Kingdom and United States, and CEO Dimon conceded that the trades were 'flawed, complex, poorly reviewed, poorly executed and poorly monitored'. Not much comfort for the investors who lost millions and are still pursuing legal action.[19]

And of course it's not just banks which fail to heed warning signals. In March 2005 an explosion and fire at the BP refinery in Texas City near Houston killed 15 people and injured 170—America's worst industrial accident in a decade. The official inquiry found six underlying causes, *all of which had been known to management.*[20] After enduring more than US$70 million in earlier fines and penalties, in October 2009 BP was fined a record US$87 million for industrial negligence, including US$31 million in 'wilful violations' of process safety management.

Similarly, a gas explosion in 2010 at the Pike River coal mine, near Greymouth in New Zealand, cost 29 lives and was one of the country's worst mine disasters. The ensuing Royal Commission found that in the previous seven weeks there had been 21 reports of gas building up to dangerous levels and a further 27 incidents of lesser gas build-up, including on the very morning of the accident.[21] The Commission concluded that the company had 'failed to heed numerous warnings of a potential catastrophe at the mine.'

Then there was the crash of an AirAsia Airbus A320 which plunged into the sea off Indonesia in 2015, killing all 162 people aboard. The conclusion of the official investigators was that the crash had been triggered by a rudder control system malfunction—a fault which had occurred 23 times in the preceding year. The BBC news report on the disaster was headlined 'AirAsia probe: Anatomy of an avoidable crash'.[22]

Finally, a little understood aspect of a notorious case arises from the 'McDonald's hot coffee incident' when an elderly New Mexico woman suffered third-degree burns after a cup of scalding coffee, placed between her legs, spilled when the car pulled out from the drive-through. The case is best remembered for the fact that a state jury awarded her an eye-popping US$2.9 million in punitive and compensatory damages (subsequently reduced to US$640,000 and eventually settled out of court for an undisclosed figure).

Less well known is that the company had received at least 700 complaints of coffee burns in the previous decade. In their analysis of the case, Alfonso González-Herrero and Cornelius Pratt concluded:

> McDonald's knew that its coffee was among the hottest—if not the hottest—in the industry. It seemed the fast-food chain also knew its coffee sometimes caused serious burns; however it did not consult experts about the issues. Both these issues were seemingly overlooked.[23]

The point of these examples is not that hindsight is useful to show what organisations *should* have done. Rather, it is to emphasise that detecting and acting on these red flags is a real challenge for senior executives. In fact, Mitroff and his colleagues concluded that the detection of such signals 'remains an enigma for most organisations'.[24]

But it doesn't have to be like that. This book sets out in detail practical ways that senior executives *can* identify potential crises early and how to take positive, planned steps within a formal strategic framework.

CHAPTER KEY TAKEAWAY
It's not a question of predicting when a crisis will happen. The goal is to be ready for when it does.

CHAPTER 5

GETTING THE LANGUAGE RIGHT

It's a challenge for executives everywhere—recognising the difference between issue, emergency, crisis and disaster, and ensuring a common understanding across the organisation.

These terms can get thrown around rather carelessly, but you're making a major mistake if you think the differences don't matter.

Let me stress that this is not some trivial debate about duelling definitions. To crisis proof your organisation you need to fully understand these terms, and people in your organisation need to know exactly what the executive group are talking about. From a management perspective, perhaps the single most important reason is that each of these terms should relate to a specific activity, with its own tools and processes.

Using the wrong tool is a sure path to failure. Think of the carpenter reaching into his toolbox and pulling out his newest saw. It's a wonder to behold, with a high-grade steel blade, hand sharpened and aligned teeth, and a polished walnut handle individually crafted to the owner's grip. A great tool indeed, but it's of no real use if the required task is to drive in a nail.

The same applies in organisations. Most managers are familiar with the 'shiny thing syndrome'—where the latest fad seems to be the answer to every problem: 'Let's focus on empowered teams to improve performance everywhere.' Or, 'Let's use 360-degree feedback throughout the whole organisation.' Or, 'Let's use the Six Sigma process for every possible situation.'

The correct way forward is to fit the proper tool to the task, and this very much applies to crisis proofing. The best possible emergency response system is little help in managing a crisis, and formal issue management is not much use in responding to a fast-developing emergency.

And there's another big problem with not properly understanding the tools. It's too easy for an organisation to put one process in place and imagine they are well covered for a whole range of needs. For example, having an up-to-date and effective crisis manual is important, but it doesn't mean you can sit back and say, 'Job done'. The manual alone—no matter how well written—does nothing to help prevent a crisis happening in the first place.

THE IMPORTANCE OF TERMINOLOGY

It's hard to overstate the importance of appropriate terminology to communicate significant distinctions in meaning. Management pioneer Edward Bernays said, 'Communication is the centrepiece of effective leadership' and it's clear that getting the language right is crucial. In fact, the impact of language on the attitude and behaviour of people is the basis of an entire formal concept known as 'verbal and linguistic behaviourism'.[1]

In modern business management, many common terms owe their origins to the military—such as mission, objectives, strategy and tactics. And there seems to be an endless flow of management books which find supposedly important lessons for today's executives from the works of historic military leaders and writers. Within that military context, an instructive example of the importance of terminology would be the important distinction between 'strategic withdrawal' and 'retreat'. While unsuccessful generals occasionally use the former as a euphemism for the latter, there is a vitally important difference. To order a true strategic withdrawal, perhaps to a new defensive line, communicates a totally different meaning from ordering a general retreat.

Crucially, that distinction is not just one of language. It will directly impact the behaviour of the officers and the troops. A genuine strategic withdrawal is a more or less disciplined military manoeuvre. A general retreat is more likely to deteriorate into panic amid a sense of every man for himself. The French even have a special phrase for it—*sauve-qui-peut*.

Within a general business context, the same important distinctions in language can be seen, such as describing a new business situation as a merger rather than a takeover. Here again, executives sometimes use merger as a euphemism for takeover, though the difference in terms of attitude and behaviour, both of employees and managers, is well recognised. And that difference typically becomes very real when lists get drawn up of who will lose their job in the newly combined organisation.

There are occasions when something may have a number of different names, but is still well understood as the same thing. For instance, when I previously mentioned Hurricane Katrina and Hurricane Pam, I didn't need to explain that I was using the language most commonly applied in the Western Atlantic and Eastern Pacific. The same weather feature is referred to as a cyclone in the Indian Ocean and the South Pacific, and is a typhoon in the Western Pacific. Yet the phenomenon is exactly the same, irrespective of terminology (except that it rotates anti-clockwise in the northern hemisphere and clockwise in the southern hemisphere). By contrast, with 'issue' and 'crisis' it is not simply such a difference in terminology but rather a more fundamental difference in accurately characterising each phenomenon.

SOME DEFINITIONS

Defining key terms is never easy, and when it comes to contentious concepts such as issue and crisis, even experts can fail to agree.

Sometimes there is legitimate disagreement and sometimes it seems to be driven mainly by professional jealousy and scholarly rivalry. Unfortunately, none of that is at all helpful for busy executives and serves only to increase practitioner suspicion of academics.

The underlying problem is that issue and crisis are genuinely hard to define. The American Robert Heath has observed that no definition of issue management has yet achieved consensus,[2] and the British crisis expert Denis Smith went so far as to say that crisis is one of the most commonly misused words in the English language.[3] It's a bold claim, and Smith explained that the word crisis is often trivialised to the extent that its use 'borders on the bland' and that there is yet no real collective acceptance about a precise meaning.

However, despite such misgiving, we must have a basis for discussion and Table 5.1 is my best effort. The most useful advice my father ever gave me was, 'Have a go. It can't be *that* hard.' That's why I embarked on writing an international *Dictionary of Battles and Sieges*, which took me 10 years and eventually became a three-volume work of 600,000 words.

In exactly that same spirit, my purpose here is not to attempt any definitive answer but rather to provide working definitions of the key terms which form the foundation for discussion throughout this book. Crucially, my table also describes the nature and purpose of these management activities.

Table 5.1 Definitions of key terms

CHALLENGE	MANAGEMENT ACTIVITY	KEY FOCUS
ISSUE Any trend or development—real or perceived—usually at least partly in the public arena, which, if it continues, could have a significant impact on the organisation's financial position, operations, reputation or future interests and requires a structured response	**Issue management** A coordinated cross-functional effort to identify, prioritise and actively manage towards resolution those developments that most impact the organisation and where there is a capacity to make a difference	To utilise resources across the organisation to make a difference and work towards planned, positive outcomes
	Issue communication An element of the broader issue-management process that contributes to and supports the development and implementation of the strategic plan, including message development and effective delivery	To ensure all communication meets stakeholder needs, and supports and is consistent with the strategic plan
EMERGENCY An unplanned or unwanted event that impacts the organisation locally and calls for immediate action. It has a low potential for adverse impact beyond the initial event, but if badly managed could become a crisis.	**Emergency response** An immediate action plan to identify and manage the emergency. Local management is in charge and risk to reputation and media interest beyond the nearby area are low.	To bring the emergency under control and to prevent it from escalating

CHALLENGE	MANAGEMENT ACTIVITY	KEY FOCUS
CRISIS An event or development that can focus unwanted visibility on the organisation and is likely to endanger health or the environment, or seriously impact the organisation's reputation or ability to do business. There's a high potential for adverse impact beyond the initial event.	**Crisis management** A coordinated action that mobilises many functions to respond to the crisis, to assess the potential impact, to provide resources, to minimise physical and reputational damage, to manage all stakeholders, to protect the organisation, and to capture post-event learnings	To use resources from throughout the organisation to bring the crisis under control as quickly and effectively as possible and to minimise damage
	Crisis communication What gets said by the organisation during and after the crisis. It also provides insight into societal concerns to help develop and communicate strategy.	To prioritise concerns among key stakeholders to ensure consistent, accurate messages, and to help protect organisational reputation
DISASTER A major adverse event that affects the broader society, such as natural disasters (e.g. floods, earthquakes or storms), social unrest (e.g. riots or political upheaval) or infrastructure breakdown (e.g. power outages). These may trigger a specific crisis for individual organisations.	**Disaster management** A coordinated response, often managed by statutory or territorial authorities, that mobilises diverse forces. While the event may affect individual organisations, they face less risk to reputation and there is less focus on direct blame or accountability.	For government authorities, to protect people and property. For individual organisations, to protect people and business, with a focus on restoring normal operations and how to play a role in assisting the community.
	Business continuity Coordinated action to ensure an organisation's ability to do business during and after a crisis or disaster. Includes effective back-up and redundancy systems, and key stakeholder communication.	To restore physical operations or to sustain supply to customers

How these key concepts relate to each other and the role of senior executives in the overall process is covered in detail in the next chapter. But we need to spend a little time here talking about the two most important elements which play a critical role in crisis proofing—namely, issue management and crisis management. I call them the conjoined twins of management, and it's impossible to understand either without understanding its relationship with the other.

ISSUE MANAGEMENT

It's important to state at the outset that issue management is not about spin. It's not about image creation. And it's not about using smart communication to put a gloss on poor performance or to hide mistakes. It's a proven executive discipline that aligns with strategic planning and contributes directly to the business bottom line.

It's an effective way for organisations to proactively engage in social, regulatory and political debates which have the potential to inhibit business or damage both individual and corporate reputations. Most importantly, best practice around the world demonstrates that effective issue management requires the involvement and support of leaders and top executives across many functions, departments and businesses in order to deliver the organisation's strategy and to develop and safeguard its good name.

The definition in Table 5.1 describes issue management as a coordinated cross-functional effort to identify, prioritise and actively manage towards resolution those developments that most impact the organisation, and where there is a capacity to make a difference.

In the context of crisis proofing, issue management is a core executive activity to detect problems early, and to take positive planned action to prevent issues developing into crises. While issue management has many purposes, none is more important than crisis prevention.

Two upcoming chapters are devoted to how to implement issue management as a practical process, and the role of executives in using it to help crisis proof your organisation. Those chapters also emphasise that issue management is not just an activity for public relations and communications professionals. Communicators often have 'ownership' of the process and can play a significant role in strategy development and implementation. But issue management truly is a top executive responsibility which cannot be delegated downwards.

For the present I need to introduce two basic aspects of the definition, one trivial and one more fundamental. The trivial aspect is what we should call this executive discipline. Some people call it *issue* management and others call it *issues* management.

This might not seem to be an important distinction, but it cries out to be resolved. Howard Chase, the man who first coined the term and is regarded as the 'father' of the discipline, once quipped that it should be *issue* management not *issues* management in the same way that it is *brain* surgery not *brains* surgery.[4] I would add that in the same way it is house renovation, not houses renovation, and bank reform, not banks reform. Howard Chase knew what he was talking about, so let's have no argument on that subject.

The other, more serious, definitional challenge is to distinguish between a legitimate issue and a day-to-day problem. Issue management is not an all-purpose problem-solving tool, and is too important to be devalued for that purpose. Indeed, understanding the difference between a problem and an issue can have a real bottom-line impact on the way organisational resources are deployed.[5]

Issue management is certainly useful for addressing some problems. But not all problems are issues in terms of requiring a detailed issue management strategy and full mobilisation of resources. And not all issues are problems. Some even represent genuine opportunities.

However, executives generally are expected to handle a wide variety of problems. Indeed, it's been said that problems are the *lingua franca* of business. But a key to successful management is to use the correct problem-solving tool for each challenge. For instance, to understand the financial implications of a proposed project, the correct tool might be *cost–benefit analysis*; to examine in detail why an incident happened, the correct tool might be *root-cause analysis*; and to analyse and assess an organisation's communication capability, the correct tool might be a formal *communications audit*.

In these and many other areas, there is a recognised and well-established management tool to address each particular type of problem. Issue management as a tool is no different, but it's frequently misapplied through careless use of the word 'issue'.

Some managers tend to describe any problem they face as an 'issue', be it market share, staff retention, interest rates, competitive pricing, timing a product launch, cash flow or getting a new advertising campaign completed on schedule. But the distinction between problem and issue has an important implication for top executives and is critical for crisis proofing.

Mislabelling a problem as an issue may simply be careless. Yet it can also be deliberate. Sometimes subordinate managers will characterise a problem as an issue (or even as a crisis) simply to create attention, to free up resources, to access budget or to facilitate change. It's seen as a way of making them or their problem appear more important and maybe trying to get help reaching a decision they are paid to make on their own. But it's a misuse of the language, and maybe they need a sharp reminder of proper process and responsibility.

Using the right language and the right tool is no trivial discussion. One of the essential skills and responsibilities that generally separate executives from other employees is a capacity to identify problems, and to solve them effectively.

Broadly speaking, *problems* are day-to-day challenges that functional or departmental managers need to just get on and deal with. By contrast, *issues* warrant the application of a formal, cross-functional issue management process, and typically have some particular qualities.

CHARACTERISTICS OF ISSUES

Issues typically:
- involve external parties (and are thus at least partly beyond the organisation's direct control)
- have no black and white or 'right' answer
- may involve public policy or regulation
- are driven by emotions rather than hard data
- happen in public or in the news media (conventional or online)
- may be controversial, with strongly held contending opinions
- are likely to attract interest beyond the immediate stakeholders
- have a moral or ethical component
- have the greatest potential risk in the event of failure
- and, most crucially for crisis proofing, if left unmanaged have the capacity to become a crisis and threaten the entire organisation.

I once heard this important distinction neatly expressed as: Problems are *solved*, but issues need to be *resolved*. This is much more than simple semantics or a clever maxim. To take a dictionary definition approach, to *solve* is to explain; to find the answer or solution—for example, when solving a mathematical equation, completing a crossword puzzle or calculating the load characteristics on a new bridge. You know there's a right answer. You just need to find and present the solution.

To resolve is quite different. The Oxford English Dictionary says to *resolve* is to separate a thing into its component parts or elements; to reduce by mental analysis into more elementary forms, principles or relations; to change from discord to harmony; or to determine on a course of action. It may sound more complicated than it really is, but pursuit of resolution is very much the hallmark of issues. There is seldom any ready-made solution or 'right answer'.

In this way, unlike a problem, which can be solved, an issue has to be resolved. This means seeking out and developing a balanced way forward from a range of possible actions, all of which may have conflicting risks and rewards. Furthermore, the absence of a single 'right answer' reinforces the need for a process that helps to define and clarify the issue; to set a clear, agreed objective; and to develop and implement effective strategies and tactics. This is where issue management delivers its essential value—providing a framework and a management discipline to establish a process as part of crisis proofing.

Let's use a hypothetical scenario to illustrate the difference. You own a property where you want to build an office block, but the site is rather shady with limited natural light for much of the year. This *should* be defined as a problem, because it's technical, with recognised solutions which can be found in the architecture design handbook. It's based on demonstrable fact, and the results can be measured, either in a computer model before construction or in real life after the building is complete. Moreover, this is an impersonal discussion, balancing costs and benefits, which takes place in the privacy of the architect's office.

Now imagine that the design for the proposed development has been made public and it is vehemently opposed by nearby residents. They say the building is ugly, inappropriate and unsympathetic to the local environment.

What you have on your hands now is not a problem but an issue. It's no longer technical, but emotional. It's no longer simply based on demonstrable fact, but depends heavily on opinion. What is 'inappropriate'? Values are hard to measure. How do you measure ugliness? It no longer relies on technical solutions but solutions that have to be negotiated, and not just with impersonal professionals but also with angry residents who have personal commitment to uncompromising positions. And, of course, it's no longer being resolved in private but at angry public protests, on the high-profile picket line, in the news media and in politically charged planning hearings. It's gone from being a private problem to a highly contentious public issue which could threaten the reputation of the developer and could cause costly delays and modifications. And if it was sufficiently delayed or even blocked by planners, it could trigger a financial crisis.

While this is a simple example, the list and variety of possible issues an organisation might face is seemingly inexhaustible. Here are just a few potential scenarios which meet some or all of the criteria listed above to constitute a legitimate issue—that is, they involve external parties, have no 'right answer', are driven by emotion rather than hard data and so on. Such scenarios could include:

- addressing regulatory concerns over use of an environmentally sensitive chemical
- recognising public awareness about identify theft to position new security technology
- anticipatory planning for adverse public reaction to scheduled plant closures or job layoffs
- ongoing accusations of racial or sexual harassment or discrimination, or workplace bullying
- responding to online rumours of faulty products or rude service
- meeting community opposition to controversial zoning proposals
- addressing hostile response to foreign buyout of an iconic local brand
- promoting public acceptance of nuclear power generation
- combating parental resistance to vaccinating babies against childhood diseases
- reacting to charges of worker exploitation by contractors in the developing world

- managing hostility to introducing recycled water into a town drinking supply
- responding to an internet campaign alleging that charity donations have been misspent
- facing anger over demolition of historic buildings to make way for a new highway
- preparing for reputational damage from upcoming high-profile litigation
- countering claims that product packaging comes from endangered rainforest timber
- encouraging legislative support for wind farms.

Not all issues are as obvious as these, and obvious issues are sometimes deliberately ignored. But any one of the issues listed here has a very real potential to become a crisis—operational, financial, legal or reputational.

CRISIS MANAGEMENT

That takes us from issue management to the second of the important elements which play a critical role in crisis proofing—namely, crisis management. The broad definition in Table 5.1 says a crisis is an event or development that can focus unwanted visibility on the organisation and is likely to endanger health or the environment or seriously impact the organisation's reputation or ability to do business.

But there are some other very important characteristics of a crisis which distinguish it from other organisational risks. Like Taleb's Black Swan events (introduced in Chapter 4), a crisis is a low-probability, high-impact event, which may or may not emerge from an issue. In fact, one of the easiest ways to capture the defining characteristics of a crisis is to compare and contrast it with an issue.

It's a major mistake to treat issue and crisis as interchangeable terms. Not only do they have distinct meanings, but they also need a different management response. Of course, they are closely related. Issues can be the warning signs that a crisis is possible. And issue management can be regarded as a powerful tool for crisis prevention. In fact, a crisis can be described as an issue that *wasn't* managed.

However, issues and crises are very different in nature and need to be managed in different ways. Let me put it this way: issue management is steering the ship out of troubled waters, while crisis management is trying to save the ship after it has struck an iceberg. In other words, it would make no sense at all to order a change of course to avoid icebergs if the ship was already sinking and people were drowning.

In a management context, that difference—and why it is important—falls under eight key categories.

EIGHT DIFFERENCES BETWEEN ISSUES AND CRISES

(1) Choice
Issue management is designed to allow you to explore all possible choices, weigh the benefits of each option, and make an informed decision. Typically, the more you explore the issue the more possible choices open up. For example, you might analyse the communication benefits of a media release versus a press conference versus a one-on-one interview, and the options of newspaper versus radio versus television versus social media. In a crisis, the choices become fewer as the situation deteriorates. When a television news crew and the media pack are waiting down at reception, discussing the options of media release versus a press conference versus a one-on-one interview is no longer relevant.

(2) Certainty
When facing an issue, you can research every possible fact, analyse the views of key stakeholders, and obtain independent expert opinion to ensure nothing has been overlooked. In a crisis, you often have to make decisions without knowing all the facts—when it is still unclear exactly what happened and why, let alone who was responsible and what it will cost. But you still have to go with what you know.

(3) Urgency
Closely related to choice is the question of time pressure. In issue management you usually have time to fully assess and make the best decision. In a crisis you are frequently under pressure to make a decision right now. In fact, the best decision in a crisis might well be the one you *should* have made 30 minutes ago.

(4) Cost
When you are facing an issue, potential cost is typically an important consideration in deciding how to proceed. It might, for example, be cheaper to simply cease manufacturing a troublesome product than to publicly defend the product or to implement restrictive new regulatory requirements. However, it's pretty much inevitable that as an issue deteriorates, potential costs will increase. Your own issue management plan, implemented in your own time frame, will almost invariably be less costly than the plan imposed on you by regulators. By contrast, cost is usually not a main consideration when facing a crisis. For example, if heavy equipment is needed to rescue men from a mine collapse, or if you have to undertake costly scientific tests, or if you need to hire a bulldozer to stop leaking chemicals reaching a river; no one will say, 'but there's no provision for that in this year's budget'. It's only when the crisis is over that lawyers and accountants will start to argue about the dollars and cents.

(5) Continuity
Issue management is a normal executive activity, done according to schedule in office hours while business continues. A crisis, by definition, is outside normal experience. It causes top executives to drop all other priorities, and it may severely disrupt continuity of the organisation's core activity.

(6) Duration
Issues can extend over months, years or even decades. Take, for example, the seemingly endless issue of anti-smoking efforts, or the sustained campaigns against whaling or rainforest destruction. By contrast, crises generally have a more explicit time frame and eventually come to an end. Although it may not seem like it at the time to the people involved, crises—like emergencies—do tend to have a beginning, a middle and an end. However, the impact of the crisis, particularly financial or reputational, may persist for much longer. Think of the *Exxon Valdez* disaster in Alaska in 1989, which remains today a blot on the company's reputation almost three decades later, or the *Deepwater Horizon* oil spill in the Gulf of Mexico in 2010, which will likely affect BP's reputation for an entire generation.

(7) Impact
An issue is an identified event or trend which could have a significant impact on the organisation. That impact is often measured in terms such as market share, reputation, community concern, licence to operate, recruitment, financial cost,

regulatory compliance, stock price, capacity to retain and expand business, and so on. A crisis may have some of those same impacts in the longer run, but in the more immediate term a genuine crisis is an event which threatens life, property or the environment, or threatens the capacity of the organisation to carry on business or achieve its strategic objectives.

(8) Outcomes

It's when you consider intended outcomes that the difference between an issue and a crisis becomes most stark. The purpose of issue management is to identify potential problems early and develop proactive plans to work towards planned outcomes which are positive for the organisation. By contrast, despite the theorists who claim a crisis is both a threat and opportunity, the reality is that a crisis typically endangers the entire organisation, and the primary objective during a crisis is to minimise damage and help the organisation survive. Or, as I said before, the difference between planning to avoid danger at sea and scrambling desperately to save the ship after it has started to sink.

LANGUAGE AND POSITIONING

Crisis management is a coordinated action that mobilises many functions across the organisation to identify potential crises and to develop an effective plan to respond in order to minimise physical and reputational damage. But beyond that basic definition, there is one crucial distinction which underlies the whole principal of crisis proofing—namely, that tactical crisis response is not the same as strategic crisis management. One is about what to do when it all goes pear-shaped. The other also incorporates ways to prevent crises happening in the first place and how to manage the consequential risks that arise once the triggering crisis event is over. Or, as it has been vividly described, *crisis management* is not the same as *crash management*—which is what to do when everything falls apart.[6]

Before I expand on this crucial distinction, I would like to mention one further reason why it's essential to get the language right. An important role of senior executives is to determine the management structure of the organisation. Properly understanding crisis and issue management leads to how the two functions are positioned within the organisation.

Crisis management can be structurally positioned in a number of different ways; for example, alongside security and emergency response and assigned to operational managers and technicians; within the CEO's staff and aligned with strategic planning; or positioned primarily as a communication role within the public relations function. Each of these models, and others, can be found within current practice; each derives to a large extent from the way the discipline is internally defined and perceived; and each has direct implications for the way resources are allocated. This important organisational decision is a key executive responsibility.

The same question of organisational structure also applies to issue management, which may be positioned primarily as a communication role within the public relations function; positioned as a strategic activity within businesses; positioned wholly within the government affairs function; or shared between communications practitioners 'owning' the process and businesses and functions 'owning' the issue. Again, each approach has implications for the way the discipline is resourced and perceived, both within the organisation and in relation to external stakeholders. And again, it's a key executive responsibility.

Across these and similar applied models are overlaid other important organisational perspectives, such as whether issue and crisis management are seen primarily as head office or regional responsibilities; whether the most senior executives are directly involved; and, most critically, the degree to which functional silos and turf wars hinder coordination between disciplines.

In terms of operational practice, there are many different models, and the optimal structure will vary for different organisations. But whatever the organisation, everyone in it needs a common understanding, and that requires meaningful, unambiguous language.

In the mid-1960s, in a US Supreme Court case about whether a particular movie should be classified as obscene, Justice Potter Stewart famously wrote: 'I shall not today attempt to further define the kinds of material I understand to be embraced [as 'hard core pornography'] ... But I know it when I see it.'

When it comes to issues and crises, it's no use the CEO saying that he or she will 'know it when they see it'. Everyone in the organisation needs to have the same understanding of the nature and parameters of each discipline, how they interface and how each function or division is involved. The next chapter demonstrates these interfaces and reinforces that crisis proofing demands the different activities form part of an integrated process, owned and driven from the top of the organisation.

CHAPTER KEY TAKEAWAY
There's no value in worrying excessively about competing language and definitions. However, you need to know exactly what you mean, and so does everyone else in the organisation.

CHAPTER 6

FITTING IT ALL TOGETHER

One of the most important aspects of crisis proofing is recognising how all the different elements fit together.

My relational model which follows has two central purposes. The first is to illustrate the relationship between the core activities which produce effective crisis proofing and the role of senior managers in these activities.

The second purpose is to reinforce that crisis proofing is an integrated cycle which involves top executives long before the triggering event and continues through the post-crisis phase and beyond.

In Chapter 1 I briefly introduced the broad idea that crisis proofing demands four interlocking steps—crisis preparedness, crisis prevention, crisis incident management and post-crisis management. The model details each of these phases.[1]

This approach highlights that crisis management is not a stepwise, linear process, but comprises clusters of related and integrated disciplines. While these may be undertaken in sequential fashion, some of the activities may operate simultaneously. In fact, two of the major quadrants—crisis preparedness and crisis prevention—most often *should* happen at the same time. What this means is that getting prepared for a crisis striking, and taking action to help prevent a crisis, need to happen in parallel.

Finally, the model illustrates two other important aspects of crisis proofing. First, that it's divided into two distinct elements—pre-crisis management (what to do before a crisis strikes) and crisis management

FIGURE 6.1 EFFECTIVE CRISIS MANAGEMENT: A RELATIONAL MODEL

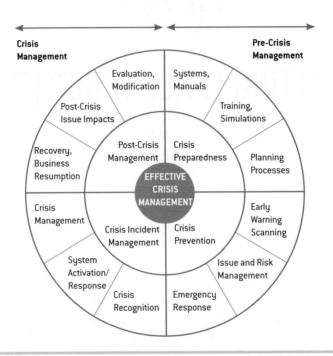

(what to do during and after a crisis). And second, that the flow of activities circle back to deliver learning and continuous improvement.

There is a disappointingly large volume of literature about why and how organisations fail to learn from crises. Effective crisis proofing needs organisations to learn not only from their own crises but also from crises which strike other organisations—maybe in the same industry or the same area. As some wise person is supposed to have said: 'It's always cheaper and less painful to learn from other people's mistakes rather than making them all yourself.'

CRISIS PREPAREDNESS QUADRANT

Crisis preparedness is the group of activities I previously compared to taking out home insurance. These activities don't prevent a crisis striking, but they do help prepare your organisation to respond well and to minimise any damage.

The first important aspect of the crisis preparedness quadrant focuses on systems, manuals and other crisis-management infrastructure, such as having equipment in place, a 'war room' established, resources allocated and documentation prepared. Key items in being well prepared typically include selection and induction of the crisis management team; agreement on reporting and authority lines in the event of a crisis; functional checklists; pre-prepared materials such as approved media statement templates, organisational information, product data sheets and executive profiles; staff and stakeholder contact lists; and logistical resources for the centralised crisis management centre, such as phones, radio, television, computer access and back-up files of all material. (We'll come to discuss these items in later chapters.)

This group of activities might seem rather tactical or procedural, but it demands executive suite oversight. Some items can properly be delegated to functional specialists, such as putting the crisis manual together, preparing the 'war room' and developing checklists and written materials. However, other activities, such as appointing the crisis team members and agreeing on crisis reporting lines, demand leadership and direction from the top. Later we'll cover the preferred make-up of the crisis management team and how the team works under pressure. But there should be no misunderstanding that the preparedness phase of crisis proofing needs top executive input and leadership.

Obviously none of this preparation is of real value without hands-on familiarisation programs such as table-top exercises, live simulations and communication system testing, which comprises the second important aspect of crisis preparedness. While most organisations regularly practise emergency response—such as fire drills and office evacuation—experience shows the crisis management manual is often left unrehearsed in a dusty three-ring binder. As a result, when a crisis strikes, the team is unprepared and the manual itself proves to be out of date. To be properly prepared, crisis management response should be formally exercised at least once, if not twice, a year.

This demands time and commitment from busy managers, and it's top executives who have to insist on participation. Having run scores of exercises and simulations, I know only too well that some crisis management team members will always have 'good reasons' for not attending, with a raft of other things taking higher priority. Can we schedule a different date? Why do I have to be involved? Can I send my deputy? Is this really business-critical?

As I always tell any reluctant participants, if it was a real crisis you would drop everything and clear your diary—for days or even weeks. So why can't you allocate one day or even a half-day to help make sure you are properly prepared if a crisis strikes? Ultimately, though, it is the CEO or crisis team chairperson who needs to set an example and enforce participation.

The third aspect of crisis preparedness is establishing firm planning processes, and the elements of how to develop and implement a crisis plan are described in detail in Chapter 10.

Organisations are often loath to talk about crisis preparedness (or lack of it) and I have already mentioned the high cost of not being prepared. While it's not so easy to find examples of how preparedness provides specific dividends, one high-profile instance of effective crisis planning is the case of financial services giant Morgan Stanley.

A LESSON IN THE VALUE OF PREPAREDNESS

Morgan Stanley was the single largest tenant in New York's World Trade Center. Following the 1993 terrorist attack on the building, when it took four hours for company employees to evacuate, VP of Security Rick Rescorla upgraded the company crisis plan and evacuation procedures, including establishment of a back-up site 22 blocks away.

More than eight years later, when the first hijacked plane hit the World Trade Center on 11 September 2001, Rescorla immediately started evacuating almost 3000 Morgan Stanley employees, even though the public address system was telling occupants to remain in place. Within 20 minutes the company's back-up site had been activated and senior management had established a command centre at a second back-up site.

Thousands died when the twin towers collapsed and over 500 businesses in the buildings were destroyed. But 2687 Morgan Stanley employees were safely evacuated and only six lost their lives, including Rescorla himself who went back to rescue other people. The man was a hero in life and in death.² When the New York Stock Exchange resumed a week later, the company was fully functioning.

CRISIS PREVENTION QUADRANT

It's axiomatic that the best method of crisis management is to take steps to prevent the crisis happening in the first place. Unlike the crisis preparedness quadrant of the model—which focuses on getting ready to respond when the triggering event has occurred—the activities and processes within the crisis prevention quadrant are designed to help reduce the likelihood of the crisis occurring at all. This quadrant also highlights the preventive role of *other* management disciplines and how they fit into the context of crisis proofing.

The first step is early warning and scanning. This involves a range of processes which should be well known to managers. They include audits, preventive maintenance, issue and environmental scanning, social forecasting, anticipatory management and future studies. All of these can play a major role in the crisis prevention phase.

However, simply receiving a warning or advance information is clearly not the same as doing something about it. We have previously met examples of crises where 'red flags' were ignored, including the Pike River mine disaster in New Zealand and financial scandal at the French bank Société Générale.

In the infamous demise of Enron, one of the seminal moments was when the board agreed to waive the company's code of ethics to accommodate dubious 'partnerships' promoted by the CFO Andrew Fastow. Nell Minow, founder of the board watchdog group Corporate Library, later called it 'a red flag the size of Alaska'.³

Another costly crisis where warning signs were ignored arose after Victoria's Black Saturday bushfires in February 2009, one of Australia's worst natural disasters, which resulted in 173 deaths in a single afternoon. In the extensive inquiries and court cases which followed, it was revealed that there had been clear warnings about allegedly inadequate maintenance of power lines, which caused at least some of the fires. The power company and its utility manager (and their insurers) eventually agreed to pay out close to A$700 million 'without admission of liability'.[4]

Taking action on early warnings is where the established disciplines of issue management and risk management—the second part of this quadrant—link directly to other management tools and processes. Both are strategic activities with significance far beyond just early warning for crisis prevention. They provide a framework to help identify problems early, and to effectively manage those problems to reduce the chance of them becoming a crisis. Moreover, each of them requires the full involvement and support of senior executives.

The third factor of crisis prevention is less obvious, and I know from experience is more controversial—namely, emergency response. At first glance, emergency response seems like a standalone process which hasn't got much to do with crisis prevention. Not every crisis is triggered by an emergency, and not every emergency leads to a crisis. Yet the link is strong. Any emergency that is badly handled can lead directly to a crisis, especially when the impact of the emergency starts to spread, or because of perceived mismanagement, or past history.

A small fire in an electricity substation could cause a brief power blackout, for instance, and that would be classified as an emergency. But if the recovery system failed because of management cost-cutting, or the blackout spread to other areas and lasted hours or even days, then the power company could be facing a real crisis. Similarly, if a chemical factory had a moderate-sized spill it would probably constitute an emergency. But a series of repeated spills over a short period could well trigger regulatory intervention, a crisis of confidence and damaged reputation.

There's no question that organisations need effective emergency response as a core protective measure. But to optimise crisis prevention they also need training that would enable emergency responders and local managers to identify the possibility that it *could* become a crisis. They also need to have processes in place which allow the organisation to escalate in a planned way from emergency response to crisis incident management. That link is essential and it won't happen without direction from the top.

CRISIS INCIDENT MANAGEMENT QUADRANT

If you've done any reading in the area of crisis management, you'll know that much of the literature is very tactical in nature. It typically focuses primarily on the quadrant called crisis preparedness—planning, manuals and training—and then on the quadrant about managing the triggering event. Crisis incident management is certainly a critical and high-profile phase, and it deserves close attention, particularly from top management.

The first step is crisis recognition, and that is a definite skill. It requires judgement, leadership and honesty, and sometimes senior executives will try to deny that a crisis is threatening or has already happened. Take the case of former FIFA President Sepp Blatter. When the football governing body was accused of corruption in early 2011, he famously responded; 'Crisis? What is a crisis? We are not in a crisis, we are only in some difficulties and these difficulties will be solved inside our family.' Four years later, facing renewed allegations of corruption at FIFA, Blatter initially tried to blame 'discrimination and racism', but was finally forced to resign.

One of the important roles of a crisis leader is to recognise that a crisis actually exists. That might seem like an over-simplification, but it is not as easy as it sounds. There is an understandable natural inclination *not* to declare a crisis and to claim that everything is under control. This might be justified by a desire to protect the share price or to avoid damage to reputation. Indeed, it can be easier for executives to expend effort denying there is a crisis rather than dealing with the crisis itself. As the old joke reminds us: Denial not just a river in Africa.

CRISIS? WHAT CRISIS?

Senior managers sometimes seem to have a burning need to deny that there is a crisis. The crisis expert Christophe Roux-Dufort relates how he interviewed the vice-president of a French airline which had a plane crash into Mont Saint-Odile on approach to Strasbourg Airport, killing 87 people on board. Based on the fact that on the morning after the crash the level of seats reserved on their flights had not changed one iota, the airline official asserted that it wasn't a crisis at all.[5]

While absolute denial of a crisis may not be common, executives more often try to deny the extent or seriousness of the problem. Take the Ford–Firestone crisis of 2000, when 6.5 million tyres were recalled after more than 200 deaths attributed to tyre failures, over half of them involving Ford SUVs. Both Ford and Firestone had plenty of warnings from their overseas operations. Ford acknowledged it had replaced tyres on almost 47,000 SUVs in Saudi Arabia, Venezuela, Thailand and Malaysia, but claimed it was a 'customer satisfaction issue' in hot climates where tyres were more vulnerable to problems.

Despite explicit warnings from regional managers, the company insisted that tyre failures in overseas markets reflected driving conditions unique to those countries and they 'didn't immediately suspect similar issues in the US'. Firestone agreed that driving conditions in the Middle East were 'extreme and unusual'.

In the wake of well over 100 deaths in the United States and the ensuing recall, Ford CEO Jacques Nasser admitted before a congressional committee that, despite replacing tyres overseas, Ford held off taking action in the United States 'because review of its various databases assured the company there was not a problem here'.[6]

The database might have suggested 'not a problem here', but the result was one of the largest tyre recalls in history, second only to the *previous* Firestone recall, 22 years earlier in 1978.

Two separate forces are at play when senior managers attempt to deny there is a major problem. The first is a *bias towards optimism*. Doubtless you've seen graphs of sales projections which simply use this year's sales plus a fairly random percentage increase projected out into the future. The assumption is that nothing can go wrong and growth is sure to continue. Sadly, we know where that leads.

The same applied to unwary investors who convinced themselves that 'real estate values never go down'—then found themselves out on the street in the wake of the Global Financial Crisis of 2007–08.

Governments notoriously suffer the same bias towards optimism. In August 1914, at the outbreak of World War 1, the public message was 'we'll be home by Christmas'. The authorities just didn't say which Christmas, which turned out to be Christmas four years later. And the same unfounded optimism has applied to just about every war since—think Korea, Vietnam, Iraq and Afghanistan.

The second force at play is *wilful blindness*. It is the other side of the bias towards optimism, when you ignore evidence that everything is not so good at all. Like when you go to court and your lawyer tells you that you have a strong case. The other side's lawyer is telling them exactly the same, but everyone knows you can't both win. In the corporate context, this can be seen in the top executives who don't or won't hear bad news.

Following the BP Texas City refinery disaster in 2005 which killed 15 men, the then rising executive Tony Hayward said:

> We have a leadership style that is too directive and doesn't listen sufficiently well. The top of the organisation doesn't listen sufficiently to what the bottom is saying.[7]

Hayward later became BP CEO, saying he wanted to introduce a new safety culture, but failed in the face of the even bigger *Deepwater Horizon* disaster in Gulf of Mexico.

In his definitive analysis of the Texas City disaster, industrial disaster expert Andrew Hopkins said mindful leaders recognise that it is often difficult to convey bad news upwards and that they should welcome bad news. In fact, he went even further. Mindful leaders, he said, 'develop systems to reward the bearers of bad news'.[8]

A recent management report captured this broad idea very nicely: 'One of the most important things is having people around you who tell you how wrong you are.'[9]

THE CHALLENGE OF IDENTIFYING A POTENTIAL CRISIS

Most CEOs are in the center of a fortified palace, and news from the outside has to percolate through layers of people from the periphery where the action is. I was one of the last to understand the implications of the Pentium crisis. It took a barrage of relentless criticism to make me realize that something had changed and that we needed to adapt to the new environment.[10]

Intel CEO Andy Grove in the wake of his company's famous Pentium chip crisis.

A crisis is usually easy to identify when it is triggered by an emergency or major physical incident, such as a fatal mine accident or a major warehouse fire. It's much harder to identify when an ongoing problem has the potential to become a crisis, or has already become a crisis. That's when, instead of a specific triggering event, there is what's sometimes called a *creeping crisis*, such as a series of computer security breaches, persistent management misbehaviour over time, or (as in the Pentium chip case) a growing tide of product failure. This is when judgement is needed in order to activate the formal crisis management response process—the second facet of the crisis incident management quadrant.

The American Steven Fink wrote one of the most important early books on crisis management, in which he firmly positioned crisis management as a formal executive responsibility.[11] He warned:

> You should accept almost as a universal truth that when a crisis strikes it
> will be accompanied by a host of diversionary problems. As a manager,
> your task is to identify the real crisis.

Needless to say, crisis recognition alone is not enough. Response systems must be activated immediately and rapidly. The earlier discussion on Hurricane Katrina in 2005 was a brutal example of slow and inadequate system activation and response at many levels. It was also a reminder that not only should top executives know how to activate the response system, but in addition everyone affected by that system should know exactly where they need to go and what they need to do.

Beyond crisis recognition and system activation lies the central activity of managing the actual crisis—this third element of the quadrant. Managing any crisis incident has two distinct streams of activity. One is responding to the triggering event and mitigating subsequent damage. The other critical stream is stakeholder management and media response. We'll explore both of these aspects in due course.

POST-CRISIS MANAGEMENT QUADRANT

The fourth quadrant of the relational model addresses the risk of lasting financial or reputational damage that is sometimes the main concern after the crisis incident itself has been resolved. It's the area which is most often neglected, and it's an area which top management often get wrong—and suffer the consequences.

The obvious and best understood first step in post-crisis management is recovery and the resumption of operations—commonly known as business continuity. This generally sees a focus on operational resumption, financial costs, market retention, business momentum and share price protection. Many business continuity programs concentrate primarily on protecting the organisation against infrastructure problems such as power outages, computer failure and breakdown of logistics and distributions systems. Indeed, there's a rich library of resources to help implement recovery, most of it very tactical.

But it is a serious error to think that post-crisis management and business continuity are the same thing. That's so important I need to say it again. *Post-crisis management and business continuity are not the same thing.*

When I carry out process audits for companies to assess their crisis management capability and documentation, they sometimes present me with what is really a business continuity plan. Business recovery is very important and it's entirely proper that senior executives give it a high priority. However, the reality is that the risks to an organisation post-crisis can be even greater than during the crisis itself. In fact this critical period has been called the 'crisis after the crisis'.[12]

Long after the organisation has returned to 'business as usual', what remains is the very real threat of post-crisis issue impacts—the second facet of the post-crisis management quadrant. These can include coronial inquests, judicial inquiries, prosecution and litigation, which can last months or even years. For an example of long-term litigation damage, look no further than the *Exxon Valdez* oil spill in Alaska in 1989. A jury in 1994 originally ordered Exxon to pay US$5 billion in compensation to local residents and businesses, roughly equivalent to its annual profit at the time. Following what one legal expert described as 'scorched earth litigation' involving scores of petitions and appeals and over 1000 legal briefs, requests and demands,[13] that amount was progressively reduced by 2008 to just US$507 million, plus about US$480 million in interest. By then, a large number of claimants had already died waiting for the outcome and Exxon-Mobil delivered a record-breaking annual profit of US$45 billion. It was only in 2009—after 20 years of continuous legal wrangling and damaging headlines—that the company finally gave up its last line of appeal.

These longer-term, reputation-sapping risks need to be effectively planned for and managed, and there is no area of integrated crisis management where top executive involvement is more important. Furthermore, it can't be delegated to lawyers and public relations people, as I will discuss later.

This dangerous period can produce prolonged reputational damage and seemingly endless media scrutiny. And it's the period which can determine organisational survival or terminal failure.

Organisational survival is often directly related not only to how well the organisation tried to prevent the crisis and how well its plans and processes operated in response, but also to how well it managed communication to the public and key stakeholders and their *perception* of how well the organisation conducted itself after the crisis event was over.

The final element of the post-crisis management quadrant is evaluation and modification—to undertake a root cause analysis; to honestly assess the performance of management and the organisation; to review the existing process; and, hopefully, to implement change and improvement.

This phase can be difficult, because there is a very human desire to move on rather than to dwell on what went wrong. And that option is made even more attractive when you consider the conclusion of the Institute for Crisis Management that more than half of all crises are caused by management. Yet the post-crisis phase provides a genuine opportunity to change whatever helped create the potential for a crisis in the first place. It enables the organisation to identify and correct mistakes, which in turn leads right back to improving crisis preparedness and crisis prevention.

The chapters which follow explore the key elements of the relational model shown here and detail the practical steps you can take to crisis proof your organisation.

CHAPTER KEY TAKEAWAY
A crisis manual that sits on the shelf and an occasional crisis simulation are great, but doing *only* that and thinking you are fully protected can be a very costly mistake.

CHAPTER 7

ACTIONS YOU CAN TAKE TO PREVENT A CRISIS HAPPENING IN THE FIRST PLACE

Crisis prevention is a key element of the combined processes of integrated crisis management which support crisis proofing. And of all the activities associated with crisis prevention, by far the most significant is issue management.

Many experienced senior managers enact various aspects of issue management without consciously recognising that it is a formal set of tools and processes. That's because it's a fairly intuitive exercise—identifying issues and potential crises early and taking proactive, planned action to prevent them escalating into a real crisis.

Naturally there is a lot more to it, and to be truly effective it demands top executive involvement and leadership. You don't have to become an expert, but you do need a working understanding of the tools and processes of issue management and their role in crisis proofing.

Across my regular workshops and seminars, the two most frequently asked questions are: (a) Where do issues come from? and (b) How do I know which ones to work on?

These two questions are vital to crisis proofing because they form the basis of both identifying potential crises before they happen and helping prioritise effort to prevent issues from escalating into full-blown crises.

The process for identifying risk and issue threats can be as basic or as sophisticated as suits your organisation. Some executives evidently feel the need to employ long-term strategists, trend analysts, futurologists and other crystal-ball gazers. In reality, the identification process—sometimes labelled environmental scanning, horizon scanning or scouting the terrain—can be much more prosaic.

But whatever your chosen degree of complexity and sophistication—or whether you use specialist expert advisors—senior management input and involvement is essential. The model shown in Table 7.1 captures varying levels of formality used to identify issues, and summarises briefly how these approaches might operate in a real organisation.

My purpose here is not to be prescriptive about the nature of the process and the level of formality. What's more important is that the agreed methodology is appropriate for your organisation, considering factors such as its size, exposure, history and geographic spread.

In some multinational companies, such as in the issue-rich energy and chemical sector, the process is sometimes taken to very advanced levels of sophistication. Dupont pioneered the use of a Strategic Issue Council to identify emerging issues that might otherwise fall between organisational boxes. It has a cross-business/cross-functional membership, supported by a team of government affairs and issue management professionals.

For its part, Shell added another level of input, undertaking regular large-scale scenario reviews that draw on people from across its worldwide structure, not just to identify probable issues but also to 'consider a range of plausible futures and how these could emerge from the realities of today', which then feed directly into strategic planning.[1]

However, for many companies this degree of formality is neither appropriate nor necessary. But for organisations at all levels, a team approach has been shown to be very effective, especially where the team

Table 7.1 Approaches to identifying emerging issues

MORE FORMAL ↑ ... ↓ **LESS FORMAL**

Dedicated resources	Online systems or a formal monitoring group
Cross-business cross-function teams	Meet regularly to identify issues; IM staff in support to provide structure and tools
Regular inter-function review, including issue management, government affairs, public affairs and communications	Brainstorming, issue reviews and joint assessment; mainly by communication professionals
External audits, and community and corporate advisory panels	Multi-faceted commitment to an 'outside-in' perspective
Government relations scanning capability	Mainly through legislative and regulatory review and public opinion polling
Employee scanning capability and a formal process for raising issues	Particularly through public/ stakeholder interface and participation in trade associations
Electronic services	Internal or commercial monitoring of mainstream and social media
No formal process, but an integral part of public affairs/issue management	Largely based on professional experience and goal-setting

Adapted with permission from the Australasian Centre for Corporate Public Affairs

has cross-business/cross-functional participation and support. The cross-functional method has some particular benefits as it:

- reduces silo thinking
- prevents issues falling between groups
- addresses issues that cover multiple businesses, functions or geographies
- includes issues that exist primarily as a corporate function
- ensures consistency of approach and governance across the organisation.

Some organisations extend this approach by broadening the review process to involve external opinion. For example, the multinational chemical company BASF gives priority to an outside view, with a Global Stakeholder Survey scanned into what they call a materiality matrix.[2] This external element helps a company gain a diverse and sometimes critical 'outside-in perspective', particularly on contentious issues such as environment, health and safety, and sustainability.

Whatever issue scanning process you choose, useful sources of live and emerging issues are, in fact, often quite simple and easily overlooked, and don't need to rely on excessively complicated tools. As New York PR veteran George McGrath says: 'For most organisations, key issues will be found from reading headlines rather than tea-leaves.'[3]

ISSUE SOURCES

The first and most obvious source of potential issues is effectively monitoring the mainstream news media and social media. This can range from reading the local newspaper, watching the television news and using a daily online word search, right through to comprehensive professional monitoring. Often it is a combination of both.

However, I'm constantly surprised by how many organisations fail to effectively do even basic media monitoring. Case studies and news reports reveal that organisations are constantly caught unaware by issues that emerge in the media and develop rapidly. Regardless of the changing importance of traditional versus digital media, and the roles of professional reporters and 'citizen journalists', news scanning remains a crucial element in issue identification.

Later I will be discussing more fully the crisis which struck the New Zealand dairy giant Fonterra in 2013 when it announced a global recall of product thought to be contaminated with the deadly toxin botulism. The case is important for a number of reasons, none of them flattering to the company. But for the moment the key point is that their greatest single export market was China, yet they were forced to admit they had no process in place for monitoring the Chinese online services Weibo and Weichat, which were the principal forums for critical consumer backlash. The result was failure to understand the depth of the crisis Fonterra's mistaken recall had provoked.[4] (Weibo is a Facebook/Twitter hybrid and Weichat is an instant messaging system.)

SOURCES OF POTENTIAL ISSUES BEYOND MAINSTREAM AND SOCIAL MEDIA

- industry and political conferences
- scientific and trade publications
- regulatory and legislative updates
- trade association meetings and newsletters
- executive forums
- your organisation's own business/operating units
- published information from critics and opponents
- industry and business allies, and joint venture partners
- surveys of clients, customers, employees and other stakeholders
- analysis by experts
- feedback from staff who deal with external people and organisations.

Most of the less obvious issue scanning sources are relatively inexpensive. Yet they are often under-utilised, despite the fact that they can yield priceless information and warnings. And a number of these sources directly involve the executive group. When you attended an industry or political conference, or a trade association meeting or executive forum, are you alert to information about potential issues and crisis threats? Do you feed this back to the organisation? When you meet with industry or business allies or joint venture partners, is the focus solely on the procedural agenda (and good food and drink) or are you making time to identify trends and shared issues which could affect your organisation or could be a shared crisis risk? And do you have a process for feeding this information into the evaluation process? Top executives are in many respects the eyes and ears of the organisation at a strategic level and need to be an active part of the scanning and monitoring process.

There's a common saying that 'Organisations don't know what the organisation knows', and this is very important when it comes to identifying risks and issues and implementing crisis proofing. In fact, internal sources are often under-appreciated, even though an organisation's employees may be close to potential issues. For instance, a pattern of complaints received by Customer Service can signal a potential issue in product quality or customer relations, but that potential risk will be recognised only if the information is collated, reported up the organisation, and acted upon.

Case analysis around the world shows that after almost every crisis or major issue, someone inside the organisation will come forward and say: 'Oh yes, I knew about that.' Sometimes they will add: 'I tried to raise it, but no one took any notice.' What can you do to reduce the likelihood of this sort of communication failure happening in your organisation?

One answer is to ensure that formal channels exist for managers at all levels to identify and elevate potential issues. And the same applies to employees at other levels. People throughout the organisation need to know how to raise a potential issue, and be confident they will be listened to. Moreover, best practice issue management requires a mechanism to receive and evaluate that information, and to feed back to the person who raised the concern.

LINKING ISSUES AND RISK

Around about this point in the scanning and assessment process, you might be thinking: 'We have a risk management department. Aren't they responsible for this sort of thing?' That's understandable, but it's the wrong answer. Or, more accurately, it's only part of the answer.

Risks arising from issues and crises can appear in many forms, which fundamentally fall into two categories. The first is *risk as analysis*, which brings logic, reason and scientific deliberation to bear on risk assessment and decision-making. The other category is *risk as feelings*, which refers to our instinctive and intuitive reactions to danger.[5]

If your organisation employs risk analysts, my guess is that they are likely located within the finance or business development department and will tend to be focused on a relatively narrow range of risks, albeit very important, but risks which generally fall into the category of *risk as analysis*. These would normally include:

- *financial risk*—the possibility of unacceptable financial loss or loss of shareholder value
- *compliance risk*—arising from breaches or potential breaches of relevant law or regulations
- *investment risk*—vulnerability considered when assessing a new investment or possible adverse changes to an existing investment
- *actuarial/insurance risk*—mathematically calculated predictions based on measurable data related to finance and insurance
- *exchange risk*—business exposure to adverse movement in exchange rates between different currencies

In some organisations this analytical approach might even extend to include:

- *strategic risk*—threatening the organisation's ability to achieve its objectives
- *production/supply chain risk*—relating to problems in plant or processes or the supply chain
- *technology risk*—IT or e-business failures or breaches of data security
- *infrastructure risk*—vulnerability to loss of infrastructure such as water, power, fuel or transport.

There is no question that any or all of these could potentially lead to a crisis, and they all need to be properly addressed. The problem here is that the risk management/business development department, with its traditional tools and risk register, is only part of the answer.

Specifically, these conventional areas of risk don't address some of the *other* threats to the organisation, which are less dependent on data, technology and statistical analysis, and may be about perceptions and feelings, such as:

- *health and environmental risk*—real or perceived health, safety or environmental threats to workers, the local community or society
- *reputational risk*—damage to reputation and its impact on the company's ability to operate

- *human/personnel risk*—when people (at any level) do or say something dumb or illegal
- *societal risk*—risk arising from potential threats to broader society, including structural or political or social change or natural disasters
- *product/recall risk*—when products endanger, or are believed to endanger, consumer health or safety and may have to be recalled
- *online risk*—claims, allegations, rumours and reports which arise online and cause real threats.

People in the communication business say: 'Perception *is* reality.' It's important to note that we don't say is *like* reality or is *similar* to reality. The concept here is that the way people perceive things or events is real to them and they respond accordingly. Sometimes it's called their mental construct, or their construct of reality.

It's certainly not a new idea. Two thousand years ago, in the first century AD, the Greek philosopher Epictetus said: 'People are disturbed not by things but by their view of them.' The importance of perception versus reality here should not be underestimated because it reinforces that seemingly 'soft' risks, such as those I have listed, have just the same potential to become crises. Moreover, they tend to share some of our defined characteristics of issues, namely that they involve external parties, have no 'right' answer, are driven by emotion rather than hard data, and so on. In other words, risk as feelings.

It's because of these characteristics that the solution often lies less in the hands of statisticians and analysts, and more directly in the hands of effective senior managers who can provide leadership and priorities.

RISK VERSUS RESOURCES

As companies start to prioritise the identified issues, it's a very common mistake to assess issues in terms of resources available rather than the potential risk to the organisation. In other words, prioritising on the basis of 'Have we got the people to deal with it?' rather than 'How important is it and how could it affect us?' In this way, important issues may be discounted at the first pass on the grounds that they are too big, too controversial, too sensitive or demand too many resources.

A vital step here is to recognise that an organisation is rarely alone when it comes to facing an issue. There are often allies or those with a common interest who are willing and able to play a part.

The strategic use of allies in such circumstances is critical. One option is that the issue may be assigned entirely to a trade association or formal alliance, with the individual company doing no more than monitoring and assessing progress. This could apply when the organisation regards the issue as important, but does not want to have its name or brand directly linked to the issue.

Alternatively, a similar outcome might also be achieved by a more active participation; for example, being part of the industry association committee or alliance overseeing the issue or by providing expertise or even a 'loan executive' (sweat equity) to work directly on the issue but still under the trade association's identity.

Importantly, deciding about the use of alliances does not apply only to commercial organisations. Not-for-profits (NFPs) and community organisations equally can benefit from alternative participation models, which may preserve resources in order to optimise joint objectives. In fact, the NFP and activist communities can often teach the corporate world about effective use of ad hoc alliances. Broadly, however, these are all very real ways in which you can influence or even drive the issue without necessarily being seen as the active issue leader or depleting limited resources.

In addition to utilising existing structures, such as a trade association or a community coalition, your organisation can also 'share responsibility' by helping to establish a purpose-built alliance to address a specific issue of common concern.

While both business and community groups establish single-issue alliances to fight a specific campaign, such alliances must be open and transparent. There is no legitimate place for phoney front alliances to disguise an organisation's involvement in an issue (sometimes known as astro-turfing). For example, one major international shopping centre company was exposed in a court case as having set up fake 'local community' groups to oppose shopping centre projects promoted by its commercial competitors.[6]

DEVELOPING PRIORITIES

This is where the hard work starts. No amount of scanning, monitoring and resource assessment is of substantive value if it doesn't lead to action. And that demands prioritisation. At the start of the scanning process just about everything looks like an issue. A common mistake is to think that the longer the list of issues drawn up, the better prepared the company is to achieve its corporate goals and protect its reputation.

However, no organisation can actively manage every issue in its environment and, in addition to the possibility that some can appropriately be assigned to an allied organisation, other issues can safely be placed into a passive management or monitoring phase.

This might involve, for example, an individual employee or small internal group being given responsibility to track the issue and identify any change in status; a decision to passively monitor the issue and to revisit on an agreed schedule; or an informed, conscious decision to categorise as 'not an issue *for us*' or 'not an issue for us *at present*'. It is important to stress, however, that this should be a planned, *agreed* decision, not just consigning the issue to the 'too hard basket' as a default excuse to do nothing.

When it comes to full-scale proactive issue management—which involves a formal issue management team, goals and strategies, a communication plan, implementation schedules and commitment of substantial resources—even the largest organisations recognise that the number of priority strategic issues under proactive management is necessarily limited. Many experts believe six to 12 top-level issues is an optimum number, even though many others may be in passive or inactive mode.

Experience shows that any senior executive group, using brainstorming or other methods and tools, can easily come up with an extensive list of risk issues and potential crises. It might be an extension of the formal risk register; it might be a long list captured on a whiteboard; and it might be dozens of sticky yellow Post-it notes. The format is not so important. The real question is how to progress from an exhaustive list of all possible issues to a workable, prioritised list of the proactive few—and do it in a way that's logical and fully aligned with your capabilities, culture and strategic objectives.

One popular solution—which definitely is *not* the right answer—is to get participants to vote on the list. It seems simple and logical. Let's each assign votes—5, 4, 3, 2, 1—for our five top issues, and the issues which get the most votes are our priorities.

The problem with this approach is that the participants typically have no consistent or common criteria. Are we voting on immediacy or dollars at risk? Are we voting on most likely to happen or worst impact if it does happen? They may be comparing apples and oranges, or voting simply for the issue they are most interested in, or which seems to be most popular in the group.

The outcome can easily be that the top-voted priority is an issue which is important, but has progressed so far that no amount of intervention will make any difference. Or it might be an issue which is important, but the organisation either has insufficient resources to commit to it, or is unwilling to expose its name or put its brand at risk. Or it might even be an issue which simply reflects the CEO's personal interests.

None of this is at all helpful. You wouldn't make any other major business decision solely on intuition or gut feel. 'Let's make this million dollar acquisition. We haven't run the numbers or done any analysis, but my gut tells me it's a good deal.' Issue assessment and prioritisation needs to be done on a basis which can be recorded against agreed criteria; where common values are applied; and which can be subsequently replicated against the same criteria to determine whether particular values have changed.

One common issue prioritisation model is to simply look at two criteria: probability and impact. In other words, how likely or how soon could it happen, and how badly would it impact us if it did?

This *probability/impact method* is rather crude and not very helpful. If it was entirely effective, how could the same issue be a high priority for one organisation and a lower priority for another?

The difference is logically within the organisation itself. Because of this, an effective prioritisation process needs to consider not just the issue on its own, but also the organisation—its exposure to the issue, its capacity to influence the issue, and whether it's willing or resourced to exercise that influence. In other words, can the organisation actually make a difference and is it prepared to commit both resources and reputation to deliver that outcome?

A second prioritisation model considers not simply net impact, but also takes into consideration the capacity of the organisation to influence the pace and direction of the issue. However this *significance/influence method* has a weakness too—namely that it fails to address how susceptible the issue is to influence, and whether the organisation has the resources and/or the willingness to exercise that influence.

The fact is that both models over-simplify prioritisation. Issue management is a multi-faceted discipline which needs to consider not only the nature of the issue itself, but also its interaction with a wide range of factors, including the organisation, the environment, economics, politics and stakeholders. As a result, effective prioritisation requires more than just a two-dimensional approach.

My recommended method uses a printed work sheet to assign numerical values against agreed key criteria, which creates a quantified, numerical assessment. There are different ways of doing this and the selected criteria need to reflect the circumstances of your organisation. For discussion purposes, here are six different criteria I use as the basis for prioritisation assessment (each would have an assigned maximum numerical value and weighting):

1. *Impact*—the potential magnitude for the organisation if the issue is left unmanaged. Could it become a crisis?
2. *Salience/legitimacy*—how widely in society the issue is regarded as a concern. How many people care?
3. *Visibility*—the extent of coverage in the traditional and social media. Is it 'newsworthy'?
4. *Affectability*—the organisation's capacity to influence the issue. Can we make a difference?
5. *Proximity/timing*—when the issue is likely to reach its maximum impact. Soon or not for a long time?
6. *Profile*—the willingness of the organisation to expose its brand or reputation. Do we want to attract attention?

The agreed numerical value—typically totalled out of 100—then provides a firm and informed foundation on which to prioritise.

Using this approach, and the numerical total from each of the criteria, you can better understand the importance of each issue relative to other issues. And from this comes the priority for your organisation in terms of the appropriateness and level of issue management effort and what resources may be required to work towards a positive, planned outcome.

Remember, though, any resulting numerical value is not absolute. Priority is by definition a relative concept—simply, how one thing compares with another. As part of organisational crisis proofing, prioritisation is really just a formal, structured way to compare between issues in order to determine where your organisation should most effectively invest its effort.

Moreover, the strategic benefit of this process comes not simply from deriving a relative numerical total for each issue, but also from the *process* of thinking through the key elements of prioritisation and the development of a formal framework to agree on *why* some issues are more important than others. As Prussian Field Marshal Helmuth von Moltke reportedly said: 'Plans are nothing. Planning is everything.'

THE BENEFITS ISSUE PRIORITISATION BRINGS TO CRISIS PROOFING

- *Commitment*—it involves key players, ensures their buy-in and reduces backsliding and dissent.
- *Objectivity*—it demonstrates to the board and investors that a transparent process was followed and didn't rely on groupthink or someone's 'gut feel'.
- *Confidence*—it provides confidence that the organisation is not only doing things right but is also doing the right things.
- *Rigour*—it helps to resist pressure from individuals, sometimes very senior, who demand resources for their 'pet issue'.
- *Speed*—it can be achieved quickly without having to reinvent the process.
- *Efficiency*—it optimises use of resources and minimises duplication and wasted effort.
- *Neutrality*—it reduces the risk of distortion by turf rivalries or dominant personalities.

- *Simplicity*—it can be implemented by senior executives with minimal facilitation once the format is embedded.
- *Flexibility*—criteria can be easily adapted to fit the needs of different parts of the organisation, different markets or joint ventures.
- *Repeatability*—it provides a consistent objective basis for future updates to assess whether priorities or conditions have changed.

Apart from the obvious benefits, a critical procedural aspect of prioritisation is: Who decides? Issue prioritisation is not an abstract or theoretical process, or some sort of box-ticking exercise. It can lead to important decisions on investment and resource allocation. It can also have explicit impacts including reputation; capacity to do business; investor confidence; expansion and acquisition plans; recruitment and retention; compliance cost; risk exposure; and crisis prevention. These consequences are the direct responsibility of the top executive group. That's why prioritisation needs a strategic team approach, with senior management directly involved.

It's often around about this point in crisis proofing that someone in the organisation is likely to say: 'Do we really need to do all this? It seems like a lot of time and expense.' My response is to refer to Derek Bok, President of Harvard, who once said: 'If you think education is expensive, try ignorance.' To paraphrase Bok: 'If you think a planned response to issues is expensive, try enduring a crisis.'

Compared with the time, expense, business disruption and reputational damage of suffering a crisis, identifying and proactively managing issues is a great investment.

CHAPTER KEY TAKEAWAY
The best possible method of crisis management is to take proactive steps to prevent a crisis happening in the first place.

CHAPTER 8

TAKING A STRATEGIC APPROACH

The second element of 'actions you can take to prevent a crisis happening in the first place' is to develop a strategic approach to putting all that identifying and prioritising to work. Having a strong list of risk issues is great, but it's useless if it doesn't lead to planned and targeted actions.

One large company asked me to assess their issue management process and proudly presented an impressive-looking three-ring binder which listed about 80 individual issues. Each was represented by an issue information sheet which described the issue and why it was important to the organisation; a statement of what they were for and what they were against; the name and contact details for the person responsible for the issue; and some key talking points in case the news media inquired.

Not a bad start. The problem was that the so-called manual was entirely passive and reactive. There was no evident link between the identified issues and any consistent action plans designed to drive the organisation towards positive outcomes. Then there's the fact that no organisation, regardless of size, can realistically hope to proactively manage 80 different issues.

Issue information or status sheets like these are quite common—either as hard-copy documents or as digital files—and they can be a useful tool for tracking and recording. But on their own they don't deliver change. They can also be very time-consuming and even a distraction. A participant at one of my workshops told me her boss expected her to review and update their issue sheets *every two weeks*. As a result, she said, she 'didn't have time' to proactively work on their issues.

Don't mistake the tools for the task. No amount of studying the atlas, developing draft itineraries and researching timetables is a substitute for actually making the journey. The atlas, the itineraries and timetables may be essential tools, but they do not represent the objective itself.

I like to compare this approach to a beautifully produced cookbook, with wonderful photographs of delicious food. No matter how brilliant the photographs or how unique the recipes, no matter how often you read the cookbook, your hunger won't be satisfied. You need to get into action and start to prepare the meal.

The same applies to issue management and crisis prevention. Without action, no amount of analysing, prioritising and strategising will deliver an outcome. Moreover, managing an issue or potential crisis—just like cooking an unfamiliar dish—can be messy and unpredictable. That's why you need to follow a process.

I repeat *you don't have to become an issue management expert.* But establishing and driving an effective issue planning process is central to crisis prevention and it's a core executive responsibility in crisis proofing.

Since issue management began in the late 1970s, many different planning processes and models have been developed. While the labels and structure and details may vary, most such models incorporate some form of process flow, such as the flow cycle originally published by Howard Chase and Barry Jones in 1977: (a) identification, (b) analysis, (c) strategy options, (d) action plans, and (e) evaluation.

In fact, Ray Ewing, a colleague of Chase, has asserted that all subsequent published models were based on this original construction.[1] Contemporary issue experts Tim Coombs and Sherry Holladay argue that it is still regarded as the most influential model.[2]

However, over the years, some published models became so over-engineered and complex that the process itself threatened to overwhelm the objective. Chase himself later expanded his basic model into a detailed chart which appeared as a foldout in his 1984 book with 88 distinct steps, depicted in a series of concentric circles. A researcher who worked with

Chase told me many years later that this chart was intentionally made more complicated in an attempt to gain 'legitimacy' in the eyes of CEOs and boards. It is now little more than an historical artefact.

Similarly, one large multinational corporation showed me an in-house issue management work process that was built on a flow chart with 29 separate step-point symbols, supported by 18 new 'system tools' and 12 defined roles, each with its own acronym. The company later replaced this process with a much simpler and more practical approach.

The lesson here is very clear. A process is not a plan, and the planning model needs to lead to real results. As the VP of Government Relations for a major US company told an international conference of issue managers: 'It's so important not to let the process be seen as a surrogate for the actual outcome.'[3]

I am fond of the saying attributed to the American playwright and impresario David Belasco: 'If you can't write your idea on the back of my calling card, you don't have a clear idea.' Whether Belasco actually said that is not as important as the principle—that what you propose should be easy to understand and easy to communicate.

SIX VALUES OF AN EFFECTIVE ISSUE MANAGEMENT PROCESS

- *Utility*—it is useful and can be put into practical action.
- *Simplicity*—it uses unambiguous language and a minimal number of steps.
- *Clarity*—it is not only easy to follow, but also easy to explain to others.
- *Relevance*—it focuses only on what directly adds value to addressing the issue.
- *Versatility*—it is meaningful for many types of issues, regardless of scope and scale.
- *Assessability*—it allows assessment of ongoing progress as well as longer-term achievement of outcomes.

INTRODUCING AN ISSUE MANAGEMENT MODEL

While there are many different published process models, one approach is my Do-it Plan,[4] which takes its name from four sequential steps—definition, objective, intended outcomes and tactics (see Figure 8.1).

FIGURE 8.1 THE DO-IT PLAN

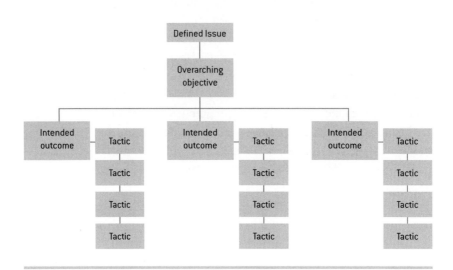

Once, when I presented this model at a conference of business analysts, one of the attendees asked a critical question. 'With respect,' he started (and you know for sure that whatever comes after that opening will not be respectful), 'With respect, isn't this a very standard planning structure?'

I replied that the four-step structure is indeed very obvious. That's exactly the point. Unlike most business decision-making, issues and potential crises often occur in a situation where emotions are running high—where perceptions outweigh facts. And, most importantly, where the challenge is outside normal experience—where there is no established process and no 'right answer'.

That's when there's a danger an organisation's actions may lack a consistent purpose. It may even fall into the trap of activity for its own sake: 'We must be *seen* to be taking action.' (Yes, even otherwise smart people really do say dumb things like that.) If the resulting actions are mainly gut response and not part of a logical strategy, they can lead to duplication, waste and even unplanned outcomes that contradict the strategic purpose.

In other words, a strength of the Do-it model is that it has only four steps, which provide a framework for cool-headed, informed decision-making at a time when structure and logic may not prevail. Let's walk quickly through these steps and see the role of senior executives.

STEP ONE: DEFINITION

Before you can start to consider the objective—'What are we trying to achieve?'—you need to clearly define the issue—'What is the problem and how does it affect us?'

I know from experience that busy managers can be tempted to think they can skip this step: 'Let's not waste time. We all know what the issue is. Let's just get on with it.'

Unfortunately, this sort of impatience can obscure the fact that, while there may be broad agreement on the outline of the problem, different parts of the organisation often perceive it in different ways. That's no surprise. It's only natural, for instance, that the lawyer will tend to see the problem in legal terms; the HR person will see it in personnel terms; the engineer will focus on technical aspects; the public relations person will look to a communication solution; and so on through the executive team.

That's just human nature and professional experience, and different perspectives are entirely to be expected. But basic ambiguity must be resolved right at the start, and the leadership group needs to insist on resolution. If the organisation's executives can't even agree on how to define the issue, how could they possibly work towards a practical and realistic objective?

My recommended method to eliminate ambiguity and accurately define an issue is to get the senior executive group to agree on a *single sentence definition* based on the following formula:

PROBLEM + IMPACT = ISSUE

In other words, you need a single sentence which encapsulates both the problem *and* its potential impact on the organisation. This approach has two distinct benefits. First, it forces the group to define the issue in a concise way that can be easily understood and communicated (problem), rather than some complex situational analysis and pages of descriptive text. Second, it drives the focus beyond just the problem itself to nail down exactly why it matters to the organisation (impact).

The importance of this definition step was highlighted for me when an organisation I was working with told me that their top priority issue was 'water'. As an outsider I had no idea what that really meant, and it soon became evident that the executive group themselves had different interpretations. After a great deal of debate it emerged that 'water' was actually shorthand for a different, more fundamental problem.

It's not appropriate here to disclose that company's real issue, but for the sake of discussion, let's use the 'PROBLEM + IMPACT' formula to develop some alternative hypothetical issue definitions instead of just 'water':

> There is a growing scarcity of water in the community where our factory is located (problem) and a water shortage would threaten our planned increase in production (impact).

Or:

> We consume a large volume of water in a low-rainfall area (problem) and local farmers claim our wells are lowering the water table and their livestock are starving (impact).

Or:

> Our production process needs to discharge large quantities of contaminated water (problem) and government regulators are threatening to close us down if we continue to pollute the nearby river (impact).

In each case, the problem and its impact are unambiguously stated, and the one sentence definition would lead directly to subsequent objectives and tactics. And in each case the identified stakeholders and the plans to address their concerns would be quite different. Furthermore, the question of stakeholders introduces another important aspect—the organisation is seldom alone in defining the issue. Government, the news media and various external stakeholders can have a significant, sometimes even decisive, influence on determining what is regarded as an issue. And it's no use at all for the organisation to simply dismiss an external view as a 'non-issue' or a 'non-problem'. As Holladay and Coombs remind us: 'If stakeholders *think* there is a risk or crisis, there *is* one.'[5]

The need for two-way stakeholder input into issue identification was well described by Canadian consultant Robert Boutilier:

> Trying to manage issues without developing relationships with the groups and people behind them is like trying to direct a movie by going online and changing the script without ever talking to the actors or crew.[6]

A classic failure to recognise the other party's view was when it was announced that shark fin soup would be on the wedding menu at the then soon-to-be-opened Disneyland in Hong Kong. Global and local environmental activist groups used the announcement to highlight the cruelty of the 'finning' process, by which the shark's fins are hacked off with a machete and the quivering body is thrown back into the ocean to be torn to pieces by other sharks. The activists called for an international boycott and, not unreasonably, Disney protested that shark fin soup is a traditional Chinese delicacy, served in high-class restaurants throughout Hong Kong and around the world. They said the issue had nothing to do with them. But after a month of adverse publicity and damage to its reputation, Disney agreed to remove shark fin soup from its wedding menu.[7]

It's a minor example, perhaps, but it vividly illustrates how external actors can define an issue regardless of whether or not it is 'real'. We'll return in a later chapter to the challenge of differing interpretations of what is 'real' and how to deal with fact versus perception.

STEP TWO: OBJECTIVE

A well-chosen and carefully worded definition at Step One establishes the firm foundation for effective issue management. More specifically, it provides the basis upon which the organisation can reach consensus on the second step—an agreed objective. Deciding on a firm objective helps avoid a very common error in issue management—to confuse 'what are we trying to achieve' with 'what do we need to do'. In other words, confusing strategic objectives with tactics.

For effective planning, there needs to be a single overarching objective. Often there are a number of possible candidates for the key objective, and my workshop participants often say, 'Can't we have two objectives?' Obviously, all the possible options must be properly weighed in terms of what is reasonably achievable and what resources are available. Yet, while there may be several possible objectives, one usually stands out above the others. Moreover, choosing just one is a discipline which truly focuses decision-making.

Consider one of the optional definitions from our previous hypothetical example:

> Our production process needs to discharge large quantities of contaminated water (problem) and government regulators are threatening to close us down if we continue to pollute the nearby river (impact).

In this case there could be a number of possible strategic approaches to determine what the focus should be:

- Buy time to substantially reduce the volume of contaminated water generated (operational).
- Call on independent experts to demonstrate there is no real adverse impact on the local river (technical).
- Argue no change is needed because the discharge is within the operating licence (legal).
- Raise questions about the risk to local jobs and taxes if the plant closes (government and community affairs).

These and other possible strategies might all be appropriate, or perhaps a combination of more than one may ultimately be implemented. But for the purposes of planning, it would make an enormous difference whether the agreed objective was broadly: (a) to recognise there is a problem and commit to make improvement; or (b) to deny there is a problem and gather evidence to support no need for change. That fundamental decision would determine the objective and lead to two very different strategic plans with different outcomes and tactics.

Beyond this hypothetical example, in broad terms a strategic objective for managing any major issue should meet the following criteria:

- There should be a single, overarching issue objective.
- The issue objective must be fully aligned with relevant organisational strategies and objectives.
- It should specifically address or respond to the issue.
- It must be clear, unambiguous and measurable.
- It must be easily stated and communicated.
- It must have top executive and board understanding, support and commitment.

STEP THREE: INTENDED OUTCOMES

The first two steps—defining the issue and agreeing on the objective—are the critical foundation and are central to crisis proofing. Without them firmly in place the whole process can fall to the ground, leaving the organisation vulnerable to potential crises. Furthermore, they are the key strategic decisions which demand direct involvement of top executives.

The next two steps are also important, but can be regarded as more tactical. Experience shows that with the definition and objective in place, the rest of the issue management plan tends to roll out more easily. As World War II US commander General George Marshall said: 'If you get the objectives right, a lieutenant can write the strategy.'

However, as emerges during the earlier steps, some issues can appear to be almost overwhelmingly broad or complex. Therefore, it is useful to divide the overall objective into discrete, comprehensible and manageable tasks, which can be called sub-objectives, or 'bite size pieces'. In the Do-it Plan, these manageable tasks are called intended outcomes. Their purpose is to partition the task and simplify the transition from objectives to tactics.

You are probably familiar with the term 'desired outcomes' as used in other management systems. But the term 'intended outcomes' has a different and more active meaning. Desired outcomes are what we would like to *see happen*. Intended outcomes, by contrast, are what we plan to *make happen*. This is not just semantics. The difference is significant as it moves the thinking from 'Wouldn't it be nice if ...' to 'What we plan to do is ...' In essence, it captures the difference between talking about it and doing it, and issue management is fundamentally a discipline about proactive, planned action.

Each intended outcome makes a positive contribution to achieving the overarching objective by identifying a specific outcome that will help deliver that objective. As a sub-objective, the intended outcome typically describes what needs to be done in a discrete area. Facing a hypothetical issue, the objective might be broken up into intended outcomes such as these:

- Government regulators understand and agree with our strategy.
- Independent experts speak out in support of our approach.
- Community leaders are engaged and their concerns have been addressed.
- Detailed information has been assembled to counter claims by activist opponents.
- A proactive media strategy ensures neutral-to-positive coverage.

While these examples are generic, they illustrate that agreeing on intended outcomes focuses effort on what must be achieved, and they provide an easily understood framework for tactics.

STEP FOUR: TACTICS

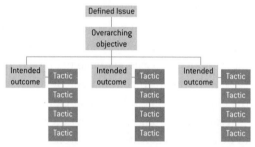

Whenever people are asked to deal with a problem, it's very human to leap from the problem itself straight to suggesting tactics. This is sometimes called working on the answer before making sure the question is clear. We've all had to deal with people like this. In my experience it's often technically trained managers such as engineers and accountants who race off listing what they think needs to be *done* while others are still making sure they're agreed on what needs to be *achieved*.

By imposing a degree of discipline, my method helps ensure that the tactics are not just activity for its own sake, but instead are focused on delivering each of the agreed outcomes, which in turn support the overarching objective. However, of the four steps in my model, identifying tactics is by far the easiest and most intuitive.

Take just one of the hypothetical intended outcomes above: 'Community leaders are engaged and their concerns have been addressed.' The detailed tactics to achieve this outcome might include:

- Identify the key community leaders.
- Decide how they will be initially approached.
- Develop briefing materials.
- Organise an appropriate forum for ongoing engagement.

- Nominate and train selected organisation participants.
- Secure mutual agreement on the engagement process.
- Listen to and record community concerns.
- Agree on how any unsolved differences will be managed.
- Develop feedback and reporting mechanisms.

This list is not in sequence and is not exhaustive. But it illustrates that the tactics usually fall very easily out of the intended outcomes. However, to be effective, each tactic must be assigned to a named individual or group responsible to implement it, along with the timeframes by which progress and completion are required.

When all the tactics are recorded for each intended outcome, what you have is a schedule of what needs to be done to deliver intended outcomes, who will do it, and by when. The cumulative result of all four steps is an issue management plan that is practical and workable.[8] It's not a massive document with over-wrought analysis and endless appendices. It is typically no more than three or four pages of well-structured text. It's easily communicated upwards in the organisation and, most importantly, it's focused on delivering an agreed objective in order to make a difference to the issue.

EVALUATION

Evaluating the effectiveness of issue management and crisis prevention is a challenge. Effort should be spent mainly on anticipating problems before they get worse, and as a result it's not easy to evaluate the impact of what *could* have happened if the issue had not been managed; or the cost of the crisis that *might* have happened, but was successfully avoided.

This conundrum was neatly captured by Australian corporate manager David Goodwin who relates the story of an External Affairs Manager who, under pressure to describe her role, says, 'I keep the elephants away.' 'But there are no elephants,' comes the reply from a sceptical CEO. To which she responds: 'See what a great job I'm doing!'

'Effective issues management is like that,' Goodwin concluded. 'Inconspicuous when it is successful, and valued most highly in its absence.'[9]

In this way, the most effective issue management and crisis prevention is often what you don't see. And in many cases it is not something you would want to shout from the rooftop. I like to think about it as being similar to cosmetic surgery. It's legal, it's ethical and it's widespread, and you are happy for people to admire the results. But you don't necessarily want them to know what work you've had done, what it cost, or in fact whether you have had work done at all. That's not a bad description of issue management.

Another distinct challenge for evaluation in this field is that strategic campaigns can sometimes last months or even years and it's genuinely difficult to assess incremental changes. For that reason I recommend evaluating against the plan. Were the assigned tactics effectively carried out, and on schedule? Did the plan achieve each of the intended outcomes, which it was previously agreed would deliver the objective? In other words, given the complexity and intractability of some risk issues, the most practical evaluation should be against the plan, not necessarily against the issue itself.

BARRIERS TO SUCCESS

Nothing is ever as easy as it looks, and implementing a plan to address priority issues and potential crises faces various barriers to success. There are four common barriers, and overcoming each one of them demands leadership from the top.

(1) Remaining in reactive mode

This problem arises when the organisation is unwilling, or feels itself unable, to make decisions and take action. Issue management and crisis prevention demands a proactive mindset rather than being in reactive mode. This barrier sometimes manifests itself as an excessive focus on minutes, memos and meetings rather than actions and outcomes. Or it becomes reflected in a feeling that the task is overwhelming and nothing can be done. Developing a plan enables the organisation to realistically assess the options and opportunities, to divide the job into manageable tasks, and to mobilise its resources to deliver planned, positive outcomes.

(2) Legal response syndrome

The legal response syndrome is seen when an organisation treats each issue as if legal considerations override all others. Many issues have a legal perspective and it is important that all legal angles are appropriately addressed. However, it is rare that any issue is solely legal in nature and all aspects need adequate attention. There is a familiar saying that an organisation can 'win in the court of law and lose in the court of public opinion'. In other words, the organisation may act in a way that is legally correct, yet results in damage to business or reputation. Effective issue planning allows top executives to develop a proper balance between legal considerations and the many other important considerations that may apply. This is a critical role for senior managers, and two later chapters of this book are devoted to lawyers and legal advice, and how decisions must reflect the overall needs of the organisation and the legitimate expectations of all stakeholders—not just the lawyers.

(3) Ad hoc management

Lack of a formal issue management structure with clear responsibility and accountability is another major barrier to success. This is typically seen when organisations are reluctant to establish a formal issue/crisis team to take command. An ad hoc approach often results when the issue is assigned to an informal group who may lack the necessary skills or resources, or to an existing group which is already heavily committed to other tasks. Simply adding crisis prevention to the end of the normal meeting agenda is just not the right answer. It's best managed by a dedicated team set up with the right people, the right resources and top executive support, and tasked specifically to develop and implement strategically aligned plans to crisis proof the organisation.

(4) Unclear goals

Of all the barriers to effective issue management and crisis prevention, one of the most prevalent is unclear goals and, with it, a lack of focus on action. This is where planning proves its value. There are planning models available in just about every area of business, and most start with a clear focus on establishing clear goals and objectives. This is regarded as the foundation of any effective plan, and exactly the same applies here.

STRATEGIC PLANNING

Emphasis on planning leads to one final topic. When senior managers are first introduced to issue management it's not uncommon to hear: 'Isn't this really just an extension of our existing strategic planning?'

It's a good question, because issue management is fundamentally an analysis and planning tool. It's also true that there are real benefits when issue management and strategic planning are integrated as much as possible in the best interests of the organisation.

In fact, US authority Robert Heath says issue management cannot have its full impact if it is not part of the strategic planning process.[10] Yet it's a mistake to think that they are synonymous or are simply two parts of the same process.

There are many differences, but they tend to revolve around the central distinction that strategic planning focuses primarily on identifying opportunities and threats to products and markets, while the emphasis of issue management is on identifying and addressing issues and concerns in the public arena which are not typically addressed in the marketplace. At the simplest level, strategic planning is about achieving business success, while issue management is largely about issue response and crisis prevention to make such success possible.

There are also important differences in the disciplines themselves:

- Strategic planning is usually scheduled in a periodic planning or budget cycle, while issue management has more flexible timing to respond to real-time developments.
- Strategic planning is accepted as a core business discipline, while in some organisations issue management is still (wrongly) regarded mainly as a communication activity.
- Strategic planning attempts to balance social responsibility with financial obligations, while issue management attempts to bring current standards of corporate social responsibility into the way the organisation deals with issues and potential crises.
- Strategic planning tends to have an inside-out focus, looking for threats and opportunities in terms of their impact on the organisation, while issue management encourages an outside-in focus, considering external viewpoints and the impact on stakeholders.[11]

But for all these differences, the two disciplines need to work together, and that's a responsibility of senior executives.

Unfortunately, experience suggests that this integrated approach to planning is more talked about than achieved. Research among major public corporations in Britain by respected experts Michael Regester and Judy

Larkin indicated that while there was an acknowledgment by corporate communication and public affairs functions of the importance of managing issues, only 10 per cent of the sample considered that their senior management proactively dealt with issues as part of the strategic planning process.[12] Furthermore, less than 5 per cent considered their organisation applied an integrated approach to linking planning, communication, regulatory affairs and other appropriate functions to assess, prioritise and plan for the impact of near- and longer-term issues on corporate objectives.

These numbers are discouraging, and there is no doubt that when the two disciplines are not working together, each is weaker. Or as George McGrath noted: 'Issue management links strategic planning with communication planning and improves the effectiveness of both disciplines.'[13]

For issue management and strategic planning to be fully operating at optimal effectiveness, any weakness must be identified and addressed at the highest level in the organisation. Only top executives have the perspective and authority to drive such change, and the drive towards integrated planning is another important element in delivering effective crisis proofing.

CHAPTER KEY TAKEAWAY
While issue management is both art and science, without proper planning and process, no useful outcome will be achieved.

CHAPTER 9

THINGS YOU CAN DO TO PREPARE FOR THE OBVIOUS CRISES

On 3 August 2013, the dairy products giant Fonterra—New Zealand's largest company and largest exporter—announced a precautionary recall of 38 tonnes of whey protein concentrate, which external tests indicated was potentially contaminated with the deadly toxin botulism. Whey protein concentrate is used in baby formula and a range of other food products.

Less than a month later, on 28 August, Fonterra announced that further tests showed the recall was a false alarm. However, the botulism scare had already sparked a global crisis for the company, which adversely affected the New Zealand dollar and badly damaged the reputation of the company and the country's products.

The full details of the case—including how the false alarm occurred in the first place—are beyond our scope here. But an independent inquiry established by Fonterra, and a separate government inquiry, exposed some crucial weaknesses in the company's crisis preparedness, culture and governance.

A CASE STUDY OF WHAT WENT WRONG

The independent inquiry revealed (among other findings) that there was only belated recognition (and delayed escalation to senior management) of the crisis; a failure to 'join the dots' between botulism, infant food products, consumer sensitivities and the company's global reputation; and that Fonterra's crisis management planning, including external communication, was inadequate for a crisis of this kind and scale.[1]

Pause for a moment to think about that—failure to 'join the dots' between product contamination, consumer sensitivity and reputation. How could there be any more obvious crisis risk for a food company? And bear in mind that this was not some small business, but a multi-billion dollar, multinational corporation, responsible for about 30 per cent of the world's dairy exports.

In terms of governance at the top level, the inquiry recommended that the board should 'explicitly accept responsibility for oversight' on progress towards system improvement, and that the board should develop its own protocol for crisis management, including the role of the chair and CEO. Here, again, it's worth pausing to reflect that a good deal of the blame was assigned not to functional operators but was aimed directly at the executive suite.

While the report was highly critical about the inadequacy of the original product testing and the fact that the company was unable to promptly and definitely track the affected batches, it was damning about Fonterra's woeful crisis preparedness. It concluded:

- While there were crisis plans at business unit and group level, 'the group plan had never been rigorously or regularly tested for one of the most likely risks, a global product recall'.
- This failure was all the more worrying given that Fonterra had recently experienced two other contamination crises—one in New Zealand earlier the same year and a previous incident in China involving its JV partner Sanlu.
- Although suspicion about possible botulism contamination first surfaced in April 2013, a Critical Event Team was not established until 22 July.
- There was no designated formal Crisis Management Team (CMT) and such a team was not created until 31 July, effectively just two days before the recall announcement.

- Despite the complexity of the business, the communications team was entirely outsourced at the time.
- No communication team member attended the initial CMT meeting, and a newly appointed Group Director of Communication began in this role just one day later.
- There was no effective social media strategy. The recall announcement was released at 20 minutes past midnight on a Saturday morning, but it was not uploaded to the company website until Monday because the only people with website access were contractors who were not working over the weekend.
- There was no consistent crisis management spokesperson.

Broadly, the report found that Fonterra's crisis management planning was entirely inadequate and the inquiry was satisfied that better crisis management processes and planning within Fonterra, including rehearsals and a designated crisis (or incident) management team, 'would have made a substantial difference'.

The subsequent official government inquiry reached its own blunt conclusion:

> The ill-prepared inevitably pay a heavy price in a crisis. Fonterra was not ready for a crisis of this magnitude and lacked an updated, well-rehearsed plan to implement, as well as a crisis management team that could spring into action.[2]

Fonterra wasn't the first big organisation to be found wanting in the face of a crisis, and certainly won't be the last. But it is not often that a lack of crisis preparedness becomes so public and is so costly. Moreover, it's not often that outside organisations are presented with such an opportunity to learn from the failure of others, in terms of inadequate crisis preparedness and poor crisis leadership.

PLANNING VERSUS THE PLAN

Many organizations want to routinize crisis management. They want to reduce it to a set of preset formulas and procedures. Many organizations often believe, erroneously, that they are sufficiently prepared if they have a formal set of crisis plans and

> procedures they can 'pull off the shelf' during the heat of a crisis. This ignores the fact that no crisis ever happens exactly as it was planned for. This does not mean that formal plans and procedures are useless, but as organizations have had to learn in the area of strategic planning, the process of planning is often more important than the final, end plans themselves. It is the process of thinking, the act of learning, that is the true important end. It's precisely here where corporate culture is decisive.
>
> Ian Mitroff and colleagues[3]

The sorry story of Fonterra's failure highlights one of the common reasons organisations give for *not* having proper crisis preparedness in place. Every crisis is so different, they argue. You can't prepare for *every* eventuality, so therefore it's a waste of time to prepare for any crisis.

This argument fails on a number of levels, not least because it's sometimes simply an excuse to do nothing. But as President John F. Kennedy said: 'There are risks and costs to a program of action. But they are far less than the long-range risks and costs of comfortable inaction.' Crisis proofing leaves no room for 'comfortable inaction'.

UNDERVALUING THE IMPACT OF A CRISIS

It's true that crises come in all shapes and sizes. But in the context of crisis proofing, I am using the term 'crisis' in its conventional sense of a high-impact, low-probability development or event which can genuinely threaten the organisation's long-term reputation or its ability to do business. And, in the case of Fonterra, a product contamination incident *should* have been at the top of the list of possible crises.

Within business and society, the word 'crisis' has been seriously devalued by overuse, until it is now sometimes used to describe just about any embarrassment or minor problem. When the keynote speaker fails to turn up at your conference it is embarrassing and awkward, but it is not a crisis. When a CEO inadvertently utters a profanity during a national television interview, he or she might be revealing something about themselves, but it isn't a crisis. And, contrary to a report I read in an IT magazine, when someone misplaces the piece of paper with the computer admin access passwords, it isn't a crisis (unless perhaps the passwords fall into the hands of a competitor, or a hacker determined to destroy the organisation's entire database).

This is certainly not what I am talking about. Every expert has their own list of crisis categories, but to make sure there's no misunderstanding about what constitutes a real or potential crisis, I have built my own list.

CATEGORIES OF CRISES

1. *Operational crises.* Generally these originate in plant or operational facilities, and typically arise from physical incidents such as spills, leaks, fire or explosions, but might also result from sabotage, a workplace shooting, social unrest, riots or even terrorism.
2. *Environmental crises.* These sometimes emerge in the aftermath of an operational incident and may include community exposure to pollution, or release of toxic substances into the environment, such as chemical emissions into the air, poisons discharging into lakes or rivers, or contamination of underground sources of drinking water.
3. *Management or employee misconduct crises.* These typically arise from moral or ethical lapses, such as misuse of company money, corruption, bribery, scandalous misbehaviour, nepotism, industrial espionage, theft or other criminal activity. These can occur at all levels of the organisation, right up to and including the executive suite.
4. *Management/legal crises.* Negative structural decisions—such as layoffs, shut-downs or offshoring—can be a cause of potential crises, along with allegations of business-related managerial wrongdoing, such as: price-fixing; tax evasion; trademark, patent or copyright infringement; or claims of unfair or improper competition.
5. *Technological crises.* These usually result from a technology failure or breakdown—including collapse of computer systems, hacking, breaches of privacy and loss of data—or infrastructure breakdown, such as a prolonged loss of power.
6. *Product crises.* Crises directly affecting products can be deliberate (such as product tampering or extortion) or accidental (such as contamination or manufacturing error, or a design fault which causes illness, injury or even death). Product crises can lead to recalls, boycotts or product liability litigation.
7. *Labour relations crises.* These may arise from specific industrial disputes, such as a strike or lockout, or from allegations of wrongful behaviour towards employees, such as racial or sexual discrimination, bullying, wrongful dismissal, or unfair or dangerous working conditions.

> 8 *Social concerns.* Organisations sometimes find themselves facing an operational or reputational crisis because they are caught up in a social concern, such as animal testing, use of genetically modified organisms, packaging derived from endangered rainforest, or suppliers who use exploited labour or underage workers.
> 9 *Natural disasters.* Crises may strike in the form of natural disasters such as floods, earthquakes, cyclones and bushfires, but (as shown in Table 5.1, earlier in this book) disaster management is a standalone discipline usually implemented at a societal level. This means it's different from the response to organisational crises, though a natural disaster can trigger an operational crisis for an individual organisation.

While this list captures the broad range of potential crises, you need to recognise that, depending on severity, some of the examples given would not necessarily develop into a full-blown crisis. They may be successfully dealt with earlier as an incident, an emergency or even an issue. That's why crisis prevention is a critical element of crisis proofing.

When you look at this list it might be rather daunting, and you can understand why an organisation might say: 'You can't prepare for all of them so let's not prepare for any.'

'NATURAL' CRISES

Every organisation has its 'most likely' crises, but there is no agreed name for these events. I call them 'natural' crises. That doesn't mean they result from natural disasters. These are the crises which are natural to the organisation. In other words, they are the industry-specific or organisation-specific crises which are reasonably predictable and should be clear priorities. For example:

- A chemical company would be expected to plan for a possible major fire or explosion.
- An airline must rehearse for the event of a plane crash.
- A car-maker should have a plan in place for a major vehicle recall.
- A mining company should know how to respond to an underground cave-in.
- A hotel must be prepared for a highly publicised outbreak of food-poisoning.

- A bank should be ready to deal with customers in ski-masks making very large unauthorised cash withdrawals.

Every organisation has equivalent natural crisis risks and, as so dramatically demonstrated by the Fonterra case, every major food manufacturer should be expected to have strong plans in place for a major product contamination or recall. For Fonterra there could have been no more obvious natural crisis, but, as subsequent inquiries showed, they were not prepared even for that most likely eventuality. Similarly, there could hardly be a more obvious crisis for an oil exploration company than a major spill, yet in the wake of the 2010 *Deepwater Horizon* oil spill in the Gulf of Mexico, BP CEO Tony Hayward admitted their contingency plans were inadequate: 'We were making it up day to day.'[4] Really, Mr Hayward?

HOW PREPARED IS 'ADEQUATELY PREPARED'

Cyber-security breaches are now almost a commonplace crisis risk, especially for organisations which depend on huge databases. But when unknown persons hacked Sony Entertainment in late 2014—doing huge damage to the company and its reputation—CEO Michael Lynton argued that the crisis was 'unprecedented'.

The cyber attack was alleged to be the work of North Korea in retaliation against the (then) upcoming movie *The Interview*, about a fictional plot to assassinate North Korean leader Kim Jong-Un, and experts argued the Sony IT system was poorly protected. Yet Mr Lynton tried to present the breach as a complete surprise and the company as a helpless victim:

> We are the canary in the coal mine, that's for sure. There's no playbook for this, so you are in essence trying to look at the situation as it unfolds and make decisions without being able to refer to a lot of experiences you've had in the past or other people's experiences. You're on completely new ground. We were adequately prepared, just not for an attack of this nature, which no firm could have withstood.[5]

Sony shareholders and Hollywood celebrities compromised by the hack must have wondered how a cyber attack was 'new ground', and how a major corporation could have 'no playbook' and still be 'adequately prepared'.

Kurt Stocker at Northwestern University, Chicago, has a depressingly pessimistic view of this problem. 'When you look at the majority of crises … what happened should have been on or near the top of the list of possible events. Why wasn't anyone prepared?'[6]

You must identify and prepare for these natural crises. However, for the present discussion I'd like to focus more broadly on crisis planning in the sense of preparing the organisation to respond to any sort of crisis across the whole range I have just listed. This idea was well expressed by Intel CEO Andy Grove:

> You need to plan the way a fire department plans. It cannot anticipate where the next fire will be, so it has to shape an energetic and efficient team which is capable of responding to the unanticipated.[7]

My purpose in the next chapter is to concentrate on the planning needed to help build such an energetic and efficient team in order to crisis proof your organisation and to prepare it to 'respond to the unanticipated'.

CHAPTER KEY TAKEAWAY

You may not be able to prevent every crisis, but there is a lot you can do to be better prepared.

CHAPTER 10

PUTTING THE CRISIS PLAN TOGETHER

This book is not a textbook nor is it a comprehensive manual. Yet it's helpful to understand the form and content of a basic organisational crisis plan if you are going to appreciate the role of senior executives in this aspect of crisis proofing.

Developing a crisis plan and setting up and training the Crisis Management Team (CMT) are the central elements of crisis preparedness. The typical crisis plan—sometimes called the crisis manual—is in fact often a crisis readiness and response plan. Therefore, it is generally confined to the activation and response phase (including crisis communication) and does not include other phases of crisis proofing, such as crisis prevention, business continuity, operational recovery and post-crisis risk.

While a crisis management plan must be a formal document, it does not need to be a complex production, and you can put the basics in place relatively simply and cost-effectively. Simplicity and useability should be the goal. We've certainly moved beyond the four-inch-thick binder that hardly anyone ever refers to, and is most likely littered with the names of long-departed executives and functional managers. Best practice today is a practical, relevant and up-to-date 'living document' that reflects the needs of the organisation and focuses on practical guidelines and information rather than flow charts and needless data.

Furthermore, the plan is not only brief but ideally is also developed as both a printed document and a digital version, which can be stored in mobile devices and accessed remotely. This is critical if you are working away from head office or remote from the crisis site, or when the crisis itself forces evacuation of your office.

> ### IS ONE PLAN ENOUGH?
>
> The Institute for Crisis Management in Denver, Colorado, advocates three crisis plans:[1]
> 1. the *operational crisis plan*, which covers the actions needed to mitigate the crisis and keep the organisation functioning during that time
> 2. the *business continuity and recovery plan*, which covers the actions needed to get the organisation back to normal following a crisis
> 3. the *crisis communication plan*.

There is no one-size-fits-all crisis plan. In fact, some experts believe each element requires its own plan (see 'Is one plan enough?' box). However, there are some common elements in any good crisis management plan, which should be seen as a standard management tool and not as a shelf ornament. From a senior executive point of view, there are seven key elements and I will discuss each of them in turn:

- appointing a designated Crisis Management Team
- activating the team
- determining the crisis management location
- articulating clear roles and responsibilities
- compiling contact lists
- generating pre-approved information
- undertaking crisis training.

DESIGNATED CRISIS MANAGEMENT TEAM

Probably the single most important action in developing a crisis plan is to appoint a Crisis Management Team (CMT) *made up of the right people.* This critical decision usually lies entirely with the senior executive group. It may not be as easy as it looks and cannot be delegated. As we saw with the Fonterra case, sometimes even large and powerful organisations don't set up a formal CMT until it's too late. And, some organisations I have worked with have a designated team which very clearly is *not* made up of the right people.

Hopefully, you won't be surprised to hear that the CMT should not be just the executive team under another label. It should comprise the people who will be of the most help in a crisis, some of whom may not be regular members of the executive team.

The main criteria for inclusion should not be rank and status. I have seen designated teams where some members are there because they thought they were important—that being on the team was a privilege of status—and no one was willing or able to argue to the contrary. Such people can be a real hindrance when it comes to making hard decisions under pressure.

On the other hand, it's important that whoever is included should have sufficient seniority and influence to take responsibility and get things done without unnecessary delays waiting for approval. In other words, the team should be chosen for what they bring to the task, not just because of their job titles. The way I like to think about selecting the CMT membership is to ask: 'Who would you most want alongside you in the trench when the bullets are flying?' That test sometimes rapidly discounts the manager who has braid on his shoulders, but loves to talk and won't make a decision. Such selection decisions call for diplomacy and tact, but they pay off when the pressure comes on.

Because of the range and complexity of possible crises which may strike, a common practice when appointing a CMT is to designate a core team (sometimes called the central or inner team), which assembles regardless of the nature of the crisis. While every organisation has its own specific needs, a typical core CMT might include representatives from corporate leadership, PR/communications (including social media), legal, finance, human resources, operations, business and administration (to provide documentation and facilities support).

Specialists can then be added to bring their particular skills and knowledge as needed, depending on the nature of the crisis. These additional functional or specialist CMT members (sometimes called the supplementary or outer team), might include logistics, transport, IT, health/medical, environmental management, emergency response and security.

Given the modern demands of travel and other business commitments, many organisations also have a roster of designated alternates or deputies, who are available to step in if one of the main team members is absent. It has been said that good crisis management needs 'a culture of deputies', and to be effective these alternates or deputies must be equally well equipped and trained.

Moreover, all these people—core CMT members, supplementary members and deputies—must know who they are. It seems obvious, but I have facilitated crisis simulation exercises where some of the people in the room didn't even know they were officially designated as part of the process until they got the memo about the scheduled training.

This brings us to the crucial question of appointing the CMT chairperson. This may or may not be the CEO. Sometimes in a crisis the CEO is more valuable dealing with strategic stakeholders such as politicians, business partners, the community or the news media, rather than personally leading the CMT. While it goes without saying that the CEO will be intimately involved with key decisions, that's different from leading the team on an hour-by-hour, day-by-day basis. Whether the CEO should be the spokesperson during a crisis is a different question again, and we'll come to that in the next chapter.

Clearly, the CMT chairperson needs leadership skills as well as a high level of understanding of the organisation and the nature of the crisis itself. I recommend having alternative chairpersons; for example, one person if it is a business crisis and another if it is an operational or technical crisis. As well as ensuring subject matter knowledge, this dual-leader approach also provides an experienced back-up if either person is not available. In addition to leading the CMT, the chairperson is often also the person who takes or delegates responsibility to mobilise the team and activate the process, and that in itself is a key role.

ACTIVATING THE TEAM

Just like appointing the right people to the CMT, another critical responsibility of senior executives is knowing when and how to summon the team. Although it seems obvious, some crisis management plans lack a clearly defined process for activating and assembling the team.

There should be a clear statement and policy about *who* is responsible for summoning the team and *how* it is to be activated, though this needs to be flexible enough to cope with extraordinary situations.

Conventionally, this authority lies with the CEO or the CMT chair, but the process has to be robust enough to work even when key people are absent or out of contact. Moreover, the activation process needs to work not only during normal business hours but also at night, or at 3 p.m. on a Sunday afternoon, or during public holidays.

If you are the executive who is required to make this decision, you need a very clear idea of *when* to call the team together. And it's not that easy. Harvey Pitt, former Chairman of the US Securities and Exchange Commission,[2] once said: 'One of the most difficult problems executives face is confronting the fact that a crisis actually exists.'

Experience shows that a common mistake is to delay activating the team to 'wait for more information' or to 'avoid looking as if we are over-reacting'. These responses are understandable, but are potentially very dangerous. After all, a crisis is by definition a situation which is outside the normal and where decisions must be made, even when not all the facts are known.

It's important to remember here that activating the CMT does not necessarily mean a crisis has been declared. The team might meet and decide it is *not* a crisis and assess that existing response systems are working well. Or the team might decide that it is not a crisis *yet*, and reschedule to meet again later in the day to review developments, while ensuring that key people remain on standby and available at short notice.

Either way, the activation process needs to work well—most commonly by direct phone calls or e-alerts—and the team members summoned must know what to do and where to go.

CRISIS MANAGEMENT LOCATION

Every organisation needs a clearly identified location where the CMT will go when they are mobilised. It does not have to be a sophisticated 'war room' or 'crisis control centre', but it does need to be equipped with at least the basic requirements, including multiple telephone and internet connections, conference call capability, computers, television, radio, photocopiers, maps, contact lists and copies of key data. It should also have access to service facilities such as catering and restrooms, and a separate, nearby room to meet and brief the news media.

Crucially, it should not be the office of the CEO or CMT chair, as those rooms will almost certainly be needed for other purposes during a crisis.

Of course, all the participants must know where the location is, and have 24/7 access to it. This *should* go without saying, but is not always the case. In one crisis simulation exercise I managed, the client liaison manager agreed that the participants would be told to meet at the Crisis Management Room at a set time, but the meeting notice would not state the location. At the same time, the CEO's secretary was instructed not to tell the people who inevitably phoned asking for a reminder where to go. For that organisation it was a reality check that so many of the people involved had never bothered to look at their manual, where the location was clearly identified.

Finally, I highly recommend having a pre-planned back-up location, usually offsite, in the event that the regular location is not available; for example, if it is damaged or unavailable because of the crisis. The back-up site may be as simple as a conference room in another building, or at a nearby hotel or hall, but the team members need to know where it is and how to gain access.

CLEAR ROLES AND RESPONSIBILITIES

It is not enough to simply designate the CMT and their deputies. The crisis management plan should spell out the roles and responsibilities of all the people concerned, making it clear that these may be different from their day-to-day duties.

In addition, the usual reporting lines for individual CMT members may be different when there is a crisis. They may temporarily be reporting exclusively to the chairperson or another team member, not their usual boss. This can be a sensitive issue and demands executive endorsement of the plan to ensure there is no conflict.

Moreover, the CMT members are there to contribute to the team in all respects, not just for their own line or functional role. For example, the organisation may not have a full-time in-house public relations professional, so the business unit representative may be designated to act as contact point and liaison with an external communications expert. Similarly, the organisation may not have an in-house lawyer, so the human resources representative could be designated to oversee any legal aspects and liaise with external counsel.

These supplementary roles are not necessarily complex, but they should be clearly stated in the plan and understood well in advance. Role clarity is always important, but never more so than in a crisis, and you need effective leadership to ensure the best possible operation of the team.

CONTACT LISTS

When your organisation is facing a crisis, you *must* have an up-to-date and comprehensive contact list, not just of senior managers and local emergency services, but also of the many other people and organisations you may need to contact in a hurry. Every organisation will have different needs, but your list might also include government agencies and regulators, political and community leaders, key customers and suppliers, news organisations, major shareholders and joint venture partners.

Naturally, the list must be prepared in advance, must be up to date and must work at any time, not just during business hours. After BP's notorious *Deepwater Horizon* oil spill in the Gulf of Mexico, Jon Stewart on the comedy news program *The Daily Show* compared the spill response plans of the top oil companies and found they were virtually identical. They all contained the name and phone number of the same independent expert oil spill specialist. Unfortunately, as Stewart revealed, that expert had *died some years earlier*. Relying on an out-of-date list may be even worse than having no list at all.

PRE-APPROVED INFORMATION

When a crisis occurs, there is typically confusion and lack of accurate information about the event itself. There's not much you can do about that in advance. What you can do in advance is make sure someone assembles reliable information about your organisation which can be called on immediately. This might include background such as organisational size and history; principal products; biographies and photos of top executives; and copies of key documents such as values or mission statements. In addition, the information might include location maps, site layout diagrams and technical data about products. Finally, it should include pre-written and -approved media statement templates (with blanks to be filled in), a list of media contacts and a list of frequently asked questions (FAQs), with pre-approved answers.

The rise of social media has seen the emergence of another important element of pre-approved information: the 'dark website'. This is a micro-website formatted and prepared in advance, waiting to be activated very rapidly in the event of a crisis. The dark site is not cluttered with the usual homepage organisational messages and material, but is focused purely on the present crisis. When activated it would typically include:

- relevant but brief organisational background
- basic information about the crisis
- what the organisation is doing to deal with it
- copies of any media statements that have been issued
- advice about when updated information can be expected
- contact information for the news media
- contact information for the public who may be affected.

A dark website, like other aspects of advance preparation—such as contact lists and pre-approved information—may be regarded as tactical. Yet they all need top executive involvement to ensure they are in place and up to date.

Before moving on to what to do and say in a crisis, there is one further critical area of pre-crisis preparation which lies directly within the responsibility of senior executives, and that is training the CMT.

CRISIS TRAINING

The crisis management plan is of little value if it sits on a shelf gathering dust, or if the people concerned are not familiar with its contents and don't know what is expected of them.

Indeed, the fact that there is a plan and a trained CMT should not be kept as some sort of 'state secret'. Some companies I have worked with are reluctant to tell staff about crisis preparedness, because they imagine it might cause unnecessary concern. But I think employees could be legitimately concerned if they felt their organisation was *not* well prepared to protect them and their workplace in the event of a crisis.

That's not to say that the full crisis plan should be publicly posted online, especially if it contains private details. But employees at all levels *should* know there is an effective plan in place and be confident that it's regularly tested.

A survey of financial analysts and investor relations officers at companies across Canada and the United States found that while many companies are mindful of the potential damage crises can cause to their sales, reputation and share value, few have an effective crisis management plan in place to deal with negative scenarios—and if they do, it is likely out of date.[3] Of responding analysts, 85 per cent said a corporate crisis had the greatest negative impact on a company's value, yet over 50 per cent said their company plan prepared them only for an operational crisis, and 50 per cent didn't even know if their company conducted crisis simulations.

There are many different form of crisis training. The most familiar is a *table-top simulation*, when the CMT are presented with a 'surprise' hypothetical scenario built around a developing operational or management crisis. It's designed to test the formal plan and is conducted under time pressure to assess the team's ability to perform their assigned roles and work together towards clear outcomes. A key focus is on timely internal and external communication. While the simulation is typically confined to the CMT (with or without deputies), a more advanced model can include participation by 'actors' playing the roles of external stakeholders, such as angry neighbours or excessively inquisitive reporters.

The other popular training model is a *full-scale exercise*, which deploys extensive resources outside the CMT, including, for example, actual representatives of emergency services and law enforcement, plus regulators, community leaders and news media (complete with tape recorders and video cameras). These high-profile exercises can be costly and time-consuming, but they have an added advantage of helping build working relationships with external stakeholders.

Other options are a *command post or war-room exercise*, designed mainly to test the effectiveness and operability of the designated location, or the back-up location; and *war games*, where competing teams are established to work through alternative response strategies.

HOW TO OVERCOME THE PROBLEM OF 'CRISIS TRAINING FATIGUE'

1. Avoid repetitious scenarios about predictable operational crises such as accidents, infrastructure breakdown and disasters. Mix it up with realistic managerial scenarios; for example, a cyber-security breach or real or perceived executive wrongdoing. Research shows these crises are typically high on the list of what's most probable.
2. Involve different people in the exercise beyond just the core team, such as designated deputies or alternates. There's always a high chance that some key players will be absent when a real crisis strikes. It will also improve 'bench strength'.
3. Spring a surprise exercise rather than scheduling it weeks in advance. Real crises don't fit neatly into any executive timetable. Will the activation systems work at night or at the weekend?
4. Instead of a conventional hypothetical scenario, get the team to workshop a real-life crisis or near miss which has happened to another organisation, perhaps in the same area or same industry. The principal purpose here is not to criticise what the other organisation did, but to honestly assess: 'What would we have done?' 'Would we have performed any better?' 'What can we learn from what happened to others?' and 'Do we need to makes changes to our own processes or preparedness?'

The form of training your organisation chooses is a decision for senior executives, based on what's appropriate for you, and may vary between different models. However, crisis simulation exercises in general have one major problem. Some executives seem to have the false idea that once they've completed a scenario drill, the job of getting ready for a crisis is done; that it's the finale to complete the process—a box-ticking exercise done and set aside until next time someone thinks crisis management is important.

This is a dangerous misunderstanding, because the team simulation is not the end of the journey to crisis preparedness. It's simply part of the beginning.

While the exercise helps test the process, validates plans and capabilities, and develops leadership skills,[4] a key outcome of any crisis simulation is also to identify gaps and weaknesses in organisational preparedness. Problems need to be remedied and the whole process exercised again, not just adjusted in the hope that it will work better in the face of a real crisis.

At the end of a crisis training exercise I usually get the team to assess: (a) Did the hypothetical simulation reveal any weaknesses in our knowledge of the scenario subject? and (b) Did it expose any practical, real-life problems? For example, in one exercise, the company had a well-equipped, secure cupboard in the crisis response room which contained all the pre-planned material, but on the day no one knew where the key was kept. As a result they subsequently lodged one key with the security office and another in a small 'break the glass' box alongside the locked cupboard.

At the very least, formal exercises should take place no less than once a year and preferably more often. Greater frequency may be appropriate if there has been recent management change; for example, appointment of new leadership, restructuring of functions or personnel, a merger or acquisition, or moving to a new location.

Regardless of timing and format, good crisis training should test the team's capacity to:

- make decisions against the clock
- work with incomplete or uncertain information
- maintain a high-level strategic perspective
- keep calm under pressure
- ensure key actions or communications don't get overlooked
- make effective use of the checklists
- balance competing priorities
- work as a team.

Crisis leadership is a learned skill which comes from practice. Your options are make mistakes and learn during training, or to make mistakes in a real crisis when everything is going wrong and the world is watching. Simulation exercises are essential for crisis preparedness, but they need to be fresh, relevant and, above all, regular.

CHAPTER KEY TAKEAWAY
A strong plan to get ready for a crisis is essential, and so is practising to make sure it works.

CHAPTER 11

HOW TO MINIMISE DAMAGE WHEN A CRISIS STRIKES

When you attend your local gym to learn self-defence, it's usually not because you are planning to fight anyone. More likely you train in order to get fit and in the hope that your new skill will reduce the chances of someone else wanting to pick a fight. But at the same time, you train in the knowledge that you'll be well prepared in the unlikely event that some ill-intentioned person actually does decide to attack you.

In the same way there are two sides to crisis proofing. The first is to take every possible step to try to prevent the crisis happening in the first place. The other side is to minimise the damage caused by any crisis which does happen. To properly understand the full scope of crisis proofing, both aspects need to be considered in parallel.

Much of my emphasis so far has been on the proactive mode—getting prepared before the crisis strikes, and taking steps to prevent it happening at all.

The focus now moves to the reactive mode: what to do when the crisis does happen; the role of senior executives in a crisis; and how effective crisis response helps to minimise damage—financial, operational and reputational.

Some people say that crisis management is an oxymoron—a contradiction in terms. That you can't 'manage' a crisis. That a crisis by its very definition is beyond conventional management experience and structures. That its unpredictability trumps regular processes.

To some extent all of that's true—if you think of managing in terms of order and control. But the key distinction here is that we are talking about crisis *response*—what you do and say when it all goes wrong—not crisis *control*. Sure, this is one of the most unpredictable and risky areas of crisis management. Yet how a company responds to a crisis often has a far greater impact on reputation and recovery than the crisis itself.

In the wake of the General Motors vehicle recall crisis in 2014, CEO Mary Barra wrote to all employees: 'Our company's reputation won't be determined by the recall itself, but by how we address the problem going forward.'[1]

One reason for this dilemma is that when a crisis strikes, external scrutiny is at its peak—by the public, news media, regulators, investors and other stakeholders. As the great comedian Spike Milligan once wrote, you will be 'scrutinised with an intense scrute'.

All this adds up to the central challenge of crisis response—that you have to do the right thing and say the right thing; and you also must be *seen* to do and say the right thing. And, crucially, you have to do and say the right things when the situation is confused; when you don't have all the facts; when regular roles and responsibilities may no longer apply; when you have to choose the 'least bad' option; and when the most important decision may well be the one you *should* have made 30 minutes ago.

This brings us to crisis communication. There is lot more to crisis management than communication, yet there is no denying that communication is a critical factor in how the management of a crisis is perceived.

In fact, 40 years ago, long before the rise of the internet, the Canadian scholar Joseph Scanlon wrote: 'Every crisis is also a crisis of information. Failure to control the crisis of information can ultimately result in failure to control the crisis.'[2]

In my experience, the notion of trying to control the crisis itself is at best optimistic, and at worst futile. But attempting to control your own crisis communication is absolutely a legitimate objective. Moreover, responsibility rests very clearly in the executive suite. And communication is a critical element of crisis proofing.

THE IMPACT OF BAD COMMUNICATION

As I mentioned before, the perception of how a company responds during a crisis often has a far greater impact on reputation and recovery than the crisis itself, and failed crisis communication can have a devastating and prolonged effect.

Look no further than the long-lasting damage to reputation caused by the misjudged statements from CEO Tony Hayward after the notorious BP oil spill in the Gulf of Mexico. It will probably be a generation before people forget his infamous plea that he would like to 'get his life back'. The *New York Times* called it the 'sound-bite from hell'.[3]

Sadly, there is a roll-call of bad crisis communication which has served to undo any good work or make a crisis worse.

Consider when faulty 'see-through' yoga pants sold by the American sports apparel company Lululemon caused a major hit to reputation and share price in 2014. A product recall was implemented but chairman Chip Wilson gave an interview in which he tried to 'explain' the excessively sheer pants problem by saying: 'Quite frankly, some women's bodies actually just don't work for them.' Facing a predictable backlash, he issued a much-criticised mea culpa, which ABC News suggested might be 'the worst apology ever'.[4] The result was a genuine reputational crisis and he soon resigned from the company he had founded.

Or consider Edward Burkhardt, Chairman of the Montreal, Maine & Atlantic Railway. In 2013, one of his company's trains, loaded with petrol, ran out of control downhill and virtually destroyed the small Canadian town of Lac-Mégantic through a deadly fireball which killed 47 people. After waiting four days before going to the scene, Burkhardt failed to show sufficient sincere sympathy and empathy for the victims and their families and friends; tried to blame fire fighters and a company employee before the cause of the disaster had been investigated; and tried to present himself as a victim because of his financial loss through the company's plunging share value. It's small wonder he was heckled and dubbed the most hated man in Lac-Mégantic. Contrary to his assertions, the official inquiry subsequently concluded that 'no one individual or single factor' caused the derailment and that the railway had a weak safety culture and no functioning safety system to manage risks.[5] The company later sued for bankruptcy and was sold.

This importance of communication in a crisis leads to two critical questions which directly involve organisational leadership:

1 Should the CEO be the spokesperson?
2 Should the CEO go to the scene to take charge?

Both of these questions are far more complicated than they might appear. In particular, the role of the spokesperson, and who plays that role, is vital to effective crisis communication.

THE ROLE OF SPOKESPERSON

Before you can even consider who should speak for the organisation, and whether it should it be the CEO or another executive, you need to think about the qualities that make a good spokesperson. Some of these can be taught—and that's where good media training is essential. Some of them are more about character and personality.

DESIRED QUALITIES OF A CRISIS SPOKESPERSON

- Capacity to communicate empathy as well as authority
- A good understanding of the crisis and organisational response
- Enough technical knowledge to avoid embarrassing mistakes
- Authority to make commitments on behalf of the organisation
- Ability to stay calm under pressure
- Previous experience with news media and other stakeholders
- Capacity to operate in a highly fluid and unstructured situation
- Ability to avoid jargon and corporate speak
- A willingness to listen as well as talk

In addition to this list of qualities of an effective crisis spokesperson, one other important factor comes into consideration; namely, that the individual who is a great spokesperson in normal times may not be the right person in a crisis. After all, a crisis is, by definition, a high-stress, high-risk situation which is most definitely not 'business as normal'. The executive who is professional and respected when announcing business results or a new corporate takeover to an audience of shareholders and financial analysts may appear very uncomfortable or even uncaring when speaking to the families of people killed in a terrible accident; or when talking to angry community leaders about a chemical leak which has poisoned the local town water supply; or meeting distraught mothers frantic about a faulty product which they believe has endangered their children.

What the spokesperson says, *how* it is said and *where* it is said are all critical elements in helping to determine the public perception of how well—or how badly—your organisation is responding to a crisis.

The spokesperson also has another very important role, which is setting the *tone* that will apply across the whole organisation's response. Although oil spills provide some high-profile and well-known examples of what not to do, let me share an example from the same area which demonstrates how real leadership can set the proper tone.

When a newly rebuilt oil tank at an Ashland plant near Pittsburgh, Pennsylvania, failed and collapsed, spilling one million gallons of diesel oil into the Monongahela River, Ashland CEO John Hall went to the scene and took charge.[6]

The company hired two air force C-130 transport planes to fly in Coast Guard oil pollution clean-up specialists. Within a week they presented Allegheny County with its first cheque for clean-up expenses. Furthermore, Ashland knew they faced legal action, so *encouraged* people to submit claims so that they could make advance payments.

The company also decided to publicly admit every mistake. 'What we didn't want to happen was for some outside investigation to reveal unpleasant information. Then, charges of cover-up could undermine the company's credibility.'

CEO Hall later said: 'Our attitude was: Hey guys, we've made a mess here. We've got to clean this thing up and we've got to try to do anything we can to help the people who have been inconvenienced.'

Even though the spill was entirely the company's fault, PR expert Paul Holmes concluded: 'Ashland came through the crisis better-known and better-respected than it went in.'[7]

I will return to the subject of the CEO setting the tone for communication during a crisis in a later chapter.

SHOULD THE CEO BE CRISIS SPOKESPERSON?

Choosing the right spokesperson is always important—and never more so than when an organisation is facing a crisis.

Yet despite the evident importance of the crisis spokesperson, many organisations simply revert to the default position that 'the CEO is our only spokesperson' without properly understanding whether that really is the best option.

It seems to be a case of yielding to conventional wisdom, and the position of the CEO can further promote this idea. It's very natural that the CEO feels a need to show leadership in a crisis, and to be seen to be taking responsibility for the response strategy—that when the stakes are so high, the buck stops at the top. However, that's not the same as being the spokesperson or, more accurately, not the same as being the primary or only spokesperson.

So, all other things being equal, should the CEO be the crisis spokesperson? The problem here is that the question itself is easily misunderstood. Absolutely the CEO should be visible and speak when there is a crisis, especially to address issues of policy and to show the organisation cares.

That does not mean the CEO should be the *only* spokesperson; nor does it mean they should speak on each and every aspect of the crisis on a 24/7 basis. The CEO should speak to demonstrate compassion and underline commitment to fixing the problem. Yet it is entirely appropriate—and often desirable—to have different spokespersons to talk about technical or operational details, or to provide routine media updates. Or a different person to address internal, as opposed to external, audiences.

Having qualified and well-trained alternative executives speaking on specific matters, or to specific audiences, is an effective way to help reduce the risk of over-exposing the CEO, and also allows the CEO to focus on providing leadership to manage the crisis. Furthermore, it allows the CEO to be held 'in reserve' to step in if things start to go wrong, or a dispute arises.

A conventional argument against this approach is the idea that, in the event of a crisis, the organisation must 'speak with one voice'. That is true, but here's the crucial distinction: speaking with one voice does *not* mean having only one spokesperson. That's a common misunderstanding. Speaking with one voice actually means consistency of message. It means that while new facts may emerge about the crisis, the overall message doesn't keep changing from hour to hour. And it means that the message remains unchanged across all the designated spokespersons—a calm, consistent and qualified voice.

SHOULD THE CEO GO TO THE SCENE TO TAKE CHARGE?

The importance of the CEO being visible builds on a reality I have already mentioned; namely, that the CEO must not only *do* the right thing, but must be *seen* to do the right thing. And in the fast-moving world of social media, the answer is not only about being seen to do the right thing—but increasingly also about perception and reputation. This leads to the second of my two critical questions: should the CEO go to the scene of the crisis and take charge?

Although it might seem like a tactical question for crisis planning, it is one of the more contentious issues. In fact, the pioneer US crisis expert William Small declared that no other issue has been debated so much as the role of the CEO in the first few hours of a crisis, and whether he or she should race to the scene.[8]

In some ways this question is almost unanswerable, and it links closely to the previous discussion about the CEO as spokesperson. At one level the solution seems quite simple: the CEO should be where he or she can do the most good for the organisation—perhaps out in the field comforting victims; perhaps in the board room directing recovery; or perhaps at external meetings to reassure investors, regulators and other stakeholders.

One of my favourite quotes is from the satirist H. L. Mencken, who is supposed to have said: 'For every complicated problem there is a solution which is clear, simple and wrong.' That is certainly the case here. It's one of those questions which seems obvious ... but isn't.

US President George W. Bush was famously attacked for failing to go to New Orleans soon enough after it was ravaged by Hurricane Katrina, even though it was claimed he was in Washington with his experts closely monitoring and managing the situation. Similarly, BP Chief Tony Hayward was bitterly criticised after being photographed at a yachting regatta in Britain during his company's Gulf of Mexico oil spill disaster, despite the fact that he had been constantly on call for the media for weeks.

It's an easy criticism, particularly in politics. Take Russian President Vladimir Putin who came under attack for remaining on holiday on the Black Sea for four days during the crisis over the sinking of the submarine *Kursk*. Or British Prime Minister David Cameron condemned by the media and his political foes for failing to return from a luxury holiday in France as the Global Financial Crisis unfolded.

Then of course there was CEO Lawrence Rawl of Exxon. When the tanker *Exxon Valdez* ran aground off Alaska, causing one of the worst oil spills in the United States, he didn't fly to the scene but stayed unseen in his office for six days. He then emerged to give a disastrous TV interview in which he blamed the captain for being drunk and blamed the US Coast Guard and Alaska state officials for delays in the clean-up.[9]

Three weeks after the spill, the CEO finally went to Alaska, where he was asked why he didn't go sooner. The hapless Mr Rawl told a news conference:

> I'm technologically obsolete. Getting me up there would have diverted our own people's attention. I couldn't help with the spill; I couldn't do anything about getting the ship off the rocks.[10]

This tone-deaf statement demonstrated that the CEO had no real understanding of his role. Of course he wasn't expected to help get the ship off the rocks. But he did need to show a personal commitment to the people of Alaska. This statement also reflected his suspicion and antagonism towards the media, which was legendary.

William K. Reilly, then head of the Environmental Protection Agency, said later that Rawl 'provided a casebook example of how not to communicate to the public when your company messes up'.[11]

Contrast this with Warren Anderson, Chairman and CEO of Union Carbide, who was praised for flying to India immediately after the chemical leak at Bhopal in 1984 to take charge on the scene. However, he was promptly arrested on arrival and spent almost a week cut off from proper communication in an Indian prison, leaving the company leaderless at a critical time. Right intention, wrong outcome.

It's not easy and the window of opportunity for the CEO to do the right thing in a crisis is very narrow. Moreover, it's sometimes extremely hard to know what *is* the right thing to do. However, from my research there are many, many more leaders criticised for *not* going to the scene than those who went and it proved the wrong decision. Broadly, I believe there are good grounds to argue that the CEO *should* go to the scene of a crisis, even if for no reason other than to be visible and to show that the organisation cares.

SO, WHAT TO SAY?

Communicating in a crisis is in some ways unlike any other area of communication. Indeed, unlike just about any other area of senior executive responsibility, it frequently requires making decisions and developing and conveying messages under pressure of time, when the information available is confusing or incomplete, and when emotions are running high.

None of that will be a surprise. But for organisations facing a crisis there is another challenge, and that's the credibility gap. Many CEOs and other senior executives cling on to a firm belief that what they say is heard and believed. Unfortunately, data suggest this is a case of sadly misplaced confidence. Repeated research in many different countries shows that when it comes to public perception of the ethics and honesty of professions, business executives are well down the list, along with journalists, politicians and used-car salespeople.

A Harris Interactive poll in the United States found that just 15 per cent of those questioned had a great deal of confidence in those running major companies, and 27 per cent said they had hardly any such confidence at all.[12] In a similar vein, a major study for the Public Affairs Council found that only 61 per cent of the public had a favourable view of major companies, and only 50 per cent thought CEOs possess high honesty and ethics.[13] Public Affairs Council President Doug Pinkham said at that time that considering the results of their study, companies might need to reconsider whether it's smart to use the CEO as spokesperson.

In fact, CEO credibility is under challenge even within top management. A major international study of C-Suite executives (excluding the CEO) found that 74 per cent reported that CEO apologies in general are genuine.[14] Which leaves a rather worrying 26 per cent who thought that CEOs in general are 'rarely or almost never' genuine in their apologies. Is it any wonder that the public have their doubts?

However, while I've already outlined the options for who should face the media and when, the reality is that it's big business, not just the CEO, which has a credibility problem, and in the end someone has to speak on behalf of the organisation.

There is a very extensive library of books and articles on the generally accepted techniques of how to communicate in a crisis. The truth is that some of this advice makes the task seem much easier than it is in real life. The book you're now reading is not intended to be a tactical how-to manual, but it is worth taking up just a little space to review some of the basics.

Given the data on public scepticism regarding corporate communication, and given the fact that the pressure and emotion of a crisis makes effective communication even harder, the task is not easy. And that should never be underestimated.

A high level of public and media scrutiny is a fact of life in any crisis and some dos and don'ts set the framework for success.

DOS AND DON'TS OF CRISIS COMMUNICATION

Do
- Respond quickly
- Speak with one voice
- Be informed and accurate
- Admit what you don't know
- Demonstrate empathy and caring
- Stop rumours; correct misinformation
- Focus on what you are going to say
- Say when more information will be available

Don't
- Speculate about cause or effect
- Lie or stonewall
- Be 'unavailable'
- Treat media as the enemy
- Say 'No comment'
- Apportion blame or point fingers
- Let legal considerations dominate
- Use jargon or acronyms

Needless to say, there is much more to it than that. Yet these 'golden rules' will serve any senior executive well. Are these rules new or original or revolutionary? Absolutely not. Are they fairly obvious? Yes. But, as I like to say, the obvious is always obvious when someone else points it out to you.

There is a litany of bad crisis communication exposed in the media, and I'll warrant that in just about every case you'll see a failure to comply with at least one of these basics.

While they are all important, none is more important than the need to demonstrate empathy and caring. As I write these words, there has just been a news report on television about a major multinational which sacked about 100 port workers. Each of the people affected was sent a text message at 30 minutes before midnight telling them not to come to work and to check their email for 'a letter regarding redundancy programme notification'.

I have no doubt there were logistical challenges and problems of timing. And I'm sure some smart lawyers were consulted about whether this was in breach of employment law. But it certainly didn't demonstrate empathy and caring, and was almost certain to make a bad situation even worse.

There is no really 'good' way to lay workers off, but this close-to-midnight method could only be described as a reputational crisis in the making, and my television is showing me pictures of angry workers blocking the port gate and union leaders calling for a nationwide strike. I will watch with interest to see how the company spokesperson explains this crisis communication. And I'll bet it's not the CEO who speaks but some lower executive sent out to face the music.

Every crisis is different and, as I said earlier, that fact is sometimes used as a 'reason' not to commit resources to crisis planning. Yet while specific circumstances vary for every crisis, I believe effective crisis communication can be built around five key *initial* steps, which apply in just about every crisis situation.

It is important to note that these five initial steps do not include blaming, justification, explanation or recovery. There will be plenty of time for that later, when the initial shock is over. But cover these five basic communication requirements right at the beginning and you will go a long way towards crisis proofing your organisation and avoiding disaster.

FIVE INITIAL STEPS FOR EFFECTIVE CRISIS COMMUNICATION

1 *Briefly state the facts as currently known.* Don't speculate and don't guess, but recognise that you need to address false rumours and perceptions as well as what actually happened.
2 *Apologise.* To be effective, any apology must be swift and sincere. Apologies that are only grudging or reluctant, or are really non-apologies, can be worse than no apology at all.
3 *Express sympathy.* Those affected by a crisis not only need to hear that you are sorry for the crisis, but also that you are sorry for how it has affected them personally. As the old maxim goes: 'People don't care what you know—they want to know that you care.'
4 *Express empathy.* You need to show those affected that you know how they feel. Crises are about feelings as well as facts. Demonstrating empathy shows you are human, not just a brand or organisational figurehead.
5 *Focus on actions.* Describe what actions you have already taken and what actions you plan to take to deal with the problem and prevent it happening again.

CHAPTER KEY TAKEAWAY

How a company responds and what it says during a crisis often has a far greater impact on reputation and recovery than the crisis itself.

CHAPTER 12

WHAT TO DO AFTER THE CRISIS SEEMS TO BE OVER

In the wake of any organisational crisis, the first order of business is typically: How do we restore operations? How quickly can we get back to business as usual?

It's natural and it's entirely understandable. But it's only part of what is needed in the post-crisis phase, and executives who fail to operate across the broad picture may be exposing their organisation to fresh risk.

Of the four phases of crisis proofing introduced in my integrated model (crisis preparedness, crisis prevention, crisis incident management and post-crisis management), post-crisis management is by far the most contentious and one of the most neglected areas of executive responsibility.

One reason is that it's not at all clear what actually constitutes the post-crisis phase. Some experts suggest that how to explain and how to apologise is the key post-crisis activity. There are established academic processes which support this approach,[1] but they tend to suggest that the main emphasis is on discourse and communication rather than operational action. In other words, explanations, apologia and image, rather than getting things done and proactively addressing post-crisis *events*. Moreover, the explanation/discourse approach is essentially short term and doesn't fully address the longer-term risks to the organisation.

CHAPTER 12: WHAT TO DO AFTER THE CRISIS SEEMS TO BE OVER   123

So when does the crisis end and post-crisis begin? It's a good question, and there is no definitive answer—experts and non-experts cannot even agree about what specifically is meant by 'post-crisis'.

The truth of the matter is that the crisis itself can evolve, and its impact can also evolve across time. Take, for example, the prolonged post-crisis legal process which followed the *Exxon Valdez* oil spill crisis in 1989, which was not finally settled until 2009. The company lawyers were probably rather pleased with themselves for hugely reducing the eventual payout, but it came at the cost of 20 years of continuous legal wrangling and reputation-sapping headlines.

Or the similar post-crisis marathon which faced BP after its notorious oil spill crisis in the Gulf of Mexico in 2010. Long after the worst of the spill had been cleaned up, and after years of seriously damaging publicity, in 2015 BP finally settled its liabilities to the US federal, state and local governments by agreeing to a US$18.7 billion settlement of economic and environmental claims. This took its total pre-tax charge for the spill to US$53.8 billion.

BP's CEO at the time said the settlement meant they could now 'plan the company's future', and the announcement had a positive effect in the BP share price.[2] But BP still faced numerous lawsuits from shareholders and other affected parties who opted out of the 2012 class action settlement. The *Wall Street Journal* reported many US investors expected spill-related litigation to drag on for decades.[3]

In both these cases, when did the crisis end and the post-crisis phase begin? Both were first an environmental crisis (a major oil spill); then a management crisis (slow and inadequate response); then a management/legal issue (sustained legal and public scrutiny of management response); and finally a damaging reputation issue which may persist for a generation. It's this prolonged and sometimes very dangerous transition from crisis to post-crisis to issue which is the focus of this chapter.

To keep all of these competing activities aligned, I'll return to the fourth quadrant of my integrated model—post-crisis management—and consider each of the key clusters of activity;

namely recovery/business resumption; post-crisis issue impacts; and evaluation and modification. These are the three areas of activity which need to be pursued after the crisis *seems* to be over, and it's a serious mistake to do one and not the others.

RECOVERY/BUSINESS RESUMPTION

Of all the post-crisis activities, the cluster under the heading of recovery/business resumption is undoubtedly the one which gets most attention. As mentioned earlier, it includes concepts such as operational recovery, market retention, business momentum and share price protection, and comes with a variety of names, including business continuity and turnaround management.

The immediate tasks here, in a broad sense, are strongly tactical rather than strategic. There is a large body of literature presented as crisis management, or sometimes post-crisis management, which is in fact primarily about operational requirements such as data recovery, customer and supplier management, and restoring IT and communication, and essential services such as power, gas and water. In fact, some commercially offered 'business continuity programs' concentrate almost entirely on protecting the organisation against infrastructure problems such as weather events, power outages, computer failure and breakdown of logistics and communication systems. One of the problems this approach creates is that the terms 'crisis management' and 'business continuity' can become interchangeable. Indeed, I've been invited to speak at conferences on crisis management which turn out to be solely about operational continuity.

There's no question that business continuity is important and that operational recovery is essential in the wake of a crisis. The real danger is that when the executive group put their effort solely into recovery, the short-term results may feel satisfying and productive, yet can mask emerging new threats to business and reputation.

Crisis management and business continuity are not synonymous. When business has been restored—when all the explaining and apologising is done—is when new crisis risks can assail the organisation and its reputation.

POST-CRISIS ISSUE IMPACTS

In the immediate aftermath of a crisis, when blame and operational responses might be the main focus, and when the natural desire is to move on, leaders may be unwilling or unable to make more objective judgements about the ongoing risk to the organisation, and about the need to change management processes. While many aspects of operational recovery and business resumption are largely tactical activities, the task of identifying and managing post-crisis issues lies unambiguously at the door of the CEO and top executives.

The reason for this responsibility is equally unambiguous—namely, that the risks to the organisation can be far greater *after* the crisis than *during* the crisis itself. The Dutch academics Paul 't Hart and Arjen Boin captured this idea very well when they coined the term, the 'crisis after the crisis', which they said existed in the 'long shadow of post-crisis politics'.[4] Similarly, the British crisis writer Norman Phelps warned: 'When the dust begins to settle, the aftershocks are often more devastating and costly to the organisation over the long term than the original crisis.'[5]

> **DANGER IN THE TUNNEL**
>
> The light of resolution the manager begins to see at the end of one crisis tunnel may very well be the prodromal light of an oncoming crisis. That would be bad enough if it were not also for the acute whistle of another crisis sneaking up behind the manager in the same tunnel.
>
> Louisiana academic John Darling[6]

No matter what words are used to express it, this phenomenon is very real and represents a serious risk to the organisation which may persist long after the return to 'business as usual'. We have already discussed the terrible long-term costs of a crisis in terms of share value, reputation and even corporate survival, and it's very evident that much of this risk lies in the dangerous post-crisis phase—the so-called 'crisis after the crisis'.

The reality is that the endpoint of a crisis is sometimes not 'resolution' but a fresh or renewed issue or crisis. John Darling refers to the *illusory nature* of crisis resolution and admitted that it is often difficult to see where one crisis ends and another one begins, especially where the ripple effects of one crisis set off fresh issues or another crisis within the organisation.

One of the authorities on this elusive transition is my hero, Bob Heath, a Texas academic who I first met when he visited my home town a few years ago. We spent the day visiting nearby wineries, and he helped me with his understanding of issues and crises and the link between the two.

Bob is one of those genuine experts whose writing aims to explain concepts in a way which is intended to inform the reader rather than to impress through convoluted language and supposedly advanced vocabulary. He is also one of the most prolific writers in his field. His ideas on post-crisis risks are set out in a piece which has the typically whimsical title *After the Dance is Over*.[7]

There he poses a very important question: 'What conditions lead to an issue becoming a crisis? Likewise, what elements of a crisis result in its becoming an issue?'

Any organisation which fails to consider this question, and fails to manage the crucial transition beyond conventional crisis response, faces a substantial risk to business and reputation. Or, from an executive attention viewpoint, in thinking single-mindedly just about crisis response and business recovery, you may not give proper attention to longer-term threats to your organisation.

Identifying such post-crisis impacts is usually not a difficult or complex task. Most often they are fairly self-evident, even if they are not contextualised as part of post-crisis management. Typically, they include legal proceedings such as inquests, coronial inquiries, civil and criminal prosecution, litigation, licence reviews or class action lawsuits. They might even extend to formal public hearings, such as Commissions of Inquiry or Congressional Investigations.

Whatever the framework, such developments demand top executive attention and must not be simply delegated to the lawyers and public relations people. The great French statesman Georges Clemenceau said,

'War is far too important to be left to the generals' and the equivalent sentiment can be paraphrased for post-crisis management.

There is a long and disquieting history of post-crisis events which have damaged or even destroyed reputations. For example, I have referenced the Congressional Inquiry into Hurricane Katrina and its damning conclusion that, while there was no failure to predict the inevitability and consequences of the monster hurricane, there was a failure of initiative to get beyond design and organisational compromises to improve the level of protection afforded. Later I described the investigation into the crisis which struck the New Zealand dairy giant Fonterra, and the devastating official report which concluded the organisation had failed to 'join the dots' between product contamination, consumer sensitivity and reputation.

Moreover, it's a political reality that official inquiries and post-crisis investigations are frequently established not just to determine the facts but also to find someone to blame. Sadly, the person or persons blamed are sometimes 'victims' of the situation who are offered up as scapegoats while the true 'villains' may be those responsible for the crisis-prone culture which helped promote the event in the first place.

THE CAUTIONARY TALE OF ADMIRAL JOHN BYNG

At the start of the Seven Years' War in 1756, French forces in Toulon threatened the Mediterranean island of Minorca. After considerable delay, the British Admiralty despatched Admiral Byng with an undermanned and badly maintained fleet, and 700 men from Gibraltar, to secure the island. But they were far too late, and when he arrived the French had already overrun Minorca and besieged the garrison at Fort St Philip. After suffering heavy damage in sea-battle against a larger and better-armed French fleet, Byng and his commanders agreed to withdraw.

You might think Byng would be praised for trying to save his ships and the lives of his men, but you'd be wrong. Partly to deflect attention from its own delays and lack of preparedness, the Admiralty court-martialled Byng for 'failure to do his utmost' to prevent Minorca falling to the French. The findings of the court-martial were a foregone conclusion, even though Byng had requested and been refused the reinforcements he needed to carry out his mission. The condemned

> man was executed on the quarterdeck of his own flagship in Portsmouth Harbour in March 1757. Not only did he lose his life, but his reputation was also destroyed and his name became a byword for cowardice. Indeed, as recently as 2013, the British Ministry of Defence refused a family appeal to review the case and grant him a posthumous pardon.[8]
>
> Commenting on this notorious case, the French satirist Voltaire wrote: 'In England it is sometimes wise to shoot an Admiral from time to time to encourage the others.'

In today's corporate world, the penalty for failure in a crisis is less final than for Admiral Byng, but the hunt for someone to blame and the impact on reputation is just as strong. Many a modern executive has been sacrificed 'for the good of the organisation' in the aftermath of a crisis, though today they are more likely to leave with a comfortable package rather than facing a firing squad.

Similarly, post-crisis changes in senior personnel and the ever-popular 'restructuring of management' may be claimed as an effort to address the culture which helped precipitate the crisis. However, that's often little more than an effort to calm the market and reassure anxious stakeholders. In fact, the hunt for someone to blame can actually make future crises *more* likely, because individuals and departments may be less willing to raise the alarm about red flags and other warning signals.

This challenge is not new, and the writers Elizabeth Morrison and Frances Milliken coined the useful term 'organizational silence' to describe a situation where employees deliberately withhold information about potential problems and issues.[9] This is especially pertinent when it comes to potential crises.

Of course, it's easy to be wise after the event and to sit in calm judgement on those who had to make decisions under the stress of a crisis, with incomplete information and sometimes inadequate resources. But that's exactly what happens when behaviour in a crisis is examined in a courtroom months or even years after the event. And that's exactly why crisis proofing is so important—to help reduce the likelihood of a crisis happening in the first place, and to equip senior executives to make better decisions under pressure.

RESPONDING TO POST-CRISIS ISSUES

So, how to navigate the transition from crisis response to post-crisis issues? It isn't particularly hard. It just needs discipline and process, and the preferred process is the one I introduced earlier—namely, issue management—to clearly identify the risk, to set agreed objectives, and to put in place tactical plans of action.

Formal issue management can enable the organisation or industry to move beyond the conventional defensive processes normally associated with post-crisis response and recovery, in order to take a planned, strategic approach to the longer-term issues.

However, there is a problem here which needs executive-level intervention and leadership. Most crisis management plans have an established process to activate and mobilise the crisis team. But it is much less common to find an established process to stand the team down when the crisis is 'over', and to step away from crisis-response mode.

I have already described how it is not always easy to characterise when a crisis ends and when the post-crisis phase begins. In exactly the same way, it is not easy to describe how and when the crisis team stands down and when the subsequent issues get handed off to an experienced issue management group.

Believe me, this is not at all a trivial or bureaucratic question. It's about the best use of organisational resources and the way to achieve a planned, positive outcome; to protect reputation; and to potentially save your company from disaster.

Just as a crisis demands different skills and competencies from those which are adequate during 'business as usual', so, too, post-crisis issue management has its own requirements.

A designated crisis management team is typically focused on crisis response—deciding what needs to be said and done to deal with an immediate threat to the organisation. The team's strengths are to a great extent operational, with a skill set for making key strategic and tactical decisions to bring the crisis under control, to interact with stakeholders, and to restore operations as quickly as possible with the least long-term damage.

But that's not the same skill set, and maybe not the same group of people, needed to identify and manage those dangerous post-crisis issues which might last weeks, months or even years. The crisis management team might be likened to the fire brigade putting out the fire and making the people and fire ground safe. By contrast, issue management specialists might represent the team investigating post-crisis questions such as the cause of the fire and dealing with insurance claims and the inquest into the deaths of those who perished in the flames. In other words, the people who deal with the 'crisis after the crisis'.

The hand-off from crisis mode to post-crisis issue mode might appear to be fairly basic and procedural. Yet experience shows that it is easy and common for disconnects to open up, and for critical strategies, policy, stakeholders and momentum to be lost in that gap.

The time when the crisis *seems* to be over is the very time when executive leadership is needed to ensure people don't relax and fall into the trap of self-congratulation. If it is true—as Norman Phelps says—that the aftershocks are often more devastating and costly to the organisation over the long term than the original crisis, then executive management must take decisive steps to maintain momentum to help avoid the organisation falling victim to fresh crises or fresh issues.

EVALUATION AND MODIFICATION

The same need for executive leadership also applies to the third area of the post-crisis phase—namely, evaluation and modification.

Some of the best experts in the field have called this phase 'an opportunity to change those aspects of the organisation which helped create the potential for crisis in the first place'.[10] Nothing *should* be more obvious and self-evident. Yet the task of evaluation and modification is not only frequently neglected, but is sometimes deliberately ignored or minimised.

Given that the majority of crises are caused by management, and given that more than two-thirds arise from 'smouldering crises' which could have and should have been identified in advance,[11] it's no surprise that some top executives are reluctant to examine too closely their own management failings.

Naturally they don't express it like that. They use convenient phrases such as 'Let's not dwell on the past' or 'Let's keep focused on the future' or 'Let's renew our commitment to our core values'.

The good news is that it doesn't have to be like that. Soon after Mary Barra took over as CEO of General Motors in 2014, the company was plunged into a crisis when it was revealed that they had ignored faulty ignition switches for over a decade, and hid the danger from regulators. Barra followed a textbook approach when she apologised, admitted they had done wrong and committed to putting it right. But her communication about the crisis went much further than just this conventional response. She constantly highlighted that she did not want GM to 'move past' or 'put it behind them'. Quite to the contrary, she said she did not want this to be a bad memory that faded into the background. Instead, she wanted the crisis to 'remain a constant reminder of what happens when people don't do the right thing, and to use it to change the culture of the company'. It's little wonder that *Fortune* magazine dubbed her 'Crisis Manager of the Year'.[12]

The post-crisis phase has been described as a critical period of learning readiness, but, regrettably, Ms Barra's response at GM is likely the exception rather than the rule. More often a number of management defence mechanisms kick in which can easily block or inhibit post-crisis learning. These might include management denial that the crisis was as bad as it seemed at the time, or reconstruction and distortion of events to cover up their own vulnerability.

A stark example of this was captured by Lisa Tyler, who examined in detail the equivocal language used by Exxon in the wake of the infamous *Exxon Valdez* oil spill. She concluded that company executives who insist that the spill was an unavoidable accident surely are less likely to work to prevent such accidents in the future:

> If corporate executives insist that the accident would not have occurred if Exxon rules had been followed, they have less reason to examine corporate policies and procedures, and more reason to perceive themselves, unreasonably, as victims of the situation.[13]

Indeed, the importance of management culture in incubating the potential for crisis within an organisation was highlighted by the British writers Denis Smith and Chris Sipika, who were in no doubt at all about its impact. One of the main barriers to post-crisis learning, they said—apart from the generalised belief that 'it can't happen here'—is the 'core values and assumptions of senior managers'.[14]

The influence of management culture, and failure to learn from crisis, are especially evident when organisations not only have a crisis but then have the same crisis all over again. Such things don't often happen, though when they do, serious questions may finally get asked. But as Matthew Syed boldly asserts in his 2015 book on black box thinking: 'Failure to learn from mistakes has been one of the single greatest obstacles to human progress.'[15]

One of the best-known examples is the *Challenger* accident in 1986 when the space shuttle exploded just seconds into its flight, killing all seven crew. NASA initially tried to deflect blame, but the subsequent inquiry showed that NASA culture and groupthink was a key contributing factor that led to warnings being ignored. Tragically, the right lessons were not learned, which led to disaster in 2003 when the space shuttle *Columbia* broke up on re-entry into earth's atmosphere, again killing all seven aboard. Following the second disaster, one analysis asked the crucial question: 'Can a culture be lethal?'[16]

The same sort of questions could have been asked following the badly managed Firestone recall of 6.5 million tyres in 2000 after more than 200 deaths were attributed to tyre failures. It was one of the largest tyre recalls in history, second only to *another* badly managed Firestone recall in 1978, and repeated many of the same mistakes.[17]

Another example of a repeat crisis was when more than 1600 people died in a crush during the Hajj pilgrimage to Mecca in mid-2015. Sadly, this tragic event followed 1426 pilgrims killed in a similar stampede in 1990; 270 in 1994; 1198 in 1998; 251 in 2004; and 362 in 2006.[18]

However, post-crisis lessons are not just about repeating mistakes, but also may be about not learning from what went well. In 1955, the Japanese dairy products company Snow Brand was struck by a food poisoning outbreak which became an example of a crisis well controlled and well managed. But when a second bacteria-borne outbreak occurred in 2000, the company appeared to have learned nothing, and the result was what became Japan's worst ever food poisoning incident, with well over 10,000 people affected.[19]

A similar failure to learn was one of the causes of the Hillsborough Stadium disaster in Sheffield in 1986, when 96 football fans were killed and a further 776 were injured in a terrible crushing event, one of the world's worst football stadium disasters. It was later revealed that a near identical set of circumstances arose at the same location a year earlier, and tragedy was averted through a simple intervention by an experienced police officer. However, failure to conduct an effective debrief after this near miss prevented the first officer from transferring his knowledge to the police team in charge of the game the following year. This lack of learning, combined with other circumstances associated with the event, led to the subsequent disaster.[20]

While this sporting tragedy was still being investigated almost 30 years later,[21] what is the right process for organisations to investigate and learn from crisis?

HOW TO REVIEW AND LEARN

At one end of the spectrum is the air accident investigation model. Any senior executive who is tempted to find some excuse to avoid the possibly embarrassing review of what happened in a crisis—especially if management was at fault—should think again next time he or she walks through an airport.

The safety of today's aircraft is built to a large extent on thorough investigation of when things went wrong in the past. As you are waiting to take off, be aware that the modern standard of communication between pilots and air traffic control was massively overhauled following an investigation into the Tenerife Airport disaster in 1977, when two jumbo jets collided on the runway, killing 583 people, the worst ever loss of life in an aviation accident. And when you listen to that standard boring announcement about no smoking in the toilets, be aware that smoke detectors and automatic fire extinguishers became mandatory when an investigation into the fatal fire on an Air Canada plane in 1983 discovered the fire started in the toilet and went undetected. Only half the people aboard survived the crash-landing of the burning plane.

Or perhaps, as you lean back and enjoy the in-flight entertainment, think about Swissair flight 111 which crashed into the sea after taking off from New York in 1998, killing all 229 aboard. The investigation which followed took five years and involved reassembling a reported two million pieces of debris, before experts discovered that fire started in the in-flight entertainment system and ignited flammable insulation. It led to the introduction of new fire-resistant materials in aircraft construction.

I'm not suggesting a five-year investigation into every organisational crisis. But the air-crash model has some powerful lessons for senior managers. Avoid setting out to assign blame. Find out what really happened. Bring in experts if needed. Learn from the event and make changes to avoid it happening again.

How to undertake a post-crisis review depends very much on your organisation and the scale of the event. It might be a small management team assessment. Or it might be a technical root cause analysis. Or it might be a forensic accounting exercise. But the essential element is that it must be undertaken in a genuine spirit of trying to honestly determine the facts, not to hide or obfuscate. As the American educator and philosopher John Dewey said: 'We do not learn from experience. We learn from reflecting on experience.'

Which brings me to one other important facet of the air-crash model—the need to learn not only from our own crises but also from the crises of others. Lessons from an air-crash investigation are typically shared with other airlines, aircraft manufacturers and regulators throughout the world. The findings may lead to mandatory changes in design, maintenance or operation which are communicated through a formal process of notifications.

In a business or corporate environment, taking lessons from crises suffered by *others* is less formal but no less important. As Larry Smith, former President of the Institute for Crisis Management, says: 'You will never have a crisis someone else hasn't experienced.' I described earlier that you need a practical process to share learning via a case study simulation to consider a real-life crisis which has happened to another organisation, perhaps in the same area or the same industry, which is focused not on what other people did wrong but how you can learn.

Only by genuinely learning from post-crisis review and making any necessary changes to planning and preparedness can you close the circle on the process. In that way, evaluation and modification becomes an integral part of crisis proofing, not just bolted on as an afterthought.

CHAPTER KEY TAKEAWAY

Business continuity and recovery is important, but how a corporation responds to consequential risks after the crisis can determine the severity of adverse impacts and how long they persist.

CHAPTER 13

NO, IT'S NOT JUST ABOUT FACTS AND DATA

One of the most persistent and perplexing obstacles to effective crisis proofing is failing to properly understand the true nature of the emerging issue or crisis.

You may have defined the issue in a succinct and accurate way in terms of impact on the organisation using my formula of PROBLEM + IMPACT = ISSUE. But that's not necessarily the same as fully understanding the issue from the perspective of outside stakeholders.

It's no secret that people often *say* a problem is one thing, when the actual problem is something else. Just ask any family doctor. Or when the customer tells the salesperson 'I don't like the colour', it might in fact mean 'I do like the colour, but I can't afford it right now.' So offering a different colour doesn't address the real barrier.

The same problem can emerge when it comes to issue and crisis management. For example, a Canadian study into the motivation of campaigners against genetically modified organisms concluded that much anti-GM activism is more likely motivated by anti-corporate and anti-globalisation sentiment and desire for social reform rather than by concern for food safety.[1] That's not to say that food safety is unimportant, but it is a reminder that the stated concern and the underlying concern may be different.

So, in responding to an issue or emerging crisis it is clear that facts and data are important, yet it's a major mistake to imagine that they alone are the solution. Data is information, but it's rarely the complete answer. In fact, some stakeholders actively resist data if it conflicts with their feelings.

Social psychologists have a concept called confirmation bias, which is the tendency to search for information, or an interpretation of information, which confirms your beliefs. The flip side, of course, is the tendency to reject information that contradicts or doesn't support your beliefs, even in the face of strong data.

Take the case of anti-wind-farm campaigners who believe that low-level sound from wind turbines causes a range of illnesses. Medical experts and acousticians around the world have produced numerous scientific reports to demonstrate that wind turbines do not cause illness. But their opponents continue to claim this issue 'may be the next asbestos' and call for further studies in the hope that it will turn up something new and positive.

My friend Peter Sandman says what is happening here is that data can snatch away the basis of a belief. He uses a vivid analogy to illustrate this truth and, with his permission, I'll borrow and adapt his example.

You and your spouse are discussing where to go for dinner, and the discussion becomes an argument. You want Italian and your spouse wants Chinese. The disagreement gets a bit out of hand, so you imagine that now would be a smart time to introduce data. You throw in scientific information which shows that Italian food is more nutritious; you quote research which suggests Italian food is easier to digest; and you use a survey to show that 'people like us' tend to prefer Italian. Your spouse finally concedes and you look forward to a nice Italian dinner together.

Some hope! As Sandman points out, your spouse's level of anger hasn't gone down. It's gone up, because you have proved your spouse to be wrong. You have used data to deny his or her reasoning. And during dinner your angry spouse will doubtless find something *else* to be upset about.

Put like this, the misapplication of data seems patently dumb. But, sadly, some senior executives responsible for issue and crisis management do this all the time. Faced with a disagreement or misunderstanding, they just pile on the data.

PILING ON THE DATA

It is important to realise that this mistaken approach is not the result of malice, ignorance or deliberate misunderstanding.

Many senior executives have a technical background—such as engineering, finance, architecture, logistics or chemistry—and it's only natural that they are confident in their professional discipline. The problem is when over-confidence in the accuracy and importance of your information outweighs your capacity to see that an emerging issue or crisis is not just about facts and data.

This might seem like a somewhat abstract generalisation. So let's take a little time to consider three well-known crises where over-reliance on facts and data led to disaster.

The first of these was in the mid-1990s, when Shell UK needed to dispose of the huge disused oil-storage buoy *Brent Spar*. After three years assessing all the options, and securing legal and political backing, the company announced it would tow the 14,500-tonne facility from the North Sea to the North Atlantic and sink it in deep water. While the oil giant saw this as a logical and economical engineering solution, with sign-off from all the relevant authorities, Greenpeace characterised the plan as 'dumping toxic waste in the ocean' and vowed to fight it.

To highlight their perspective on deep-sea disposal, Greenpeace used a dramatic and media-savvy occupation of the abandoned platform. The story gained enormous international attention, particularly in continental Europe, where Shell suffered damaging protests, a boycott of its products and even firebombing of petrol stations. In the face of such protest, and with political support ebbing away, the plan to sink the buoy was abandoned and *Brent Spar* was eventually scrapped on land in Norway.

Looking back after the event, Christopher Fay, Chairman and CEO of Shell UK, told the BBC:

> We covered all the scientific angles. We covered all the technical angles and we certainly very much covered all the legalistic angles. That
> was maybe a bit inward thinking. We hadn't taken into account hearts and emotions, where people are coming from, which is in part today's debate.[2]

The following year, Cor Herkstroter, Corporate Chairman of the Royal Dutch Shell group of companies, conceded they had failed to recognise that the issue was symbolic as well as technical:

> For most engineering problems there is a correct answer. For most social and political dilemmas there is a range of possible answers, almost all compromises. So starting off with a strong, scientifically grounded mindset, we tended to misjudge some of the softer issues and consequently made mistakes. We misread some of the situations.[3]

Mr Herkstroter's honest assessment of the dangers of the so-called 'engineering approach' was also starkly illustrated in another high-profile case, which occurred around the same time.

This was the notorious Intel Pentium chip crisis, where computer users raised concerns about the integrity of a new memory chip, and were largely ignored. After weeks of denial and mounting criticism, Intel finally agreed that the computer chip fault was more serious than they had admitted and announced a recall, accepting a one-off charge against earnings of US$475 million. Intel CEO Andy Grove later summarised the wellspring of this disaster:

> We got caught between our mindset, which is a fact-based, analysis-based engineer's mindset, and customers' mindset, which is not so much emotional but accustomed to making their own choice.[4]

My third example of this problem focuses not on engineering but on science and technology. The US corporation Monsanto had been highly successful in applying biotechnology to food production in the United States, and in the late 1990s attempted to introduce what they called 'genetically improved' crops to the United Kingdom and the rest of Europe. Monsanto expected their product would be equally welcome across the Atlantic, but they had gravely misread the social and political environment in Western Europe. Their arrival triggered a eruption of objection and protest, with consumer groups accusing the multinational of 'biocolonialism'.

With their reputation in tatters and the share price starting to plummet, Monsanto was eventually forced to accept a merger with Pharmacia

Upjohn, which subsequently sold off Monsanto's biotechnology division. In a remarkably frank discussion of the debacle, CEO Bob Shapiro noted:

> We started with the conviction that biotechnology was useful and valuable but we have tended to see it as our task to convince people that we were right and that people with different points of view were wrong. We have irritated and antagonised more people than we have persuaded. Our confidence in biotechnology has been widely seen as arrogance and condescension because we thought it was our job to persuade. But too often we forgot to listen.[5]

What a damning confession: 'We forgot to listen.' British PR risk expert Judy Larkin memorably quipped: 'By the end of 2000 Monsanto had wrecked an entire industry as well as its own brand.'[6] And the brand impact was certainly persistent. Fifteen years later, the annual Harris poll of America's Most Hated Companies *still* placed Monsanto in fourth place (behind Goldman Sachs, IAG and Dish Network).[7]

The key pitfalls for Monsanto—as well as for Shell and Intel—were not listening to important stakeholders and fatal over-confidence in their own technology. Such errors cannot be permitted if your crisis proofing is to succeed.

Stakeholders will soon enough tell you whether there is a crisis. It has been argued that a crisis can be viewed as the perception of an event that threatens important expectancies of stakeholders and can threaten your organisation's performance. Crises, therefore, are largely perceptual, and if stakeholders *believe* there is a crisis then the organisation *is* in a crisis, unless it can persuade stakeholders that it is not.

WHAT'S A FACT ANYWAY?

It's a serious mistake to attempt to persuade by over-reliance on facts and data. It's a seductive thought that a fact is a fact is a fact. But that idea is an illusion. In the same way that one person's terrorist is another person's freedom fighter, so, too, one person's 'fact' is another person's 'propaganda' and yet another person's 'matter of opinion'.

This is a reasonably obvious proposition, but it seems to come as a surprise to some senior executives raised in a technical discipline where facts are regarded as indisputable, and where certainty is the cornerstone of decision-making. Everything in their training leads them to the belief I have often heard expressed in this way: 'While our opponents might lie and bend the truth, if we just stick to the facts we can't go far wrong.'

This approach is particularly prevalent when it comes to the sort of emotive and contentious situations which often underlie issues and crises. So we need to dispel the notion that having the facts on your side necessarily means you'll win the day—that facts are immutable pillars with which to build a crisis-proof organisation.

FACTS ARE CHANGING ALL THE TIME

In the early 1960s the Austrian-American economist Fritz Machlup coined the idea of the 'half-life of knowledge'.[8] Drawing on the notion of the half-life of radioactive particles (i.e. the time it takes for particles to decay), it is argued that the half-life of knowledge is the amount of time it takes before half of the knowledge in a particular area is superseded or shown to be untrue. More recently, this idea was expanded and popularised in the best-selling book *The Half-Life of Facts* in which the mathematician Samuel Arbesman argues that in every discipline, facts change in a predictable and quantifiable way.[9] In other words, everything we know as a 'fact' may eventually be overturned by new knowledge.

Apart from the rather unsettling proposition that facts keep changing, it is also the case that facts sometimes get overwhelmed not by new knowledge but by non-facts. And these non-facts have a habit of 'becoming' fact. This idea was promoted by Vladimir Lenin, one of the founders of modern communism. Lenin said: 'A lie told often enough becomes the truth.' The source may undermine this sentiment, but it's a genuinely valid idea.

I am a hopeless movie buff and this same conclusion was beautifully illustrated in the John Ford Western *The Man Who Shot Liberty Valance*, which is about the mistaken identity of the gunman who killed a notorious outlaw. At the end of the movie, the local newspaper editor realises the truth and says: 'When the legend becomes the fact, print the legend.'

Moving from the cinema to real life, one of my favourite examples of how a non-fact 'becomes' a fact was how we managed the turn of the century. Experts such as the Royal Observatory at Greenwich and the US Navy Institute were unanimous that the new millennium began on 1 January 2001. But popular belief was that it began on 1 January 2000. That false idea 'became' a fact and governments and communities around the world organised and funded massive millennium celebrations on the 'wrong day'. Needless to say, the few brave souls who dared to point out the error were accused of being pedants and curmudgeonly spoil-sports. As the wonderful fantasy fiction author Terry Pratchett wrote: 'Just because things are obvious doesn't mean they're true.'

Now, you might argue that this 'mistake' did no harm and had no real cost. Contrast that with the so-called Millennium Bug, or Y2K Bug, which we were told would shut down computers and cause life-threatening chaos at midnight on 1 January 2000. As a result, business and governments invested an estimated US$300 billion to pre-empt the crisis. It is generally agreed that problems on the day turned out to be relatively few and minor, which, according to supporters of the claimed threat, showed it was money well spent. However, there are many others who believe the Millennium Bug scare was the world's most over-managed non-event, and may have been based on a non-fact.

So, what has this got to do with crisis proofing the organisation? Which day the millennium actually clicked over, or whether the Y2K bug was real, is generally not very important in the big picture. But when it comes to facts and data about questions such as 'Is the earth really warming and if so by how much?' or 'Will global sea levels really rise and if so by how much?' the correct answer truly is critical to business and society.

Debate over climate change highlights a key challenge for executive use of facts and data. Not only do facts change over time—and non-facts can 'become' facts—but major stakeholders also may have a suspicion or even outright antipathy towards the science and technology which typically generates such information.

Look no further than the study in early 2014 which showed almost half of Americans believed in medical conspiracy theories, including a broad belief that the government is deliberately preventing the public from getting natural cures for cancer and other diseases because of pressure from drug companies.[10] The belief might not be based on reality, but it has very real consequences, with people being less likely to rely on their family doctor, less likely to have life-saving vaccination, and less likely to follow conventional medical advice. As usual, Mark Twain had something wise to say about this. 'It ain't what you don't know that gets you into trouble. It's what you know for sure that just ain't so.'

Understanding society's level of scepticism and its misdirected opinions and concerns is critically important for senior executives trying to manage issues and crises. Moreover, excessive reliance on facts and data leads to the logical next step—namely, a belief that if something is not a fact then the truth will eventually prevail. It's a comforting thought, but it's about as useful as simply standing there pleading 'but it isn't true' as a crisis crashes around you.

TRUTH DOESN'T ALWAYS PREVAIL

Just because something is not true—even if you have the facts and data to disprove it—doesn't mean it won't have an impact. In an earlier chapter I described examples where hoaxes or rumours had a dramatic effect on a company's share price and reputation, though in each case the false information was quickly disproved and the impact just as quickly dispelled.

However, it's not always that simple. The impact of false allegations can persist and cause long-lasting damage. Take, for example, accusations that began circulating in the early 1980s that the 'man in the moon' logo used by Procter & Gamble for over 100 years was a secret Satanist symbol, and that the company had helped fund Satanist groups. The charges were completely without foundation, but the company spent years defending itself before the controversial logo was eventually dropped in 1995. However, even then the damage was not over, and as recently as 2007 Procter & Gamble was awarded over US$19 million in a lawsuit against former Amway distributors who spread Satanist rumours about their competitor.[11]

Another company which faced a groundless but potentially harmful allegation was Nike when they produced a new range of footwear, which featured a logo on the heel and sole that incorporated the word 'Air' in a design intended to represent flickering flames or heat rising from the pavement.

Some Muslim critics claimed the logo could be interpreted as the word 'Allah' in Arabic script. Despite Nike reportedly receiving independent advice from respected Islamic scholars that this was a misinterpretation of the logo, the company decided this was a cross-cultural debate it could not 'win'.

As a result, it recalled more than 30,000 pairs of the offending shoes and ceased distribution of the remainder.[12] It also agreed to build several playgrounds in Muslim communities as part of the apology. Predictably, Nike was attacked by some critics for giving in to a 'noisy minority', but the company took a business decision in recognising the concern, and averted the threat of a global boycott and prolonged reputational damage.

Similarly, rumours have circulated for years that if you read Coke's Arabic logo backwards (or in a mirror or upside down), it allegedly spells out an anti-Muslim slogan. It's not true, as Coke's website spells out in painstaking detail.[13] But unlike Procter & Gamble, Coca-Cola shows no sign of even thinking about changing its multi-billion-dollar trademark. Yet, as a story in the *Economist* points out—under the rather depressing heading 'Denial is useless'—this and other supposedly anti-Muslim rumours help explain why Coke does worse than Pepsi in Arab countries.[14]

Finally, a notorious case of an unreal crisis which caused very real corporate damage was in California when a customer claimed to have found the tip of a human finger in her bowl of chilli at a Wendy's restaurant. Initially, the company tried to play it down, but the story generated massive media coverage and became the subject of late-night talk shows and comedians' routines. Wendy's then launched an ill-timed new sales promotion to divert attention, but sales continued to fall. When a US$100,000 reward was offered for information, a tipster rang the company hotline to identify the man who had lost his finger in an accident. He sold it for US$100 to the husband of the hoaxer, who cooked it before placing it in her chilli. While the couple pleaded guilty and went to prison, Wendy's had meantime been forced to lay off staff and reduce hours in some restaurants, and lost US$2.5 million in sales, equivalent to nearly a 3 per cent drop in quarterly earnings.[15]

What's important about all of these cases is that truth is not necessarily an adequate defence, even if it is supported by facts and data. Also that untruths and non-facts used by critics or opponents can have a tangible and sometimes devastating impact on business and reputation.

There's one other problem with your facts and data—namely, that they are *your* facts and data. Earlier I referred to numerous studies around the world which show that public trust in corporations and big organisations is low, and this makes communicating facts and data even harder. As a spokesperson for a large multinational over a number of years, I had to get used to being told: 'Well, you would say that. It's what you're paid to say.'

In addition, the public has been brought up exposed to the idea of 'lies, damned lies and statistics', and they often have an inbuilt suspicion of numbers. Moreover, basic numeracy among the public in general, and many specific stakeholders, is often low. When you are trying to explain numbers, it is crucial to remember that many in the public, and the news media, have no real understanding, for example, of the difference between *a mean, a median and a mode*; or what is meant by ten to the minus six; let alone being able to comprehend the scale of parts per billion or parts per trillion.

This is not to argue that the public broadly are ignorant or uneducated. However, it does highlight that while statistics may be valid and correct, statistics alone are not the answer.

WHAT'S THE SOLUTION?

So how best to use facts and data to help crisis proof your organisation? What's needed is accurate and consistent information which is sufficient to the task.

The idea of information sufficiency is important—that people have enough information to make an informed and appropriate decision, but don't feel overwhelmed by so much detail that they suspect you are deliberately trying to confuse them.

A TALE OF INFORMATION SUFFICIENCY

Think of the four-year-old girl who asks her mother, 'Where do babies come from?' You can either give her an illustrated lecture on the finer details of gynaecology and the female anatomy, or you can say: 'Babies grow inside mummy's tummy.' It's not a question of which is more accurate. It's a question of which is more appropriate at the time. However, the answer might of course be entirely different if the question came from a girl who wasn't aged four but 14—not because the facts have changed but because there is a different level of information sufficiency.

The issue of information sufficiency, and a limited public understanding of numbers, is not in any way an argument in favour of lies or spin, or fudging the facts. But it's a warning not to use facts and data to impress rather than to accurately communicate information.

I can only repeat that executives responsible for issue and crisis management often get this wrong. They mistake facts and data for a persuasive argument. And they overestimate their own ability to communicate said facts and data.

In summary, when you *need* to use facts and data to help crisis proof your organisation, there are some key things to remember:

- Don't overestimate the public's capacity to understand and interpret statistics.
- State the facts in language the audience can identify with.
- Avoid jargon, acronyms and corporate speak.
- Use independent, third-party experts to reinforce your position.
- Recognise there can be more than one legitimate interpretation of many facts.
- Listen to your audience's real concern before hitting them with facts and data.
- Speak with compassion and humility.

CHAPTER KEY TAKEAWAY

While the facts and data are critically important, most issues and crises also revolve around human qualities and empathy.

CHAPTER 14

NO, IT'S NOT JUST ABOUT THE LAW EITHER

Everyone has heard the expression: 'You can win in the court of law, yet still lose in the court of public opinion.'

It's never more true than when you are facing a crisis or emerging issue. But it's not always constructive. It seems to suggest that one area is necessarily more important than the other. Resolving this apparent clash is critically important in crisis proofing your company.

It's no surprise that lawyers occasionally recommend decisions which unwisely place legal considerations above all others. Yet there are legitimate occasions when a legalistic approach can be the right answer.

This chapter is about the perceived conflict between legal counsel and public relations counsel; how to make the best use of lawyers; how the CEO sometimes needs to act as a 'referee' between different sources of advice; and how executives can make optimal decisions in the best interests of the organisation as a whole.

First, let's get one thing out of the way immediately. Some people like to argue that lawyers and public relations people are 'natural enemies', destined always to disagree. That's outright bunkum. They typically have a different approach to what should be done and said, but the idea that they can't work together is just plain unhelpful—and untrue. Indeed, one large study of public relations practitioners concluded that, while there has been considerable discussion about the turf war within this 'oil and water' team, lawyers and PR people do in fact enjoy 'relatively harmonious and collaborative relationships'.[1]

Second, I need to make it clear what this chapter is *not* about. I don't plan to spend time on litigation PR, sometimes called litigation journalism, which is the communication process by which plaintiffs and prosecutors use the news media in pre-trial publicity to swing public opinion towards their side. (The famous criminal lawyer Melvin Belli called this 'the opening statement before the opening statement'.) Or, during the trial, those carefully rehearsed but seemingly impromptu prejudicial comments made by lawyers for either side when addressing TV cameras on the steps of the courthouse. Both strategies can, of course, be used to promote or respond to organisational crises.[2]

Nor will I spend time on legal PR, sometimes called law-firm PR, which is basically a marketing exercise. Its purpose is to promote the reputation of one law firm over the others in order to recruit plaintiffs for a proposed class action suit. We've all seen those supposed news stories about some recent crisis featuring a worried-looking 'legal expert' expressing concern, which actually constitute free publicity for lawyers trying to lure plaintiffs into sharing a hoped-for pot of gold (after the lawyers have taken their generous cut, of course).[3]

Here again, while class action promotion can directly trigger brand or corporate crises, my focus is on legal and communications counsel in a crisis, and the role of senior executives in assessing that input.

CEO MUST WEIGH LEGAL AND PR APPROACHES

The often competing and adversarial approaches to problem-solving used by public relations professionals and lawyers can have a paralysing effect on the decision-making process. The decision-maker must balance the legal and public relations concerns during a crisis. If used properly, those two consultants can play significant roles in helping an organisation survive a crisis.

New York lawyer Douglas A. Cooper[4]

There's a good reason why legal considerations are important in issue and crisis management—namely, that just about every issue or crisis has a legal component. At the same time, just about no issue or crisis is ever *solely* about legal matters. I need to say that again because it underlies this entire chapter. *Just about no issue or crisis is ever solely about legal matters.* This was bluntly captured by Carnegie Mellon business professor Gerald Meyers: 'If you win public opinion, the company can move forward and get through it. If you lose there, it won't make *any difference* what happens in the court of law.'[5]

So, yes—you need to seek and listen to legal advice. But it's equally important that legal counsel isn't allowed to trump all other advice, be it operational, business, marketing, human resources, financial, public relations, and so on. As the US legal/crisis expert Richard Levick says: 'Lawyers don't drive the bus. They're only sitting near the front.'[6] In other words, get good legal advice, but the final decisions must rest with the CEO and top executives.

STRATEGY DEVELOPMENT

The first key area where lawyers can help crisis proof your organisation is in the development of strategy to respond to an issue or crisis. In this respect, lawyers and PR people have a lot in common. They are both generally good at asking questions; they can bring a valuable 'outside' view; they can be 'independent' of internal politics and silos; they have good analytical skills; they typically don't represent large functions with turf to protect; and they typically don't hold millions of executive stock options which make them hostage to quarterly reporting and the share price.

A downside of these different approaches is the tendency to give overconfident advice outside one's own area of expertise, and Peter Sandman asserts that lawyers are by far the worst offenders.

While lawyers and PR people can both bring real value to strategy development, their training can also be a challenge. Why? Because the former are trained in the law, and it's no surprise that they tend to look at every situation as if it was a legal one. And the latter are trained in communications and may feel a desperate need to communicate. Yet neither might be the right approach for a balanced management response.

Over many years of working with corporate lawyers—especially in-house counsel—I came to realise that what was most important was the question, not just the answer. I learned to make it clear whether I was asking for a 'legal opinion' or for their opinion as a lawyer and colleague.

The good lawyers—and I was lucky to work with some real professionals—understood and acknowledged this distinction. Sadly, the not-so-good ones couldn't seem to distinguish between giving their recommendation as a legal professional and writing a multi-page analysis of black-letter law and precedent which never actually reaches a conclusion.

US President Harry Truman famously asked to be sent a one-armed economist, having tired of economists telling him, 'On the one hand, this, and on the other hand, that.' Exponents of the dismal science are maybe more inclined to stick their neck out these days (being a celebrity economic pundit is a good living), but the former president's frustration can equally be applied to some lawyers.

Those are the kind of lawyers who can't see beyond the law books to the bigger picture, and lead company executives into strategies which might not pass the 'common sense test'—when a point may be won at law, but at the cost of the broader corporate interest, particularly reputation. Yet it must be said that there is a growing group of lawyers who do 'get it' and understand the bigger reputational implications. Sadly, as I am about to describe, they are not yet necessarily in the majority.

THE LAWYER'S ROLE IN CRISIS PLANNING

1. *Insist on early planning.* With worldwide communication operating on a real-time basis, a crisis allows no time to work out how to disclose information about a damaging occurrence. Lawyers can advise top management what to expect in terms of legal liability before the event occurs.
2. *Set ground rules.* Before any crisis has taken place, decisions must be made on ground rules and procedures for how information will be released, and what the role of legal counsel will be.
3. *Insist on good record-keeping.* As the crisis progresses, a trained person must maintain a log of events and keep copies of all related written documents.

4   *Don't underestimate the importance of negative publicity.* The lawyer's responsibility is to protect the organisation, but that may mean going public early to calm community concern and assuage public outrage. Lawyers and PR people need to rely on each other's expertise to understand the ramifications of media exposure and agree on the best media method to make a disclosure.

5   *Don't rely on regulatory agencies to manage a crisis.* Recognise that government processes for managing the community during a crisis typically don't work, and that legal regulations rarely provide a successful forum for managing controversial issues.

Based on analysis by Frank M. Corrado[7]

WHEN LEGAL ADVICE GOES FERAL

As so often happens in the area of crisis management, we tend to learn more from what went badly rather than what went well. So let's look at some cases where confident legal advice might not have provided the best option.

One of my favourite examples was in Illinois in 2012, when a customer alleged he found a dead mouse in a can of the caffeinated drink Mountain Dew, produced by Pepsi. Or as one of the news reports gleefully headlined it, 'A mouthful of mouse'. Now, contamination claims—real or fake—must be one of the commonest crisis risks faced by food and beverage companies everywhere, and preparation for such events should be part of even the most basic crisis proofing. However, it's the response in this case which raised eyebrows.

Pepsi said they would produce experts to testify that the dead mouse could not have been in the can because, they argued, Mountain Dew is so acidic it would have destroyed the tiny rodent's body and turned it into 'a jelly-like substance'.[8] Yep. The company's legal strategy was apparently to tell the world that their valued brand, intended for human consumption, can actually dissolve flesh. It's no secret that many soft drinks are acidic, but imagine how that strategy must have pleased the marketing department!

It might almost be one of those 'only in America' stories, but it also raises the obvious question: where were the communications and marketing professionals when someone thought this was a good idea? Alternatively, if the reputation professionals *were* giving good advice, why was it ignored or overruled?

Lawyers conventionally focus on the legal niceties and winning the case. But sometimes that flies in the face of common-sense management and damages the promotion of brand and corporate reputation. As it has been said, a lawyer's role is to defend a position, while a public relations practitioner strives to improve upon or advance a position.

A few years before the Mountain Dew mouse case, another food company seemingly allowed legal advice and a desire for financial gain to override reputation risk. That was when the makers of Pringles decided to publicly declare that their famous stacked potato chips are not actually a potato product.

In Britain, most food is exempt from VAT (sales tax), but potato chips and similar products are taxable. So manufacturer Procter & Gamble went to court to argue that Pringles 'don't look like a chip, don't feel like a chip and don't taste like a chip'. Their lawyers helpfully explained that the stackable slices are only 42 per cent potato, with the remainder made up of oil, wheat starch, maltodextrin, salt, rice flour and dextrose. A lower court agreed that Pringles are made from dough and are therefore more like a cake or a biscuit (which must have confused the heck out of legions of Pringles consumers).

A favourable decision would have saved the company about £20 million a year in taxes, but after going through three levels of the British legal system, and much argument about the 'potato-ness' of the product, three judges of the Court of Appeal finally ruled that Pringles *are* legally potato chips and *are* subject to tax. With typical British understatement, Lord Justice Jacob insisted the question was 'not one calling for or justifying over-elaborate, almost mind-numbing legal analysis'.[9] But he might equally have asked: who thought it was a clever idea to allow a 'mind-numbing' legal strategy to potentially damage the reputation of a highly profitable brand in unhelpful news reports published around the world?

In neither the Mountain Dew nor the Pringles case was there a subsequent public disclosure of any direct loss of sales or revenue, but there is no doubt that reputation took a hit, and reputation is particularly important for snacks and other discretionary consumer purchases.

Which brings us neatly to the grand-daddy of all corporate legal strategies to backfire spectacularly for a consumer brand—the notorious McLibel case, which British Channel 4 News dubbed 'the most expensive and disastrous public relations exercise ever mounted by a multinational company'.[10]

Given the rich catalogue of PR disasters over the years that is a bold claim, but the case has special interest here because of the way it exposed corporate strategy and legal advice.

The events and lessons from the McLibel case have been the subject of hundreds of articles and even books and documentaries, but to cut a long story short, in 1986 the activist group called London Greenpeace (nothing to do with Greenpeace International) published a pamphlet titled 'What's wrong with McDonald's? Everything they don't want you to know.'

The pamphlet made some highly critical assertions about McDonald's, and the fast-food giant threatened legal action against five individuals who were distributing it. Three quickly buckled and apologised, but, to the company's apparent surprise, two held firm and so McDonald's and its legal team made the fateful decision to file a lawsuit.

What ensued was the longest court trial in English history, which lasted for 313 days spread over two-and-a-half years, during which the two virtually penniless defendants represented themselves against the legal might of the multinational, whose executives spent months being forced to defend the company's practices in open court, which was enthusiastically reported by news media around the world.

At the end of the marathon trial, the judge upheld some of the statements made in the pamphlet, so the two activists claimed partial victory. But His Honour also found that other claims made were defamatory, so McDonald's also claimed victory.

When the judge ordered the two defendants to pay £60,000 in damages (equivalent to about US$86,000), they promptly said they had no money—and even if they did have the money, they had no intention of paying.[11] The damages were later reduced to £40,000, but McDonald's said it would not pursue payment and that the issue was never about the money. Which I guess is easy to say when McDonald's' own legal costs were estimated at £10 million. That is to say, £10 million to buy years of terrible publicity!

The reason this case is important in assessing a legal strategy is that the real impact had very little to do with 'winning the case' compared with the prolonged damage to McDonald's' reputation. The case proved to be a catalyst for new anti-McDonald's websites across the internet—many of which are still active today—and the pamphlet which had been handed out in the thousands in the streets of London was reprinted and downloaded in the millions across the world. In fact, it was reported that two days after the trial ended, the two defendants were back outside a McDonald's store handing out pamphlets.

Analysts and commentators are largely unanimous that the case highlights the utter failure of a heavy-handed response to what could have been regarded as a relatively minor local problem. And that's certainly the way it's most often presented. More than a decade later, the company's UK management conceded: 'It isn't a decision we would make today. We learnt from our experience and understand why it is so often used as a CSR case study.'[12]

More importantly, corporations everywhere can learn from McDonald's' experience to think very hard before accepting the advice of lawyers and proceeding down the litigation route.

LEGAL VERSUS ETHICAL

Before leaving the topic of legal input into issue and crisis-response strategy, there is one other factor which helps drive the idea of winning in the court of law and losing in the court of public opinion. It's when ethics comes into play. The problem, of course, is that what's legal is not synonymous with what's ethical.

Yes, Mr Corporate Lawyer, we do have a legal right to call in the bailiffs and evict an 80-year-old disabled war veteran who hasn't kept up with his mortgage repayments. But is that the right decision for our company? How will it be seen by society?

And yes, Ms Corporate Lawyer, we do hold a permit to build a fast-food outlet in the middle of a sensitive historic village. But do we really want to threaten individual legal action against the upset soccer mums and retirees who want to stop the development? What will that do to our reputation? Is there a better, non-litigation avenue?

However, it does need to be acknowledged that occasionally—albeit rarely—taking what appears to be blatantly callous legal action can in fact be in the best interests of the organisation, regardless of short-term reputational damage. An example might be when giant corporations take personal action against individuals who think it is 'no real crime' to illegally download music or movies. Such action invariably provokes outrage on behalf of the people who were unlucky enough to be caught, but we have to assume the big corporations are focusing on the much bigger message it sends to others tempted to do the same.

Every first-year law student learns that when you go to court you get the law, but you don't necessarily get justice. So if you are concerned about reputation rather than 'winning', legal action may well be the last resort rather than the first option.

As I always remind my corporate clients, in any David and Goliath struggle, no one ever comes out cheering for Goliath, even when Goliath is in the right. And as with the Biblical David and Goliath, no one remembers what they were fighting about, but everyone knows who won and who was the villain of the piece.

The key, once more, is the role of the CEO and the top executives. The lawyer may retreat behind the stance that it's his or her role simply to advise on the law. And no responsible CEO should proceed without understanding the legal position. But no issue or crisis is ever entirely or purely legal, and it's the role of top executives to make a balanced judgement—to decide not just what's legal but also what's ethical, what's just and what's in the overall best interests of crisis proofing the organisation.

THE FLOW OF INFORMATION

As discussed earlier, the longer-term impact of a crisis is often directly related not only to how well the organisation tried to prevent the crisis and how well its plans and processes operated in response, but also how well it communicated to the public and key stakeholders, plus the *perception* of how well the organisation communicated (or failed to communicate).

This brings us to the second key area where top executives need to judge between legal and PR counsel to crisis proof the organisation—namely, resolving the perennial debate about the flow of information.

There is a huge amount of published material built on the proposition that when trouble strikes an organisation, the PR person invariably wants the CEO to talk to protect reputation, while the lawyer wants the CEO to say nothing to protect against liability. There's an element of truth in this, but it tends to be a cliché rather than a useful analysis of the situation.

One problem here is that while the lawyer will have concerns about saying something which might compromise liability or confidentiality, the PR professional understands that the public not only wants information, but they often believe they have a *right* to information. They also know that if information provided is not adequate or accurate, rumours and lies will rapidly spread into any gaps, aided by the terrible tools of social media.

Some people claim that every word used to persuade the public is a word which can be used to persuade the judge. However, saying nothing can also be a big problem and 'no comment' is commonly interpreted as an admission of guilt. So while the legal convention is that anything you *say* can be used against you in a court of law, anything you *don't* say can be used against you in the court of public opinion.

Or, put in even simpler language, in the court of law you are presumed innocent until proven guilty, but in the court of public opinion you are more likely presumed guilty until proven innocent. In other words, silence is not golden—it's guilty. That's why the flow of information—what gets said and who says it—is critical, and legal advice can be decisive in that decision.

Despite their typical love of words—and sometimes the sound of their own voice—when things go wrong for the organisation, lawyers will almost always adhere to the maxim that the less you say the better; or that you can't get into trouble for you don't say. In fact, a 2016 survey of senior corporate lawyers in the United States found that more than half said their litigation communications were overly conservative, and nearly 80 per cent named fear of negative press coverage as a factor preventing them from communicating more aggressively.[13]

Most often lawyers in this situation will cite the risk of liability or making a bad situation worse. The problem is that when it comes to a crisis or a high-profile issue, it just ain't necessarily so.

This is one area where there is frequent and legitimate disagreement between lawyers and PR professionals, and where top executives need to make a very important judgement call. Are there risks in communicating? Absolutely. But the risks from not communicating can be even greater, and more lawyers are beginning to understand this conundrum.

The lawyer and crisis expert Richard Levick illustrates such conflict by this example:

> As a crisis breaks and you're ready to go forward with a statement laying out the facts, and what you plan to do to correct the situation, by all means, show it to legal counsel. But be prepared for her to get out her red pen. 'You can't say that,' she'll warn you. 'Three years from now someone's going to call that up and use it as the basis of a lawsuit.' Don't get angry. It's her job to tell you that. But don't tear up that statement, either. Your job is to look her in the eye and say that, without bold action, in three years you may not have a company at all.[14]

GET THE PRIORITIES RIGHT

When your client has a crisis that could put it out of business, call the crisis manager first, think about legal issues later. If you do it the other way around your client might not survive to utilise your keen legal analysis.

California lawyer Adam Treiger

LISTENING TO LAWYERS

The fact that executives tend to listen to the lawyers is not in any way a surprise. After all, CEOs and the boards they report to must be well versed in all legal obligations and requirements of compliance and fiduciary responsibility (not to mention that they may be paying very handsomely for legal advice). But that's no reason to simply default to the 'Let's go with what the lawyers say' approach. And there is some hope in the fact that some major law firms now have crisis communication practice groups which claim to provide the client the best of both worlds—namely, the careful lawyer and the wise communicator.

A statutory obligation of executives and boards is to act in the best interests of shareholders. Yet two of the most analysed cases in the history of crisis management show us two very different approaches to that obligation.

The first is the notorious *Exxon Valdez* oil spill in 1989. You just need to look back to where I described the so-called 'scorched earth legal strategy' pursued by Exxon. By fighting every possible step of the way they certainly saved shareholders millions, but at the cost of 20 years of high-profile bad publicity and bruising headlines. And in the process they made themselves the model of how not to manage a crisis. Indeed, one respected analysis of the case carried the striking title 'Exxon Valdez: How to spend billions and still get a black eye'.[15]

Contrast that with the second iconic case—the Tylenol crisis of 1982, when unknown persons spiked headache capsules with cyanide, killing seven people in the Chicago area. It's so significant that some writers argue modern crisis management actually began with the Tylenol poisoning.

I have written critically about whether the Tylenol case really is still the 'gold standard' of crisis management as it is sometimes portrayed.[16] But the approach by Johnson & Johnson to priorities in this crisis tells us a lot. The company's Associate General Counsel at the time, Roger Fine, has explained that if shareholders had been the top priority, they would not have spent US$100 million recalling product but would have tried to stonewall the media with no recall. Instead, he says, they followed the Corporate Credo which ranks customers' needs first followed, in order, by those of employees, the communities in which Johnson & Johnson has plants, and finally shareholders.[17]

Note that—the interests of shareholders ranked fourth, and in the process Johnson & Johnson became regarded by many as a model of how to respond in a crisis.

When it comes to crisis proofing the organisation there will always be many stakeholders who expect to be provided with information—of whom shareholders are just one group—and saying nothing at all is almost never a viable option.

SILENCE IS NOT GOLDEN

Although it may not be fair, corporate silence in the wake of a crisis is tantamount to an admission of guilt. And it's worth adding here that *making* no comment is not the same as *saying* 'no comment', which is the verbal equivalent of putting your hand over the lens of the TV reporter's camera.

No one today really believes that 'no comment' is an appropriate response. But if there genuinely is a good legal reason to make no comment, then there are ways it can be done to minimise reputational damage—such as 'I would like to comment but I just don't have the full facts at the moment' or 'It would be inappropriate for me to comment as this is now the subject of legal proceedings' or 'I am not in a position to comment right now but I will make a statement shortly' or 'We're still gathering the facts, but we're committed to responding when we have all the information' or 'I'm not really the right person to comment. You need to speak to [fill in the blank].'

Yet, when there is a real crisis, this sort of stalling most often won't do. Although the lawyers might be urging you to say nothing, you will realise that something needs to be said, and you need to say it.

There is a whole library of books on how to deal with the media and how to balance protecting reputation and protecting legal liability. While that level of detail is beyond our scope here, one example illustrates the very best of leadership in a crisis.

In February 1990—just months after the *Exxon Valdez* debacle in Alaska—the tanker *American Trader*, chartered to BP, ran over its own anchor off the coast of Southern California, rupturing the hull and spilling almost half a million gallons of crude oil onto the popular Huntington Beach in Orange County, causing widespread pollution.

Although responsibility lay primarily with the ship, the President of BP America, John Ross, raced to the scene and told the assembled news media: 'Our lawyers tell us it's not our fault. But we feel like it's our fault and we are going to act like it's our fault.'

It was an extraordinary statement, and we can only imagine what the corporate lawyers thought. But after a remarkably successful clean-up, the incident soon disappeared from the headlines. Six months later they polled residents and BP had a *higher* approval rating than before the spill.

Mr Ross later wrote:

> Responsibility is not the same as liability. In the case of the Huntington Beach spill, BP was prepared from the outset to assume responsibility for a swift and well-supported response ... We took the view that the early hours of the crisis were too precious to waste on bickering or waiting for someone else to be the 'responsible' party.[18]

He added:

> You will not be surprised to hear that a company's public acceptance of responsibility where liability is unclear gives its legal counsel some concern. But in these circumstances lawyers can be quick to focus on the immediate damage and too slow to perceive the larger political and regulatory costs.

This important role of the CEO in setting the tone in a crisis was shown with the example of the Ashland oil spill in Chapter 11. A more recent example is the forthright statement from Walmart boss Bill Simon after a Walmart truck crashed into the back of a limousine in early 2014, killing American comedian James McNair and seriously injuring comedy star Tracy Morgan:

> This is a tragedy and we are profoundly sorry that one of our trucks was involved. The facts are continuing to unfold. If it's determined that our truck caused the accident, Walmart will take full responsibility. We can't change what happened, but we will do what's right for the family of the victim and the survivors in the days and weeks ahead.[19]

Mr Simon was widely praised for his prompt and unambiguous response, which helps to demonstrate that a strong leader *can* balance the legal and communication needs to help crisis proof the organisation.

One of the most contentious areas of the need to balance legal needs with the broader interests of the organisation is when and how to apologise, which is the focus of the next chapter.

CHAPTER KEY TAKEAWAY

Lawyers and legal advice are essential, yet decisions must reflect the overall needs of the organisation and the legitimate expectations of stakeholders.

CHAPTER 15

WHY LAWYERS DON'T LIKE YOU TO APOLOGISE

One of the most contentious areas of disagreement that top executives need to judge in relation to legal advice is about when and how to apologise.

Apologising *ought* to be easy. After all, a good apology is fundamentally not a lot more than saying, 'I'm sorry for what I did, I commit to making amends and I will try not to do it again'.

Yet some organisations seemingly will do anything to avoid making a genuine apology and, unfortunately, it's sometimes legal advice that lies behind this reluctance.

While it's clear that lawyers have a responsibility to protect the organisation against legal liability, lawyers' professional caution, as we have seen in other areas, can lead to organisations baulking at frank communication and a genuine apology. Add to that the reluctance of individuals and corporations to admit fault and you have a recipe for non-apologies that are little more than an embarrassment. Or, as Richard Levick says: 'A lawyerly press release or public statement is often as dangerous as no statement at all.'

This challenge was captured by musician Dave Carroll in his book about the famous incident (see Chapter 16) when United Airlines refused to apologise for baggage handlers breaking his guitar and to pay for the repair: 'Sometimes saying you're sorry is not only the right thing to do, but also the least expensive.' This is certainly borne out by studies in many countries of medical mistakes in hospitals. The overwhelming evidence is that when doctors admit a mistake and say they're sorry, the patients are less likely, not more likely, to sue.

WHEN APOLOGISING REDUCES LIABILITY

This is a very rich area of research. To take some typical examples, an American study of factors which prompted families to file medical malpractice claims following perinatal injuries found that 24 per cent filed suit when they realised that physicians had failed to be completely honest with them about what happened, allowed them to believe things that were not true, or intentionally misled them.[1] The study concluded that such filings may have been prevented by an apology.

Similarly, a study of British patients and families suing doctors found that 37 per cent might not have brought malpractice suits had there been a full explanation and apology, factors which to them were more significant than monetary compensation.[2]

And, more specifically, when the University of Illinois Medical Centre introduced a new program of patient disclosure, apology and compensation, the number of malpractice suits halved in two years and in the 37 cases where the hospital acknowledged a preventable error and apologised, only one patient filed suit.[3]

There is also good evidence that when lawsuits do proceed, both judges and juries tend to appreciate apologies and look upon them favourably in terms of modifying penalties.[4] For example, when the Catholic Diocese of Dallas agreed to apologise for failing to protect young boys from abuse by one of its priests, the jury award of US$119.6 million was reduced to US$23.4 million.[5]

In other words, in some circumstances an effective apology can reduce rather than increase legal liability and it must be acknowledged that more legal advisors are beginning to understand this. While some lawyers remain overly cautious in advising against apologies, many are becoming more sophisticated in understanding the potentially positive impact of apologies.

THE EFFECTS OF APOLOGY

1 *Shaping corporate reputation.* Litigation has the potential to damage reputation and, conversely, reputation can impact the outcome of litigation. Executives should guard reputation not only as a valuable business asset but also as a valuable legal asset in the event of litigation.
2 *Facilitating forgiveness or private settlement.* In some cases the offer and acceptance of an apology can help an organisation to pre-empt accusations and negative publicity, diffuse public anger and even help avoid a lawsuit entirely. But it cannot be expected to allow the organisation to avoid punishment for what has happened.
3 *Evidence for the plaintiff (admission of guilt).* In some cases an apology may be construed as an admission of guilt, or in other cases an admission of liability. However, an apology is not necessarily an admission of wrongdoing and when plaintiffs claim wrongdoing, courts may require a higher standard of proof in order to discourage frivolous suits.
4 *Evidence for the accused (reduction of penalty).* An apology can function as a defensive tactic for the accused organisation in some circumstances, and may protect against having to pay punitive (but not actual) damages. The majority of cases in which apology has proven persuasive in reducing jury awards to suing parties have been in medical malpractice, libel/defamation and private tort claims.

Adapted from Ameeta Patel and Lamar Reinsch[6]

THE CHALLENGE OF A GOOD APOLOGY

One of the important characteristics of an effective apology is not only that it is *intended* to be genuine, but that it also must be *seen to be* genuine in the eyes of the offended party or parties. In other words, for an apology to be effective it must be focused on the other person's needs and feelings, not your own. The response by Exxon to the *Exxon Valdez* crisis (which seems to be the gift that goes on giving) is a case in point.

The public and the media repeatedly accused Exxon of not taking responsibility for the spill, despite the fact that the Exxon officer on the scene, the chairman and the president all repeatedly apologised, and an apology advertisement in the name of the chairman appeared in about 100 major magazines and newspapers.

The frustration of Chairman Lawrence Rawl was evident in an interview with *Time* magazine:

> I went on TV and said I was sorry. I said a dozen times that we're going to clean up. But people keep saying that I don't commit. I don't know what the hell that means. Do you hang yourself or hold a gun to your head and say I'm gonna squeeze it five times, and if there's not a bullet in there I'll be all right?[7]

In the same ill-advised interview he said that the thing that bothered him most about the disaster was the embarrassment: 'I hate to be embarrassed, and I am.'

Apart from the obvious fact that Mr Rawl needed some media training, it seems that Exxon didn't understand the difference between making an apology and being apologetic. I'm reminded of an unrelated headline which once appeared in the *New York Times*: 'Too busy apologising to be sorry'.[8] It wasn't that Mr Rawl and his company didn't apologise, but that society and the offended parties were reluctant to accept it as a genuine sign of contrition. And, anyway, there are some offences so egregious that perhaps no apology will ever suffice.

At a less dramatic level are the so-called apologies which are little more than an outworn formula of over-used words to avoid any sort of accountability and to 'blame the victim'. Sometimes they are called the 'non-apology'. We all know them, and sadly they sometimes reflect unhelpful legal input. For example:

- 'I'm sorry you were offended' is *not* the same as 'I'm sorry my behaviour offended you'.
- 'I'm sorry you didn't understand me' is *not* the same as 'I'm sorry I failed to make my meaning clear'.
- 'I'm sorry you feel that way' is *not* the same as 'I'm sorry I made you feel that way'.

Such unapologetic 'apologies' happen all the time. Every year brings an embarrassing new crop of individuals and organisations who find that sorry is the hardest word. Look no further than US Senator Bob Packwood, accused of sexual harassment, who famously said: 'I'm apologising for the conduct that it was alleged that I did.'[9]

Or Abercrombie & Fitch CEO Mike Jeffries who made headlines in 2006 when he told *Salon* magazine that Abercrombie & Fitch only makes clothes for 'cool, good-looking people'. When the comment came back to haunt him in 2013 because of a YouTube video, he said: 'While I believe this seven-year-old, resurrected quote has been taken out of context, I sincerely regret that my choice of words was interpreted in a manner that has caused offense.'[10]

It would seem that his interpretation of the word 'sincerely' differs somewhat from the dictionary.

Although there is a woeful catalogue of such non-apologies, for the present let's look at three examples from Australia.

The former Leader of the Parliamentary Opposition, Tony Abbott, made some remarks which were taken as offensive to the (then) Prime Minister Julia Gillard. This is how he 'apologised': 'If she wants to take offence, then of course I am sorry about that. And if she would like me to say I am sorry, I'm sorry.'[11] As his political opponents asked at the time: 'Why bother?' Some even said his words simply compounded the original offence, though admittedly it was in the heat of political debate.

Or take the explanation by the Australian political consultants Hawker Britton after they inadvertently exposed the private email addresses of about a thousand clients and associates: 'We obviously apologise if anyone is in the slightest way upset. It's a human error. We don't want them to occur, but sometimes they do.'[12]

It may be that in both cases it was carelessness rather than some planned legal strategy. But, regardless, neither response conveyed any spirit whatsoever of sympathy or contrition.

Finally, let's consider the case of controversial Sydney radio host Alan Jones who apologised on air in 2012 for calling Lebanese males 'vermin and mongrels' who 'simply rape, pillage and plunder a nation that's taken them in'.[13] His comments are widely believed to have contributed to a race riot at Cronulla, in Sydney, a few months later.

But what's extraordinary about this case is that while he apologised in 2012, his original comments were made in April 2005. After extended legal wrangling and appeals, in 2009 the New South Wales Administrative

Decisions Tribunal found that his remarks incited hatred and contempt of Lebanese Muslims and ordered Jones to apologise within eight weeks. He then launched more than two years of further legal proceedings in an attempt to overturn the decision, presumably with the support of his legal advisors.

Only when his legal options ran out did the broadcaster finally state publicly (using a script directed by the tribunal) that his comments were unlawful and that he apologised for making them. But this was almost eight years after the original offence and, remarkably, the apology was broadcast via a pre-recorded message when the man himself was on leave. By then the apology had little or no value.

It is not often that an individual or organisation will go to such exhaustive legal lengths to evade having to make an apology. However, there are many phrases executives use to avoid apologising or accepting personal responsibility. From this shameful lexicon, there are two terms which are particularly offensive and seem to be currently favoured by risk-averse legal advisors.

The first of these is 'It's regrettable', as opposed to 'I am really sorry'. My Canadian colleague Melissa Agnes, who blogs and consults in the field of social media crises, says that 'It's regrettable' puts your lawyers at ease knowing that you aren't directly admitting guilt, and it may make you feel as though you're in control.[14] However, it's not an apology. Your upset customers or stakeholders won't see it as one, and it won't help you regain control of the crisis. Moreover, she says, it truly *is* regrettable since the longer it takes you to acknowledge and admit your mistake the more repercussions your organisation will see as an outcome of the crisis.

The other horrible non-apology which has been around for longer but still retains its popularity is 'Mistakes were made'. Social commentator Mark Memmot called it the 'king of non-apologies'[15] and it was famously used by (among others) President Richard Nixon to justify the Watergate scandal; British Prime Minister David Cameron to comment on UK Middle East policy; and American General David Richards to try to explain how an air strike killed 70 Afghan civilians.

'Mistakes were made' is a champion sorry excuse for an apology, and there are some good reasons to stop using it. Apart from the fact that it tries to evade or divert personal responsibility, it conveys no compassion;

doesn't indicate any commitment not to make the same mistakes again; and it's a statement of the blindingly obvious. Of course mistakes were made. That's why you're in the spotlight. So next time an organisation or individual in trouble says 'Mistakes were made', the best response should be, 'Yes, and you just made another one'.

> **HOW TO APOLOGISE**
>
> It's not possible to capture every aspect of apologising in a few bullet points (and apologising is not supposed to be a 'tick the box' exercise). But here are some basics:
> - For an apology to be meaningful you must express remorse and empathy, and acknowledge responsibility.
> - Sometimes you need to apologise, *even when it's not your fault*.
> - The apology must be both sincere *and* perceived to be sincere by the other party.
> - Apologies are more likely to be convincing if delivered by the individual wrongdoer or a very senior executive of the offending organisation rather than by a lawyer or 'spokesperson'.
> - If there are individual victims it is better to apologise in person rather than through a media conference (for example, by visiting the injured in hospital).
> - An apology is far more effective if delivered early and voluntarily, not only after damaging media attention or under duress.
> - Deeds must match words. If the apology promises to make amends or make improvements you must deliver.
> - It's best if the apology includes a commitment to avoid such incidents in the future.
> - You must avoid corporate speak, weasel words and legalese.
> - You must avoid conditions, finger pointing and blame shifting.
> - Remember, the apology is about them, not about you.

APOLOGISING AND REPUTATION

So, can an executive apologise on behalf of a brand or an organisation without courting fresh legal liability? The answer is absolutely yes. This challenging topic has been exhaustively analysed both by legal and communication experts, and it's very clear that an appropriate apology can not only minimise fresh liability but can in fact reduce claims and reduce the likelihood of being sued.

For example, one expert analysis has referred to what it calls the 'folklore' about the legal consequences of an apology.[16] It argues that while an apology might strengthen the plaintiff's case (to the disadvantage of the apologist), the evidence suggests that an apology has an equal, or even greater, potential to make a positive contribution to an apologist's legal strategy.

It is also very clear that while apologising *may* increase legal liability, not apologising is just about *guaranteed* to increase public anger, victim resolve and even regulatory concern.

At the same time, well-considered apologies can enhance rather than diminish the reputation of an effective executive. Of course, an important legal and moral obligation of the leader when a crisis strikes is to consider and balance the rights of shareholders, creditors and employees, as well as victims and the general public. Unfortunately, the result of trying to please all parties is sometimes an equivocal, evasive apology that satisfies no one and may well make a bad situation worse.

TAKE A DEEP BREATH ...

Next time you're clearly in the wrong, take a deep breath, put aside your self-justification, your excuses, your blame, your defensiveness and simply apologise. Being courageous in this way is generally scary in anticipation. But it feels great once you've done it ... to you, and to those who you lead.

Erika Anderson, *Forbes*[17]

Although there is a huge amount of published material on when and how to apologise—some of it highly contradictory—one of the most authoritative and comprehensive studies of this question is by the American legal academic Jonathan Cohen published under the provocative title 'Advising clients to apologize'.[18]

Dr Cohen (then at Harvard Law School) wonders at the way we counsel children and adults to act when they have injured others. He says good parents teach children to take responsibility when they have wronged another—to apologise and make amends. By contrast, Cohen says, lawyers typically counsel the opposite. Most lawyers, he argues, focus on how to *deny* responsibility, including what defences a client might have against a charge, and what counterclaims. (Cohen was writing in 1999 and many lawyers have undoubtedly learned over the intervening years.)

He champions the concept of a 'safe' apology—which is regarded by *both* sides as sincere and genuine, while protecting the rights of both the apologist and the recipient. The safe apology offers an avenue for decoupling the issue of apology from the issue of liability, and as such helps to avoid needless conflict, and helps to prevent the added insult of refusing to apologise or offering a non-apology which makes the recipient even more angry.

Of course, it doesn't make the issue of liability disappear, but Cohen argues that a safe apology lets parties talk to one another without the spectre of liability overshadowing open discussion. And the record shows that far more cases are settled than are litigated.

When a matter goes to court, it is inevitable that the legal system focuses on adjudicating rights rather than on repairing relationships. When a top executive has to judge when and how to apologise in the best interests of crisis proofing the organisation, they need to seek and weigh well-informed PR and legal advice. But lying at the heart of this decision should be the objective of protecting and maintaining relationships, and balancing the legitimate needs of all parties.

CHAPTER KEY TAKEAWAY
When done appropriately and delivered well, an apology can reduce liability and enhance the reputation of the executive and the organisation.

CHAPTER 16

SOCIAL MEDIA: BOTH A STRENGTH AND A THREAT

It's a truism these days that the advent of social media has changed society in fundamental and irreversible ways. And that organisations already standing at the frontier of new media technologies 'hold a weapon of timely response and vast dissemination'.[1] This is certainly true in the field of emerging issues and crises.

Yet it's also a fact that in many organisations the social media function is *still* an orphan without a 'natural home' in the management structure. And it sadly remains true that many large organisations *still* haven't properly recognised that social media is critical in crisis proofing.

Take, for example, a 2013 survey of business continuity managers in US companies which found more than half (57 per cent) did not officially use social media as a crisis management resource and only 8 per cent believed that social media had become an enabler for their organisation to proactively identify and respond to crisis events.[2]

SOCIAL MEDIA AND THE CEO

In the meantime, it's very evident that some CEOs and senior executives have paid a high personal price for their failure to properly understand the impact of social media. Look no further than:

- US Professional Golf Association President Ted Fisher, who was dismissed in 2014 after an unwise and intemperate Facebook post in which he described a colleague as sounding 'like a little school girl squealing during recess'[3]
- Des Hague, CEO of the sports catering company Centerplate, who stepped down in 2014 after a video appeared on social media of him kicking a friend's dog[4]
- PayPal Director of Global Strategy, Rocky Agarwal, who lost his job in 2014 after abusing colleagues on Twitter[5]
- AT&T executive Aaron Slator, who was dismissed in 2015 for sending a text with a photo of an African child with a highly offensive caption.[6]

Finally, let's consider Royal Bank of Scotland Chairman Rory Cullinan who sent Snapchat messages to his daughter about how bored he was at meetings. Snapchat messages are supposed to quickly disappear, but his 18-year-old daughter captured screen grabs and unhelpfully posted them on Instagram with the message 'Happy Father's Day to the indisputable king of Snapchat'. Shortly afterwards, in early 2015, Daddy was out of his high-paying job.[7]

Are such management-level social media personal calamities typical? Maybe not. Yet they surely are a warning, and the top executives involved probably all thought: 'It can't happen to me.' And they are a reminder that social media is a human-to-human exercise, and social media in a crisis expresses values, both of the organisation and the individual executive.

It's true that some so-called 'social media disasters' are really quite trivial affairs, driven by a handful of over-excited netizens. But it's also true that the speed and spread of social media and data exchange means that genuine failures in issue and crisis management and risk communication are more likely to be exposed and more likely to create lasting damage. After all, not only is the world of social media very fast moving, but it's also extraordinarily unforgiving. And even 'trivial affairs' can have a real reputational impact. We know that internet users spend most of their time on social networks, and some research shows half of all social media users say they express complaints or concerns at least once a month about brands or services on social media.[8] That's a massive amount of potential risk.

However, for the present, our purpose is to think specifically about how social media has changed organisational crisis management, and there are a number of well-understood changes—some positive and some negative, some bringing strengths and some creating weaknesses.

HOW SOCIAL MEDIA AFFECTS CRISIS MANAGEMENT

- Organisations have better tools to monitor and identify emerging issues and potential crises.
- Communication is faster and broader than ever before.
- Issues and crises can escalate much more rapidly, but may be over more quickly.
- Multiple platforms increase media momentum and potential impact on the organisation.
- Damaging material can remain live online long after the crisis is 'over'.
- There are better opportunities for more and earlier participation.
- More stakeholders can be reached quickly and easily.
- Resource-poor organisations and individuals can drive the pace and direction of an issue or crisis.
- Scrutiny and expectation of organisational response is intense and relentless.
- Lies and rumours spread just as quickly as facts.
- The opportunity for mistakes has expanded exponentially.

THE ROLES OF SOCIAL MEDIA IN CRISIS MANAGEMENT

Beyond the more familiar broad effects, it's important to recognise that social media has three distinct roles when it comes to crisis management—as an instigator, as an accelerant, and as an extinguisher.[9]

First, social media as an *instigator* occurs in situations where, without the social media platform, the crisis would not have occurred, such as spoof sites, hacking, web security breaches or cyber terrorism. It also occurs where an ill-considered comment or thoughtless response on social media can trigger a crisis.

There is a woeful catalogue of such cases and a number of websites are devoted to collating what they call 'epic fails'. For the moment, let's remember Ashley Johnson, waitress at a North Carolina Brixx Pizza Restaurant, who posted a message on her Facebook page abusing some customers who she served for three hours and left what she thought was a measly tip. Her Facebook page was on private setting, but one of her 100 'friends' copied it to management and she was fired for breaching company policy. The result was massive online outrage, with some critics saying the punishment was excessive and others accusing the management of breaching her privacy. It was undoubtedly a reputational crisis for the company, which spread to mainstream media, but they held firm and she was not reinstated.[10]

Then there was the notorious YouTube video showing a FedEx delivery man throwing a boxed computer over a fence. That attracted almost nine million views, and might have wiped out the good reputation earned from the movie *Cast Away*, where an imaginary FedEx employee played by Tom Hanks is stranded on an uninhabited island. However, the company responded online with its own YouTube video of Senior VP Matthew Thornton issuing a heartfelt apology, along with a blog post accompanying an embedded version of the video message.[11] Another in the same video category is the much-debated Domino's Pizza brand crisis, described in the next chapter, where the problem also both began and was eventually resolved on social media. Neither the FedEx nor Dominos cases would have ever taken off as a reputational threat without social media, and in both cases the company was widely praised for its online crisis response—even if it was not necessarily swift enough.

HOW AN ONLINE JOKE CREATED SELF-INFLICTED REPUTATIONAL DAMAGE

On April Fools' Day 2010, ThinkGeek, an online retailer selling geek-gifts and joke products, launched 'canned unicorn' as 'the new white meat'. It was largely an in-joke for their followers until the National Pork Board claimed it infringed the copyright of their slogan 'the other white meat' and their lawyers issued a 12-page cease and desist demand. Company owner Geeknet apologised on their website, saying they had not intended to 'cause a national crisis and misguide Americans regarding the difference between the pig and the unicorn'.[12] They also published the lengthy legal letter, which led to jokes and mocking headlines online and in conventional media across the country, such as the NBC 'Pork Board squeals over unicorn meat'.[13] By responding with legal sincerity to a social media joke, the Pork Board created real reputational damage where none had previously existed.

There are also situations where a social media strategy which backfires dramatically can in itself create a severe hit to organisational reputation. One of the best-known examples was McDonald's' disastrous hashtag #McDstories inviting people to share heart-warming experiences about eating fast food.[14] Predictably the site was hijacked by negative responses.

But such cases seem to keep coming, like more recently when the New York Police Department invited people to submit photographs of themselves interacting with the Big Apple's finest under the hashtag #myNYPD.[15] Needless to say, the site attracted hundreds of pictures of 'police brutality' and more than 70,000 people posted comments before it was cancelled.

Or, in late 2015, when the Victorian Taxi Association in Melbourne imagined it would be smart to start a Twitter hashtag #YourTaxis to get the public sharing positive experiences about taxis.[16] Instead, they were overwhelmed by angry stories about smelly cabs and incompetent drivers, plus many more serious allegations. Sadly, no one seemed able to learn from past disasters.

Second, social media as an *accelerant* occurs where a similar crisis before the advent of social media could have taken place, but would not have spread so widely or so quickly.

Here, again, there is a woeful catalogue of cases where social media rapidly spread what would have been a crisis or potential crisis anyway. One of the most famous social media reputational crises in this category involved the Canadian singer Dave Carroll, whose US$3500 Taylor acoustic guitar was badly damaged by United Airlines baggage handlers at an airport in Omaha. For nine months the airline brushed off Carroll's claim and denied him the US$1200 repair bill, at which point he could have gone to any newspaper and the result would have been a passing reputational crisis for the airline. Instead, Carroll created a song called 'United Breaks Guitars' and posted it on YouTube.[17]

Within weeks the clip had been seen by more than three million viewers, and millions more were exposed to criticism of the airline when Carroll appeared on TV chat shows across America. United Airlines belatedly changed its mind and agreed to compensate Carroll, but he refused the money and the airline instead made a US$3000 donation to the Thelonious Monk Institute of Jazz. But this modest 'goodwill gesture' was dwarfed by the wider reputational and financial impact of the incident. The *Times* of London reported:

> Within four days of the song going online, the gathering thunderclouds of bad PR caused United Airlines' stock price to suffer a mid-flight stall, and it plunged by ten per cent, costing shareholders $180 million. Which, incidentally, would have bought Carroll more than 51,000 replacement guitars.[18]

A respected business website commented: 'Can United's $180 million loss be chalked up entirely to a song on YouTube? Probably not. Did the song have a very real and very negative effect on United's brand equity? Absolutely.'[19] At last count, the YouTube video has accumulated almost 15 million views and Carroll wrote a book on his experience and on the power of the internet.[20]

Another company which felt the impact of social media as an accelerant was Canadian juice maker Lassonde Industries, producer of the Oasis brand, which took legal action against a fledgling local soap-maker called Olivia's Oasis. After a prolonged legal battle the Quebec Superior Court found that the claim of trademark infringement was groundless and ordered the juice-maker to pay businesswoman Deborah Kudzman's legal costs. The case received fairly routine mainstream media coverage, but when Lassonde won an appeal in 2012, leaving Ms Kudzman to pay her massive legal bill—said to be around US$100,000—it faced an online reputational crisis. Popular TV host Guy A. Lepage tweeted to his more than 100,000 followers that he would boycott Oasis in protest. In the face of a massive backlash on Twitter and Facebook, the company immediately reversed its legal strategy and promised to cover the soap-maker's legal costs. Ms Kudzman commented: 'I spent seven years fighting this, and within basically 48 hours, because of the outpouring of support, it was resolved.'[21]

More recently, when troubled British entertainment retailer HMV had to lay off 190 employees, it was always going to be a conventional hit to reputation. But while staff were getting the bad news, one redundant employee, Poppy Rose, who had access to the corporate Twitter account, started live tweeting about the layoffs, describing the process as a 'mass execution'. A steam of negative tweets continued for almost half an hour—reportedly because no one in senior management knew the Twitter password to stop the flow—and the story became news around the world.

On her own Twitter account, the 'hijacker' wrote: 'I wanted to show the power of social media to those who refused to be educated.' But, as *Forbes* concluded, the rather obvious lesson for employers in all of this is take control of your social media accounts, change the passwords, and restrict access *before* you let go of the employees who run those accounts.[22] (A rather more serious example of a crisis made worse by social media is the Qantas A380 near-disaster described later in this chapter.)

Thirdly, social media as an *extinguisher* occurs where social media is used effectively before, during or after a crisis to mitigate the damage, and in some cases actually eliminate the crisis.

While this role is less common, a good example was when some animal lovers claimed online that the Procter & Gamble fabric freshener product Febreze could poison pets. The false claim was promptly and effectively dealt with by the company using supporting statements from the US Humane Society and expert veterinary authorities. Most importantly, their counter-offensive relied almost entirely on online sources and the rumours died down within a few weeks.[23]

The 'extinguisher' role has a particular relevance where the audience is likely to be net-savvy and active on social media; for example, those in the gaming community. A few days before Sony announced a delay in the launch of PlayStation 3, some bloggers were already commenting critically about the product, largely on the basis of speculation and innuendo. By closely monitoring social media and rapidly correcting rumours which might be perceived as fact, Sony was able to largely shut down the potential crisis and prevent it spreading to mainstream media.[24]

Communications advisor Charlie Pownall proposes that social media shapes reputation in three ways. Specifically, social media:

- *ignites*—where someone does something online which triggers a reputational threat
- *amplifies*—where it reflects and amplifies what people think and feel about you
- *sustains*—where discussions on social media ebb and flow, and expand and contract as people enter and leave the fray, which means it can be sustained for weeks, months or even longer.[25]

The language used to define the different roles of social media may differ, but each poses a threat to crisis proofing, and each needs to be identified and managed. While a huge amount has been written about the impact of social media, much of it comes down to two key characteristics—speed and perceived loss of control—and I will focus on those critical areas as they have special relevance to crisis proofing.

MONITORING AND RESPONDING

It's blindingly obvious that organisations need to monitor social media to know what's happening and what people are saying, and to be able to respond very quickly. But it's also blindingly obvious that many organisations fall at that hurdle.

Following a near-disastrous engine fire on a Qantas A380 shortly after take-off from Singapore in late 2010, the social media world was alive with rumours after a blogger in Indonesia posted pictures of wreckage which had fallen down from the sky (extraordinarily, the wreckage bore the Qantas company logo). But the airline had no effective monitoring in place, and their first warning of trouble came after a financial news service picked up the rumours and falsely reported that the aircraft had crashed. Before the damaged plane could burn off fuel and land back in Singapore, the company's shares had already started to fall.

Qantas CEO Alan Joyce later told the *Wall Street Journal*:

> We were ready for traditional media and we had a press conference by 4 o'clock that afternoon, which I fronted. And we had our press statement out within half an hour of us knowing the issue. But we'd missed this whole [social media] end of communication.[26]

As a result, Qantas beefed up its media monitoring, and IATA, the international airline body, developed a new social-media-era crisis communication guide.

BEST PRACTICE IN THE AGE OF SOCIAL MEDIA

There are many lists of how to use social media in a crisis. The IATA communication manual for airlines, airports and manufacturers in the wake of an aviation disaster includes the following guidelines:

- Develop your social media policy in 'peacetime'—do not attempt to engage with online audiences 'piecemeal' in the midst of a crisis.
- Perform an audit of all social media channels already used by the organisation. You may find that sales or marketing staff, for example, already use sites like Twitter for sales promotions. Don't overlook sites which may be operated by overseas offices.
- Identify the audiences you wish to reach online—and then focus on the channels which are most likely to reach them. Once you have identified the appropriate social media platforms, focus only on these channels.
- If a decision is made to develop an online presence on platforms like Facebook or Twitter, ensure that these channels are fully integrated with your

ongoing communication program, so they are regularly updated and become regarded as a prime source of news and information about the organisation. This will enable you to develop a dedicated 'follower' network over time, with which you can engage in a crisis.
- Remember that any online channel (even if it appears to be password-protected) is potentially open to anyone. Your postings may also be forwarded or 're-tweeted' with added commentary.
- Include monitoring of social media channels as part of your conventional media monitoring program. There are numerous low-cost or free-to-use programs which allow you to track online conversations about your organisation, your competitors, or the industry generally.
- Include monitoring of employee union activity on social media and websites, and consider providing them with a direct feed of your statements.
- If you decide to engage with online conversations about your organisation, this should be a policy decision made at a senior level, and not left to junior staff members. Once you have decided to engage, it is very difficult to withdraw.
- Determine who will be your 'spokespeople'—in other words, which members of staff will be responsible for posting information on social media platforms, and for engaging in online dialogues on behalf of the company (if that policy decision has been made). Ensure that these staff have the appropriate training and are clear on your communication policy and messaging.
- Never hide behind anonymous user names—make clear that any postings or comments are made on behalf of the organisation.
- If you are building a social media presence for the first time, work on the assumption that you will face a major crisis on the day your sites go 'live'. In other words, ensure that you have the appropriate resources to cope with a flood of online enquiries and comments, and that you are prepared to track and correct any inaccurate or hostile social media postings about the organisation, from day one.
- After an accident or major incident, any online postings should appear on all social media channels operated by the company—do not overlook channels used primarily for sales or marketing purposes. Any inconsistency in your messaging or approach across different channels may be noticed and commented on by online audiences and by the news media.[27]

IATA. Reprinted with permission.

The IATA manual was published in April 2013, and is a standout example of how to synthesise crisis response in just 25 pages of simple, effective language which can be readily understood and implemented. Unfortunately, it seems that at least one major airline didn't get the message.

Just a few months later, flight 214 of the Korean airline Asiana crashed on final approach to San Francisco International Airport, killing three passengers (one of them run over by an airport crash tender). One of the 304 survivors who escaped the crash was Samsung executive David Eun, and within minutes he posted a photo of the burning wreck on Twitter, with the dramatic message: 'I just crash landed at SFO. Tail ripped off. Most everyone seems fine. I'm OK. Surreal.'

While his post was re-tweeted more than 32,000 times, the airline itself remained silent for more than four hours. Its first bland tweet simply said: 'Thank you for your concern and support at this time. We are currently investigating and will update with news as soon as possible.'

Not only was it unhelpful and hours too late, but it also used the hashtag #SFO, whereas passenger photos and news of the crash had already circled the world, mainly on the hashtags #OZ214 and #Asiana. It was two hours later—a full six hours after the crash—that Asiana issued its first media statement. By then, of course, Asiana had completely lost control of the story. It was a woeful tale of failure to understand and respond to the crisis demands of social media.[28]

No discussion of the impact of social media in an airline crisis would be complete without mention of US Airways flight 1549 from New York to North Carolina, which was forced to make a crash landing in the Hudson River. Within two minutes bystander Jim Hanrahan had posted the first news of the incident on Twitter, and within five minutes ferry passenger Janis Krums had uploaded a picture of the plane from his iPhone to TwitPic. Within three hours the iconic photo was viewed 40,000 times online (causing the site to crash) and appeared on news networks and newspapers around the world.[29] Not only was this a dramatic example of the speed of social media in a crisis, but both men who broke the news were not professional news reporters—just regular citizens who just happened to be on the spot.

In light of such amazing speed, it is very hard for any organisation to get *ahead* of the crisis. But effective monitoring can help you avoid getting badly behind. Moreover, as the Qantas case showed, citizen journalists don't always get it right. Indeed, in the wake of a disaster, it has become almost inevitable that people will deliberately distribute false information online, or share fake or misidentified photographs. A good example occurred in late 2015, following a terrorist attack on Paris, when a photograph circulated online showing the Eifel Tower in darkness with the caption: 'Wow. Lights off on the Eiffel Tower for the first time since 1889.'[30] The mislabelled picture was reportedly re-tweeted 30,000 times, even though it was quickly pointed out that the Paris landmark goes dark *every morning* at 1 a.m.

Such incidents—either innocent or malicious—highlight the importance of every organisation having a well-managed and responsive social media capability to reduce rumours and falsehoods, and to provide the community and other stakeholders with timely and reliable information.

Sadly, it is still by no means the norm. One survey of US companies in 2014 found only 40 per cent had a social media strategy to be used during a crisis.[31] Which means 60 per cent had no such plan. How could they possibly expect to be crisis proof?

CHAPTER KEY TAKEAWAY

Social media is now central to crisis management and expands the tools available to critics as well as to corporations.

CHAPTER 17

SOCIAL MEDIA: DO IT FAST AND DO IT RIGHT

The Hollywood movie *Top Gun* popularised the catchphrase, 'I feel the need, the need for speed', and speed is a major driving factor in social media response to crises or potential crises. Yet social media is not necessarily as universally adopted as you might think.

A study published in 2003 examined 50 organisational crises in the United States over an 18-month period and reported that 64 per cent communicated about the crisis using the internet *within 24 hours of the initial media coverage*, and that five government agencies did not respond to the respective crises at all using their official websites.[1] Not exactly a speedy response.

Another study a couple of years later, which examined 92 corporate crises, found that 54 per cent of the organisations used the internet in their response.[2] It's hardly much better, as it also means almost half still didn't use social media—which is worrying.

The expectation of what is acceptable in terms of response times has escalated dramatically, and such performance should not be accepted today. But as recently as 2015, a study of local government communications in the United States found that just over 70 per cent of the government officials surveyed engage social media during a crisis.[3] Which means, of course, that almost 30 per cent of the sample reported using no social media tools during a crisis, and even for those who used the tools, the majority used only two or fewer social media platforms.

WHEN THINGS GO WRONG

For speed of response, think of the incident in 2010 when heavily built film director Kevin Smith was thrown off a Southwest Airlines flight for allegedly violating the company's safety regulations regarding passenger weight and size. He tweeted his anger to his million-plus followers, who in turn set off a storm of further criticism and the incident briefly became an international 'news story'. What's worth noting about the case is that Smith's first tweet was posted just before 9 p.m. on a Saturday night, and the airline responded within 16 minutes. How many other companies could match that? Then or today? It's a reminder that the first story told is the story most retold … and the story most believed.

The other important aspect of the Kevin Smith case was that the airline confined their response to the social media environment where the story began. Smith posted more than 40 tweets in the next few days and the airline responded almost entirely online—via Twitter and the airline's blog.

The importance of responding in the same medium as the crisis starts was a key feature of the notorious Domino's Pizza reputational crisis when two bored employees at a North Carolina franchise posted a YouTube video of themselves doing disgusting things to food in the store. The video garnered well over a million hits before it was taken down, and a national study conducted by HCD Research using its MediaCurves website found that 65 per cent of respondents who would previously visit or order Domino's Pizza were less likely to do so after viewing the offensive video.[4]

However, the company initially decided not to issue a formal press release or post a statement online; and as result came under attack, especially on Twitter, for failing to respond, and critics began to question the company's integrity.

As Domino's' PR manager Tim McIntyre told the *New York Times*: 'We *were* doing and saying things, but they weren't covered on Twitter.'[5]

With the company's reputation under assault, CEO Patrick Doyle recorded and posted a powerful and heartfelt apology and explanation on YouTube, which directly addressed the issue where it had begun.[6] The crisis soon began to die down and Doyle was widely praised for his forthright response, which is still regarded by many people as an example of how to do it well (albeit somewhat late).

The importance of choosing the right channel was also demonstrated by US home improvement giant Lowe's, who got it horribly wrong. When the company bowed to public pressure and withdrew advertising from a new reality TV show called 'All American Muslim', they unwisely decided to make the announcement via their marketing communication Facebook platform rather than on their well-controlled home page.

The result was that within days their usual Facebook information about home improvement and gift ideas was overwhelmed by a reported 28,000 posts, which became increasingly angry and hateful. Despite trying to remain 'respectful and transparent', the company was forced to shut the discussion down.[7] So yes, social media interaction with stakeholders is a worthwhile objective, but choose your channel well and manage the process.

TIPS FOR REPUTATION AND CRISIS MANAGEMENT IN THE DIGITAL WORLD

- *Listen and be present.* Most brand disasters could have been prevented by picking up online chatter early and being prepared to respond before it escalated.
- *Set the right expectations.* Be upfront about when people can expect your response.
- *Be transparent.* If you make a mistake, admit it, apologise and try to correct it. Don't delete negative posts.
- *Respond thoughtfully.* Showing you care can actually win over some critics.
- *Never lose your cool—ever.* Being rude or attacking critics in social forums is absolutely unacceptable.
- *Have a crisis team in place.* Get the right people to help craft and post a response that may quieten the chatter or help solve the issue at hand.
- *Manage access to your social media accounts carefully.* Limit access to avoid embarrassing mistakes and unauthorised posts.

- *Post moderation guidelines*. While most social media pages have Terms and Conditions, clear moderation guidelines make it simpler to remove offensive posts which violate the rules.
- *Hire experienced community managers*. Experienced managers know how to speak for your organisation and the right way to deal with online problems.
- *Remember—you will never please everybody*. Be transparent and honest, but some people will never share or accept your view. That's when your online friends and followers sometimes chime in to support your brand or organisation.

Adapted from Ekaterina Walter, *Forbes*[8]

CONTROL AND THE DARK WEBSITE

The damaging misjudgement by Lowe's brings us to the second of the key characteristics of social media, which is perceived loss of control. Your central communication objective in a crisis should be to provide the community and other stakeholders with timely and reliable information, but social media can make that very difficult. In fact, some people have argued that the advent of social media means crisis management is *never* done well any more.

That might be a rather pessimistic view, but in the face of millions of internet natives armed with mobile phone cameras and instant opinions, no organisation can ever hope to *control* the flow of information across the digital world. However, with planning and commitment, you can move a long way towards controlling *your own* messaging.

As Lowe's staff found when they made a controversial announcement via their Facebook page, which became the lightning rod for a barrage of racial hatred, they would have been better advised to communicate via their company blog where they could exercise more control.

Of course, it doesn't have to be a disaster. The Boston Marathon bombing of April 2013 is notorious for the volume of false and misleading social media activity which ensued. But the city's Police Chief provided a textbook case study of how to provide leadership in the digital age. He live-tweeted his decisions so that no one would be second guessing, demonstrating the power of human-to-human communication and his strong emotional intelligence. His department successfully used Twitter to keep the public informed about the status of the investigation, to calm nerves and request assistance, and to correct mistaken information reported by the press. The result was applause for an 'honest conversation with the public during a time of crisis' in a way that no police department had done before.[9]

One option to improve control of communication in the event of a serious crisis is to mobilise a dark site, which is a micro-website formatted and prepared in advance, waiting to be activated rapidly when a crisis hits. An overview of how a dark website works was introduced earlier, but it's important not to rush to this solution.

For 'normal crises' a dark website may be *more* than what's needed, and a well-constructed corporate blog alone can be just as effective. It typically already has company information, media contacts and links to your main website and other information. Detail about the crisis can be posted quickly, along with an FAQ section which can be rapidly loaded and updated.

However, a dark website can be the right solution for big crisis events, especially when large numbers of people are potentially affected, or where large amounts of information need to be shared and updated regularly. Examples might include the response to a natural disaster, a high-profile drug recall, an 'active shooter incident', a shipping disaster or an aircraft crash.

In fact, an airline, Swissair, has been called the poster child for dark website effectiveness.[10] When flight 111 (the 'UN Shuttle') crashed into the North Atlantic, the airline's dark website was immediately activated, and Swissair simply referred all callers to the page, explaining to both the media and the public that everything they could and would say, and all public documents relevant to the crash, would be posted there and kept up to date. A click on a button with the flight number opened the dark site and allowed interested parties to view every piece of information the airline released in chronological order. The company kept the site active for several months following the crash so people interested in the event—including relatives, employees and the media—could review all disclosed information to understand what happened, why it happened and how Swissair responded.[11] It was in the relatively early days of the internet and digital communication, but it's still cited as a gold standard for how to manage a crisis-related dark website.

Yet even a good dark site can be caught out in the detail. When Malaysian Airlines flight MH370 disappeared over the Indian Ocean in early 2014, the company quickly activated its standby site. But someone hadn't really thought about how it would look and it was published with its URL rather embarrassingly called 'Dark site', which provided needless distracting commentary.[12] Good idea—not such good execution.

ROLE OF THE CEO

While social media is still finding its full place in some organisations, there is no doubting the importance of top executive leadership to establish and maintain social media effectiveness for crisis proofing across all functions.

Executive responsibility can be summarised in some key areas and I will expand on each one. Executives should:

- authorise and resource formal 24/7 social media monitoring
- ensure open channels for escalating online concerns and issues
- demand an organisational media presence before the crisis
- get clear policies in place for who 'speaks' online
- develop a personal executive online presence
- bring social media into the executive suite
- embed social media into crisis management
- discourage talk of social media strategy.

AUTHORISE AND RESOURCE FORMAL 24/7 SOCIAL MEDIA MONITORING

I have already discussed some of the fundamentals of monitoring and the likely sources of information about issues and potential crises (Chapter 7). Social media monitoring has all those same challenges and more.

While traditional media monitoring is well established in most organisations for early warning of potential crises, social media monitoring remains a vulnerability for those companies which have yet to establish effective scanning and monitoring. I am not suggesting senior executives should be personally involved in monitoring, but they need to demand that it's in place.

One analysis reported that while study after study revealed that well over 50 per cent of executives believe that reputational risk associated with social media should be a board room issue, only around 15 per cent of companies had a program in place to capture and analyse social data.[13] Similarly, large-scale research of FTSE 350 companies undertaken in 2015 confirmed that 97 per cent of respondents agreed that reputation held commercial value, but only 16 per cent stated that they actively measured their reputational performance.[14]

ENSURE OPEN CHANNELS FOR ESCALATING ONLINE CONCERNS AND ISSUES

Monitoring without action is about as useful as an ashtray on a motorcycle. There must be a strong process by which concerns and issues are rapidly escalated to management and lead to action.

Moreover, the process needs to ensure that junior managers are willing and able to raise matters which have been identified through monitoring, and that they aren't deterred by fear of a 'shoot the messenger' attitude in the executive suite.

This requires leadership from the top and a commitment to listen to the good, the bad and the ugly. As the BP Texas City Refinery explosion in 2005 showed, when top managers don't want to hear bad news, disaster is sure to follow.

DEMAND AN ORGANISATIONAL MEDIA PRESENCE BEFORE THE CRISIS

We know from research across the world that a large proportion of news reporters assigned to a story go first to social media, especially third-party blogs and the company's online platforms. You can't do much in the short term about independent blogs, but you can demand that your organisation's own webpage, blogs, Facebook, Twitter and Instagram accounts (and other applications) are the very best they can be, with strong capacity for response in a crisis. Is it just static 'brochureware' or does it have good interactive features for the media and the public to communicate with you?

You can also ensure funds are made available to register all possible domain names which could be negative to your organisation to prevent registration and use by opponents—names such as ihatecoke.com, cokesucks.com or whatswrongwithcoke.com, plus all the other variations. And while you're at it, make resources available to build up in-house capability to develop graphic, video and audio files so that they can be distributed rapidly online when needed.

Having a strong social media presence *before* the crisis builds relationship equity, such as friends and followers who may defend you to their groups, and having a large online community also helps you to *detect* crisis earlier. The idea of interacting with stakeholders and audiences before a crisis arises is nothing new. But social media has created new possibilities for engagement. For example, corporations now need to engage with influential bloggers by responding to their postings via external corporate blogs on a range of topics, or by participating—as an organisation—in online forums or other social platforms. In that way you can answer questions and rebut rumours and, where appropriate, respond to incorrect information by firmly stating that it's wrong, and why.

Waiting to get involved with social media in the midst of a crisis is far too late. But with an established social media presence you can get your crisis messages out very rapidly to the media, public and other stakeholders, and you can be seen to be responding quickly when needed.

In addition, an established social media presence means you don't have to rely solely on old media, with gatekeepers who can distort your message. Instead, you can go direct to the public and others and, in some instances, you may even be able to bypass traditional media entirely and manage a crisis completely via social media platforms.

It goes without saying that all of this activity also means you are more exposed to critics, disgruntled customers and random web vandals. But that's the cost of openness and modern executives embrace it.

GET CLEAR POLICIES IN PLACE FOR WHO 'SPEAKS' ONLINE

You may have a clear policy on who is an official spokesperson for the organisation when it comes to the traditional media, and the training they need. But some reputational crises have been triggered by unwise, unhelpful or rude responses on social media by untrained public-facing people well down in the organisation.

You wouldn't appoint an inexperienced customer service operator to address the news media on behalf of the organisation, yet posting a tweet to a customer is equivalent to having a news conference with the world. United Airlines discovered this in the notorious broken guitar incident, and US Airways suffered a totally avoidable hit to reputation when a customer service person inadvertently attached an explicit pornographic image to a customer response.[15]

HOW A LEADER RESPONDS TO AN ONLINE REPUTATION RISK

A junior employee at appliance-maker KitchenAid posted a supposedly funny tweet about President Obama's grandmother which accidentally went out to 25,000 followers on the corporate account. Brand Manager Cynthia Soledad's response provides a case study in leadership.

> A member of our Twitter team mistakenly posted an offensive tweet from the KitchenAid handle instead of a personal handle. The tasteless joke in no way represents our values at KitchenAid, and that person won't be tweeting for us any more. That said, I lead the KitchenAid brand and I take full responsibility for the whole team. I personally apologise to President Barack Obama, his family and the Twitter community for this careless error.[16]

Genuine, heartfelt, brief and personal.

Despite such occasional missteps, one of the great strengths of social media is genuine dialogue and two-way engagement, and that must be properly managed. Top management need to set and enforce clear social media policies to crisis proof your organisation at all levels and on all platforms.

DEVELOP A PERSONAL EXECUTIVE ONLINE PRESENCE

As well as driving an organisational presence online, there is now an increased expectation that top executives will have their own social media presence, such as a personal blog or Twitter account, and this also needs policy and resources. So, if world leaders are not too busy to be active on Twitter, what excuse is there for you? (And, yes, they have staff to help them, but so do you.)

I'm not suggesting that every top executive needs to be a 'celebrity CEO'—there are few enough of them—and it's no surprise that many people are wary of social media and its risks. But demand for executive public engagement is high and is only expected to grow as more distribution channels develop and audiences fragment even more.

However, CEO participation on social media is still not extensive. For example, we know from analysis of all the top executives on the Fortune 500 list in 2015 that 61 per cent had no social presence whatsoever.[17] And that only 60 per cent of the CEOs who had a Twitter account were actually tweeting. We also know from a broader study of executive level managers (the *CEO Reputation Premium* report) that almost four out of 10 believe it is 'inappropriate' for CEOs to participate in social media.[18]

Yet with executive social media engagement comes reputational reward. As the study among executive level managers shows, highly regarded CEOs have a higher social media participation rate than average, and are about three times more likely than CEOs with weak reputations to participate in social media.

The same applies at company employee level, where one survey showed 81 per cent of employees felt that leaders who engage on social media are 'better equipped to lead a company, communicate values and shape a company's reputation in today's changing world'.[19]

Most importantly, this all has a real bottom-line value. We know, for example, that companies with a good reputation are able to charge premium prices and attract better job applicants. And from previous discussion we know that CEO reputation contributes perhaps 70 per cent of the reputation of the organisation. In addition, we know from the *CEO Reputation Premium* report that executives estimate 44 per cent of organisational market value derives directly from CEO reputation.

Moreover, a recent study in the not-for-profit sector concluded that careful and appropriate executive personal branding strategies, such as sharing value-based messages, can add to the success of corporate image and reputation, thus bolstering corporate identity.[20] So there's a clearly linked sequence—CEO social media engagement promotes reputation, and a strong CEO reputation goes straight to the bottom line.

Such online participation is also a major contributor to the CEO's personal brand, which remains with them even if they change jobs. Some examples of such personal brand include Warren Buffet and Richard Branson. Or hotel chain CEO Bill Marriott, who dictates a regular blog to an assistant. According to one expert, the octogenarian CEO's blog accounts for over US$4 million in hotel bookings.

There can be few executives with a more valuable personal brand than media magnate Oprah Winfrey. In January 2016 she posted a single tweet and link to a video in which she boasted of weight loss while continuing to enjoy bread on a Weight Watchers diet. Within a single day Weight Watchers' shares had spiked over 20 per cent, increasing the value of Ms Winfrey's personal shareholding in the company by US$12 million.[21]

While online participation is a major contributor to the CEO's personal branding, it has to be acknowledged that executive participation in social media is not without downside risk. In addition, the line between a top executive's private and professional social media is at best blurred and at worst ignored altogether.

Take the case of Ben Polis, founder and CEO of Australian energy broker EnergyWatch. He had a long history of unusual behaviour, but it was a racist and sexist rant on his *private* Facebook page that finally brought about his downfall and nearly destroyed the company.[22]

Or consider Bob Parsons, CEO of the internet giant GoDaddy, who thought it would be a smart idea to post a video of himself hunting and killing an elephant in Zimbabwe. Mr Parsons was no stranger to controversy, and when the video provoked predictable outrage he used his personal blog to explain that elephants are a major problem in some areas, and the local people had asked him to shoot the rogue bull, which was reportedly destroying their gardens.

Although the online posts were the intrepid hunter's views and not those of the company, animal activists immediately called for a boycott of GoDaddy, and business competitor Namecheap offered to donate US$1 to an elephant protection charity for every subscriber who switched from

GoDaddy. It was reported that over 20,000 customers made the switch as the company's name trended on Twitter for all the wrong reasons.[23]

CEO Parsons himself told *Time* that overall he saw it as 'a net positive' and that 'all publicity is good publicity if you are in the right'.[24] Perhaps he is an exception—I certainly hope so—but his story should not deter others from personal social media participation. It should simply be a reminder of the need to do it right.

BRING SOCIAL MEDIA INTO THE EXECUTIVE SUITE

It's a common and all too easy mistake to regard social media as a technical issue and to delegate responsibility down the organisation to engineers or operatives in the IT department. But that shouldn't be their role. You wouldn't ask telephone technicians to be responsible for what gets said on the phone, so why would you think IT people should determine what gets published on social media?

The CEO is not necessarily expected to be a social media expert. But the CEO and the executive group should have a strong working knowledge of social media and the extent of cyber risk. Unfortunately, a 2016 survey of cyber-security professionals revealed that one-third believed their CEO had major gaps in understanding of cyber risk, and almost half believed the same for their Chief Finance Officer. Chief Marketing Officers, many of whom have increasing responsibility for digital strategies, were also rated poorly.[25]

So, not only do the CEO and the executive group need to ensure adequate funding for social media preparedness, but they also need sufficient understanding to provide strategic leadership and direction where needed. For example, when the brand is under attack online, social-media-savvy executives should have the big-picture view to better understand when to respond to online criticism and when to step back in the best interests of the broader enterprise.

In the same way, the executive group has the authority make sure that overall leadership of social media is assigned to a senior manager who is also expert in communication and reputation; who is inside the executive suite; and who has the experience and authority to ensure that the focus of social media policy and implementation is not just what's technically possible, but also what's in the best interest of the whole organisation.

EMBED SOCIAL MEDIA INTO CRISIS MANAGEMENT

With the social media manager located within the executive suite, the next step is to properly use social media for those core activities of crisis preparedness, crisis prevention and crisis response.

That individual needs to be appointed as a member of the designated Crisis Management Team, and needs full support to ensure that the regular crisis training scenarios are not just about the more obvious risks, but will also include a specific e-crisis. Moreover, that appointed executive needs support and resources to set up an online dark site as outlined earlier, if that is determined as the right option.

DISCOURAGE TALK OF SOCIAL MEDIA STRATEGY

Although it might seem counter-intuitive, or even contradictory, the whole executive group needs to move beyond talking about social media strategy, especially in a crisis. What's really needed is a focus on overall organisational crisis strategy and planning. The more you allow people to separate out social media, the more you slow down the possibility of effective integration.

Such integration helps reduce the chances of an unintended social media gaffe in the midst of a genuine corporate crisis. Think no further than the Qantas marketing department inviting passengers to participate in an online competition to share their 'dream inflight experience' in the midst of an industrial dispute which grounded the airline's entire fleet.[26] The terrible feedback and damaging publicity which resulted should have been entirely predictable.

There can be no better reminder that social media has a very important role before, during and after a crisis, but it needs to be fully incorporated into the broader crisis management strategy for consistency and maximum effectiveness.

Overall, crisis proofing demands effective and up-to-date crisis strategy and response capability, and social media should be a cohesive part of that bigger picture.

CHAPTER KEY TAKEAWAY
Social media capability in a crisis demands top-level involvement and commitment.

CHAPTER 18

MANAGING CRISES ACROSS BORDERS

Crisis proofing your organisation is enough of a challenge at home. It's an even bigger challenge across borders, and international crises pose a particular threat to organisational operations and reputation.

I don't much like spending needless time over-analysing definitions. But it's important to recognise that the seemingly self-evident idea of international crisis management can be legitimately applied to at least three distinct meanings, each of which has the potential to undermine the effectiveness of crisis proofing:

- *crises spanning multiple nation states*—events which spread across different countries
- *multinational organisational crises*—events which affect an organisation in a number of countries where it operates
- *organisational crises across borders*—events which originate outside the organisation's home country.

It's worth spending just a few moments reviewing them to see not only how they overlap but also the differences between them, and why that matters to crisis proofing by executive management.

> **WHAT SETS TRANSBOUNDARY CRISES APART**
>
> The challenges faced by crisis managers who must respond to transboundary events are not different in kind from those faced in 'normal', more localized crises and disasters. What sets transboundary crises apart is that they create a need for extreme adaptation and unprecedented cooperation under conditions in which these are most difficult to achieve—when the capacity and authority for response is distributed across multiple organizations and jurisdictions and when the crisis itself creates difficult patterns of interdependence among the parties involved.
>
> Chris Ansell, Arjen Boin and Anne Keller[1]

CRISES SPANNING MULTIPLE NATION STATES

These are major events that threaten across multiple territorial jurisdictions—most often managed at a government or quasi-government level. These are sometimes called transboundary crises, and have cross-border impacts.

Typical crises across multiple nation states might include the international response to a disease outbreak (for example, AIDS, SARS or Ebola); natural disasters that affect more than one country (for example, the Southeast Asian tsunami of 2004, which killed around 230,000 people in 14 countries); or the unprecedented deadly heat wave in the summer of 2003, which killed perhaps 50,000 people across Western Europe.

These massive threats are more correctly described as disasters rather than crises. They are managed by governments rather than by corporations, and the required response between countries is better defined as 'disaster management' or 'disaster response'.[2]

While such events are way beyond the capacity of an individual organisation's crisis response systems, sometimes multinational disasters can be triggered by a corporate crisis. Take, for instance, the Baia Mare disaster in Romania in 2000.

A gold processing plant in Romania—which was a joint venture between the Romanian government and an Australian company (Esmeralda Exploration)—had a massive spill of waste water contaminated with cyanide and heavy metals into the Tisza River. It then flowed into the Danube, carrying pollution through Romania, Hungary, Yugoslavia and Bulgaria, killing fish and other wildlife and poisoning drinking water supplies. It was undoubtedly an international crisis for the Australian company and its Romanian partner, but at the same time it was also clearly a national disaster for the multiple governments concerned.

Although corporate crises creating multinational disasters are rare, two famous examples occurred in a single fateful year. April 1986 saw the notorious Chernobyl nuclear power plant disaster, in what was then Soviet Ukraine, which spread radiation across much of Western Europe and Scandinavia. (It's been said that the Chernobyl accident galvanised the development of organisational crisis management in Europe in the same way that the Tylenol poisoning did in North America.) About six months later came a fire at the Sandoz chemical plant near Basel in Switzerland, which spilled an estimated 30 tonnes of pesticides and agrochemicals into the Rhine, turning the river red. It was one of the worst environmental disasters in Europe and caused massive ecological damage downstream from Switzerland into Germany, France and the Netherlands.

Crises like these which span multiple nation states attract massive media, public and regulatory attention, but they are rare, are beyond the normal scope of organisational crisis proofing, and are not our main focus here.

MULTINATIONAL ORGANISATIONAL CRISES

These are events or developments that threaten corporate or organisational interests in many or all of the different countries where an organisation operates. They are usually perceived as a specific corporate risk and form part of the crisis proofing initiative.

They directly impact the organisation as a whole—for example, financially or in terms of corporate or brand reputation—and are typically managed from head office using standard organisational crisis response techniques, as described in earlier chapters.

The focus in these crises is most often a centralised 'command and control' model designed to ensure consistency of messaging and response across the entire corporate structure and in all countries impacted. Examples of multinational corporate crises that would have the same or similar effect across the organisation's entire international domain might include an accounting or ethical scandal among top executives; a global product recall triggered by health or safety concerns; financial losses and large-scale restructuring and layoffs; or a hostile corporate takeover.

Most importantly in this category, the crisis response is typically mobilised, directed and coordinated from head office using established tools and processes which are familiar to the executives in charge. More often than not, the same or a very similar crisis response is mandated in all countries and the crisis communication strategy is driven by corporate personnel, with a high level of top executive input and involvement.

ORGANISATIONAL CRISES ACROSS BORDERS

Unlike multinational crises, which affect an organisation in a number of countries where it operates, organisational crises across borders are where a corporation or organisation faces a crisis initiated in a foreign location outside the parent country, often removed from the culture and experience of head office executives and, more specifically, where the 'standard corporate crisis response' may not be appropriate.

This category may involve organisational operations in only one or a small number of locations, sometimes not initially seen by head office as warranting corporate intervention. However, experience shows that 'local' crises have the potential to develop and adversely impact the broader organisation, as we'll see shortly. In fact, growing globalisation of business, and the accelerating pace and spread of communication via the internet and social media, has markedly increased both the likelihood and risk of organisations becoming embroiled in cross-border crisis events in foreign countries (see examples in the next chapter).

A critical point here is that you don't have to be a multinational corporation to be threatened by a crisis which arises in another country. It might, for example, relate to problems with your supply chain, such as local accusations of child labour in your raw material supply, or unacceptable working conditions in your outsourced manufacturing.

A high-profile example is the way major international clothing brands were found to have been sourcing from the notorious Rana Plaza Complex in Bangladesh, which collapsed in 2013 killing 1130 garment workers and injuring another 2500.[3] Or the report in early 2016 that iconic Australian surfwear giant Rip Curl had sold millions of dollars worth of clothes labelled as made in China but actually made in North Korea, where factory workers were said to endure 'slave-like conditions'.[4]

The risk of such cross-border crisis threats lurking in the supply chain was highlighted by a global survey by Booz and Co of sourcing and supply executives. The study reported that the supply management organisation in many companies increasingly recognised that the supply chain faces a growing array of risks.[5] Yet they found that almost half of those surveyed had not fully evaluated the risks facing their business.

Or it might relate to misuse of your product in another country, such as the US chemical company which came under security threat because their agricultural herbicides were being improperly used by a South American government to destroy illegal coca crops. Unfortunately, powerful drug lords saw the company logo all over the drums of chemicals used to destroy their crops and assumed the company was complicit in the operation.

THE RISK OF DOING BUSINESS IN A CONFLICT ZONE

Doing business in a conflict zone is always a major risk, but the international mining company Anvil—listed in both Australia and Canada—found itself at the centre of a major cross-border crisis after reports it provided logistical support to the Congolese army in a massacre of rebels at Kilwa, near their Dikulushi copper mine in 2004. It was claimed Anvil trucks were used to transport government troops to crush the uprising, and then to allegedly take away corpses of victims of summary executions.

Three former employees of the company's Congolese subsidiary were cleared on charges of facilitating war crimes, arguing that government troops requisitioned the vehicles and they had no knowledge or control over how they were used.[6] However, human rights NGOs and officials in different countries maintained pressure on Anvil. After years of reputation-sapping controversy, it was eventually acquired in 2012 by the Chinese state-owned Minmetals Group.

While you don't have to be a multinational corporation to be threatened by a crisis which arises in another country, understanding the nature of multinationals helps identify the challenges for crisis proofing.

THE NATURE OF MULTINATIONALS

Before addressing how to manage crises across borders, it is worth considering some generic aspects of multinational organisations that influence their vulnerability to crises and their capacity to respond. These factors potentially affecting crisis proofing in multinational organisations can be grouped and discussed under some key headings:[7]

- long distances and multiple time zones
- being a 'foreigner' outside the home country
- geographic diversity
- portability of operations
- different national environments
- national employee differences.

LONG DISTANCES AND MULTIPLE TIME ZONES

Despite the wonders bestowed by modern communication technology, working across different time zones remains a constant limitation, especially in the time-critical context of a crisis. Moreover, when a crisis occurs, getting experts and specialist equipment to distant locations quickly enough, and getting sufficient information out, can be hurdles. For instance, during the notorious Bhopal crisis, with Union Carbide Headquarters in Connecticut desperate for information, it is reported there were only two open telephone lines between Bhopal and Mumbai, where Union Carbide India had its office. These days it's more likely that the volume of crisis-related traffic might crash the international communication system.

Social media has created an expectation that, during a crisis, organisational response will be virtually immediate, and it makes no difference if it's weekend or public holiday or the middle of the night in the home country. This is when the clichéd concept of '24/7 communication' becomes reality.

BEING A 'FOREIGNER' OUTSIDE THE HOME COUNTRY

It's easy to underestimate the extent of anti-foreign feeling about multinational corporations, even though the domestic subsidiary may be locally incorporated and employ local staff. Status as a foreigner in the host country almost invariably makes it more difficult to secure successful outcomes in public opinion, public policy and judicial areas, and this disadvantage is even more emphatic during and after a crisis.

Yet, long-serving head office executives steeped in corporate culture sometimes find it hard to credit that their organisation is not universally loved and respected. The impact of anti-foreign sentiment is regularly on display around the world during riots or other civil unrest when high-profile foreign banks, international airlines and multinational fast-food chains frequently become the symbolic targets of choice for protesters determined to smash windows and wreak havoc.

Anyone who doubts this liability of foreignness need only ask McDonald's, which found itself caught up in tit-for-tat retaliation between Russia and the West in mid-2014. Following Russia's annexation of the Ukrainian region of Crimea earlier in the year and the shooting down of a passenger airliner over the area, allegedly by separatist forces linked to Russia, Western countries imposed various sanctions against Russia. Not unexpectedly the Kremlin responded in kind, and banned meat, fish, vegetables and other imports from the United States.

Then the Russian government closed three McDonald's restaurants in Moscow for alleged 'sanitary violations'.[8] It had nothing really to do with McDonald's, but the fast-food giant has symbolic value as an American brand that first planted its flag in Moscow in the Soviet era. As crisis commentator Gerald Baron said at the time: 'When elephants dance, ants get stepped on, and in this case, the ants can even be large, global brands.'

McDonald's has often been subject to boycotts in various countries to oppose US actions—such as the French boycott in 2003 to protest against the war in Iraq. While there is little risk of long-lasting reputational damage, we can be fairly certain that McDonald's won't be at all surprised when it happens again.

GEOGRAPHIC DIVERSITY

Operating in different countries offers some protection in a crisis when the multinational organisation can attempt to 'isolate' a problem while still maintaining full operations elsewhere. Some multinationals even operate under less identifiable names overseas to shield the parent brand. Social media and instant access to information today makes such 'separateness' harder to sustain, especially in a crisis situation. However, geographic diversity can make it easier to sell off or shut down a crisis-prone subsidiary in order to limit damage to your broader enterprise.

PORTABILITY OF OPERATIONS

Linked to geographic diversity is the capability of a multinational organisation to relocate plants or other facilities to avoid crisis risks because of operating in a particular country. One example was the high-profile social media campaign to force some US multinationals to cease operations in Burma as a protest against the government,[9] or moving operations out of countries that threaten nationalisation of foreign assets. However, moving operations can itself create a potential crisis, as was shown when Finnish mobile-phone maker Nokia announced it would close its plant at Bochum in Germany and transfer operations to Romania, resulting in mass demonstrations and a threatened boycott.[10] Or when Australian company Pacific Brands triggered national protests after announcing it would relocate production of some of the country's most iconic clothing labels to China.[11]

DIFFERENT NATIONAL ENVIRONMENTS

The general issue of a different national environment can create potential crisis risks for a multinational organisation. It can also pose additional problems when a crisis occurs, such as different levels of political, legal and social development and different standards of regulations and work practices (including maximum work hours, workplace safety standards, environmental emissions and discrimination). One effective way to address any such mismatch can be to enforce a policy of 'our standard or the local standard, whichever is the higher', which certainly makes crisis proofing and communication easier to manage.

Differences in language and culture, education systems, political and legal systems, and economic systems all create challenges for multinational organisations responding to a crisis in another country. At the most basic level, communicating with external stakeholders such as government officials and the news media is more difficult in a different language and is more prone to misunderstanding, especially in a crisis situation when time pressure, mistrust and uncertainty are high.

Moreover, the way in which government officials and the media (and other stakeholders) perceive their role in society can vary greatly in different cultures. This directly impacts how they will react in a crisis and the way they expect to interact with the foreign company. In some countries, there is an expectation that the government will step in and override the normal corporate role, while elsewhere the organisation at the centre of the crisis may be expected to manage and fund all responses, even if they are not really at fault. Similarly, in some cultures, an immediate offer of compensation for loss of life or damage to property is expected as the norm, regardless of liability and conventional legal process.

NATIONAL EMPLOYEE DIFFERENCES

Building on these broader national differences is the fact that the organisation typically works through local employees who may have very different cultural and language backgrounds. At the best of times, there may be a tension within any multinational organisation between the central push for global integration and uniformity of policies and practices versus the need for national differentiation and appropriate local adaption. This tension is never greater than in a crisis, with the country leader trying to manage the crisis on the ground within the framework of local culture while keeping head office in another country informed.

HOW LOCAL RESPONSE PROTECTED A GLOBAL BRAND

In mid-2014, pig DNA was allegedly found in Cadbury chocolate made in Malaysia, a major crisis risk in a majority Muslim country. Some products were immediately withdrawn, and temporary action was taken against Cadbury product in a number of other countries. Within Malaysia, the crisis triggered intense criticism by some Muslim groups, with calls for a national boycott, while attacks on the company and its product trended across social media. Although a global brand was potentially at risk, the parent company publicly took a low-key role and allowed local executives to manage the crisis in a way which would have been regarded as much more passive than expected in most Western countries. However, the country-local strategy was very effective in a highly charged political and religious local environment. Ten days into the crisis, fresh government tests cleared the chocolate of any contamination and it returned to sale with little apparent lasting damage to the brand.[12]

Broadly, crisis proofing requires the executive team to ensure global consistency and transparency in the crisis response, and also to manage the broader strategy and potential impact on the organisation as a whole. The result of failure can be misinterpretation, miscommunication and potential damage to reputation.

CHAPTER KEY TAKEAWAY

Social media, expanded stakeholder expectations and multinational business mean that issues and crises have to be effectively managed across borders.

CHAPTER 19

RECOGNISING AND RESPONDING TO CROSS-BORDER CRISES

As with all issues and potential crises, early recognition of the problem and prompt implementation of a response is essential. But, because of the nature of multinational organisations, recognising potential cross-border crises creates additional problems.

The first of these problems is the risk that an organisation's managers in a location far away from the parent country may try to manage the potential crisis themselves without involving head office, at least in the early stages, in order to avoid 'looking as if they can't manage their own problems'.

This is a very human response, particularly in some cultures where requesting help may be perceived as a sign of weakness or failure. However, such unwillingness to communicate early enough can be dangerous for the organisation and its senior executives, especially when local managers may lack the experience or global perspective to properly comprehend the potential adverse impact on the organisation as a whole.

Moreover, the explosion of social media means it is now much harder to 'hide' a potential crisis from head office, certainly once it has appeared in the local news media or online.

WHEN THINGS GO WRONG

The other side of the same coin is when head office recognises the potential cross-border crisis, but tries to quarantine the impact to just one country or region in an effort to protect the wider organisation. A legendary example occurred when the toxic chemical benzene was detected in bottles of Perrier water in the United States. The French parent company initially tried to argue that the problem was confined to North America and ordered a local recall. Even before the source of the contamination was confirmed, Perrier's North American arm was confidently announcing that the problem was limited to their region.

But, within days, the same contamination was found in Europe, leading to a recall in 120 countries, a temporary shutdown of the entire production process and an international product crisis that cost Perrier almost US$263 million. The proud French company never fully recovered and was eventually sold to Nestlé of Switzerland.[1]

Another example of failing to recognise the full impact of a problem overseas—and the role of the news media—was in early 2006 when the US eye-care giant Bausch + Lomb lost 3 per cent of its share value after the Singapore government announced a link between potentially blinding fungal infections and one of the company's contact lens solutions.

Bausch + Lomb withdrew ReNu solution, but only in Singapore and Hong Kong where the story had received widespread media coverage. Two months later, the Centers for Disease Control and Prevention in the United States issued a similar report and the company's share value fell by about 17 per cent in a single day. After further sustained destruction of shareholder value, the company was sold to a private equity firm. Crisis expert Daniel Diermeier reviewed the case and concluded that companies rarely have the luxury of receiving such a clear warning.[2] This lack of anticipation may have been the consequence of underestimating the crisis or not realising its full reputational impact. But, as Diermeier said, given the particular characteristics of the issue—a quality issue, possible blindness and a clear connection to the company's core competency—this is hard to believe. What more could have gone wrong?

Good question Mr Diermeier. What indeed? Perhaps Bausch + Lomb's sluggish response was influenced by the fact that the recall in Singapore and Hong Kong received little media attention in the United States.

Something similar happened in the notorious Ford–Firestone crisis of 2000, when 6.5 million tyres were recalled after more than 200 deaths attributed to tyre failures, more than half of them involving Ford SUVs. As described earlier, Ford acknowledged it had replaced tyres on almost 47,000 SUVs in Saudi Arabia, Venezuela, Thailand and Malaysia. But, despite explicit warnings from regional managers, they insisted that tyre failures in overseas markets reflected driving conditions unique to those countries and that the problem didn't apply in the United States. Bridgestone in Japan, the maker of Firestone tyres, agreed that driving conditions in the Middle East were 'extreme and unusual'.

Not only is the whole fiasco a much-studied textbook example of how not to manage a crisis, but it also highlights the importance of cross-border coordination. In addition, it highlights the importance of media attention, or lack of it, in the home country. The *Wall Street Journal*'s Japan-based reporters said another reason for silence at the headquarters of Bridgestone in Japan was that the Japanese media had shown scant interest in the story. Because there had been no reports of Japanese dying in tyre-related accidents, they said, the scope of the recall in Japan was tiny.[3]

In any potential cross-border crisis, local management and head office need to work together so that warning signs are recognised early, and so there is a mutual understanding of how events in one place can affect other locations or the parent organisation. As you can see from these examples— even though both occurred before the full blossoming of the internet— crisis proofing demands effective monitoring and strategic analysis of news media coverage everywhere you do business.

In the age of global media, you must react immediately at the highest level within the organisation to any threat—true or not—and no matter where in the world it originates.

THE FILM STAR WHO CREATED A REPUTATIONAL CRISIS

When Hollywood actress Sharon Stone was asked about a recent devastating earthquake in China, which had claimed tens of thousands of lives, she responded that it might have been 'karma' for the way China treated her friend the Dalai Lama. It was an off-the-cuff remark at Cannes Film Festival, but French fashion house Christian Dior used Stone as the face of its brand and recognised a major cross-border

> reputational threat. Dior dropped the actress from all its advertising in China, but not before a storm of outrage in China where Xinhua, the Chinese state news agency, described Stone as the 'public enemy of all mankind'.[4] The company and Stone both apologised, but it was a reminder how easily a potential international crisis can arise.

RECOGNISING CROSS-BORDER CRISIS IMPACT

While recognising a potential crisis in any location can present challenges, recognising the possible impact of a crisis across borders can be even more difficult, and can have far-reaching consequences.

Moreover, when a crisis takes on transboundary dimensions, we may expect uncertainty to deepen dramatically. The causes of a crisis become harder to understand when the crisis stretches across countries, policy sectors and time—or all three at once.

In practice, simply gaining a full appreciation of an emerging crisis across borders is not easy. Therefore, it is not surprising that the crisis management literature features some well-known and high-profile examples of how organisations misread and misjudged the impact of a crisis elsewhere.

In an earlier chapter I introduced the much-studied case of the *Brent Spar*, a disused floating oil-storage buoy in the North Sea that Shell UK decided to tow into the North Atlantic to sink in deep water. As a result of a media-savvy Greenpeace campaign, the story gained enormous international attention, particularly in continental Europe, where Shell faced opposition from politicians, church leaders, environmentalists and even the management of Shell Germany.

The case presents a vivid example of what happens when cross-border impacts shape the outcome of a crisis. After the deep-sea disposal plan was abandoned, Cor Herkstroter, Corporate Chairman of the Royal Dutch Shell group of companies, conceded:

> We found that what was the best option on the UK was not acceptable elsewhere ... We are sometimes expected to behave one way in one part of the world and rather differently in another part. We are caught in the tensions between these differing expectations.[5]

A few years later, Eric Faulds, the Shell manager in charge of decommissioning the *Brent Spar*, was even more frank about the company's failure to recognise the cross-border impact:

> There was a lack of appreciation that other countries would be interested in our plans and that they would see the issue quite differently. Shell companies across Europe hadn't foreseen how a plan that was the preserve of a sovereign UK government and of Shell UK could rouse public protest across national borders.[6]

Another company caught up in an unexpected cross-border crisis was the Danish dairy giant Arla, which became the innocent victim of an international event. As businesses globalise, so too does the vulnerability of their functions, including crisis management. For Arla this vulnerability was exposed when the Danish newspaper *Jyllands-Posten* published offensive cartoons portraying the prophet Muhammad, causing predictable outrage throughout the Islamic world.

Incensed by the Danish government's refusal to sanction the newspaper—citing the cause of free speech—Muslim leaders launched a boycott of Danish products. As a result, Arla's products disappeared off the shelves of 50,000 supermarkets across the Middle East and regional sales dropped to virtually nothing in just five days.

Despite coming under severe criticism at home for 'cowing to fundamentalism', Arla began a comprehensive strategy to distance itself from the cartoons and to work effectively with authorities in its important Middle Eastern market, and the boycott began to slowly turn around. Commenting later on the cross-border impact of the crisis, Corporate Communication Director Astrid Gade Nielsen said that before the boycott Arla would have said it was an international company that thought globally, but the crisis revealed they had not fully understood what it really meant to be a truly global company.[7]

A further example of a company unexpectedly caught up as an innocent victim of an international event was when pro-Tibet protesters attacked the Olympic Torch Relay in Paris on its way to the 2008 Beijing Olympics. Angry citizens in China launched a boycott and street demonstrations against the French supermarket giant Carrefour. The campaign gathered enormous support online in China, but despite a slow and misjudged start,

Carrefour eventually responded effectively, though undoubtedly suffered serious reputational damage.[8]

Finally, we can consider the case of the decommissioned French aircraft carrier *Clemenceau*, which was dispatched to the ship-breaking yard at Alang on the west coast of India. While over 4000 ships had been broken up there, Greenpeace launched a campaign to focus on the huge vessel, which was reportedly full of asbestos and other toxic material. The French Government was completely unable to respond to the crisis of legal, political and media publicity which broke out in India and had to recall the ship. It was eventually broken up five years later in the United Kingdom.[9]

RECOGNISING CULTURAL DIFFERENCES

While it is important to recognise the threat of an international crisis and also to recognise its potential to spread and have unexpected impacts across borders, the more difficult challenge is to actively manage a crisis in another country, with its different norms and expectations.

It goes without saying that a one-size-fits-all approach is never going to work, and most of my colleagues agree that you need to balance strategic consistency with cultural sensitivity. But that's easier said than done, and ignoring this important element of crisis proofing may lie behind some of the epic fails of cross-border crisis management.

There are many high-profile examples of misjudging situations and attitudes across national borders, and we already met the example when Monsanto wrongly assumed—with disastrous results—that their success with GM food in the United States could be replicated in Europe.

About 15 years later, the company finally admitted defeat in the struggle to persuade the Europeans to see it their way. In July 2013, Monsanto announced it was withdrawing all of its EU applications for approval for new crops. Given that the EU had not approved a new GM crop for cultivation in Europe since 1998, the company concluded with masterly understatement that 'as the EU today is effectively a conventional seed market, we have been progressively de-emphasising cultivation of biotech crops in Europe'.[10] An American friend of mine would call that a BGO—a blinding glimpse of the obvious.

Another famous example of a US multinational assuming that policies and processes that apply at home would be equally applicable in Europe involved the response by Coca-Cola to a claimed product contamination in Europe.

When around 200 schoolchildren in Belgium and France became ill and blamed 'tainted' Coca-Cola, the initial response of the company was to deny responsibility and to suggest it was a case of mass hysteria. But after it was claimed that the cause was defective carbon dioxide in some drinks, and that other products had been contaminated by chemicals from wooden shipping pallets, government officials in Belgium, France, the Netherlands, Germany, Luxembourg, Switzerland and Spain imposed bans or partial bans on Coca-Cola products. The drink-maker eventually ordered a recall amounting to an estimated 15 million cases, but delayed a week before issuing a public apology. And it was 10 days before CEO Douglas Ivester arrived in Europe to address the emerging crisis, which was later acknowledged as the worst health scare in the company's history.

Although independent tests eventually showed the symptoms were largely psychological and the product did not contribute to illness, it has been claimed that the crisis impact resulted not so much from the tainting and the company's delayed communication and perceived 'arrogance', but from its inability to accurately understand and react to the complex cultural dynamics of the European marketplace.

The company misjudged that European regulators were acutely sensitive to food contamination issues, having very recently been severely embarrassed by a widely condemned poor response to a scare involving dioxin in the food chain. They also underestimated the impact of European sentiment against foreign multinationals and 'Americanisation' of European culture, which I previously described as the burden of foreignness. Comfortably based in Atlanta, Georgia, where Coke invests heavily in civic and community causes and enjoys a stellar reputation, the company failed to properly gauge long-term issues relating to the differences between conducting business globally versus the domestic US market. And they were certainly unprepared for the idea that government officials would react so swiftly against a global brand in response to a perceived threat to public health.

> **THREE LESSONS FROM COKE'S INTERNATIONAL CRISIS**
>
> 1. Cultural variability is a fact of life and understanding it may help organisations better predict how international publics will respond to organisational messages.
> 2. International organisations need people from host nations to act as 'cultural interpreters'.
> 3. Organisations need to avoid a one-size-fits-all (ethnocentric) approach. The belief that what works in Atlanta will work in Brussels can no longer guide successful organisation–public relationships.
>
> Maureen Taylor[11]

Another more recent example of failure to appreciate cultural differences in a cross-border crisis was seen during criticism in China of SK-II cosmetics, when Chinese authorities detected toxic heavy metals in SK-II products, made in Japan for the US multinational Procter & Gamble. The company had recently provoked concern and an online protest in China by insisting on using as brand spokesperson a Taiwanese model who was an outspoken advocate for independence for her home island, a highly sensitive political issue in mainland China. Now the company further offended China by rejecting the findings of the country's quality authority and declining to apologise.

When Procter & Gamble finally agreed on a recall of some SK-II products, the company closed its 97 sales counters across the country and instituted a refund process that was so limited and complex that near-riots broke out as angry consumers stormed Procter & Gamble's specified locations in China. About one month after the product recall, Chinese authorities confirmed the traces of any metals in the SK-II product were harmless and the cosmetics returned to sale in China.[12]

However, Procter & Gamble undoubtedly suffered significant financial and reputational damage. One problem was it tried to treat the crisis as a global issue of product testing standards rather than addressing China's perceived concerns. The company also failed to recognise the way in which Chinese media influence the regulatory system, not to mention the undeniable fact that Chinese housewives tend to trust their government far more than companies, especially foreign multinationals.

Of course, it's not just US multinationals which sometimes fail to properly assess crises in another country. I have already mentioned the 2010 Toyota recall, when the company came under sustained attack because of its apparent lack of communication, and CEO Akio Toyoda was widely criticised for going 'missing in action'. The Japanese carmaker's strategy apparently made sense in Tokyo, but they misunderstood the Western expectation of corporate crisis response, and it was only after the CEO finally apologised to the satisfaction of his US political and media critics that the brand began its recovery.

Sadly, there are many more such examples involving organisations in all parts of the world. The simple truth is that while crisis management is never easy, managing international crises is even harder.

CHAPTER KEY TAKEAWAY

Managing crises across borders brings special new challenges, and organisations need to balance corporate and local needs.

CHAPTER 20

IT'S ALL ABOUT LEADERSHIP

Right at the start of this book I described crisis proofing as the creation of a mindset at the top of the organisation. An example of such a mindset is the concept of mindful leadership, which has been explored by the disaster analyst Andrew Hopkins.

Mindful organisations structure themselves so that they are better able to notice the unexpected in the making and halt its development. People at the front line of such organisations have an expanded awareness of risk, and leaders of mindful organisations display what Hopkins calls a 'chronic unease about the possibility of things going disastrously wrong'. He says mindful leaders lie awake at night worrying about the possibility of a major accident, and they welcome bad news.[1]

While it's an acknowledged role of leaders to recognise external threats, there's also another critical leadership role in crisis proofing and that is to recognise and remediate the challenges *within* management, which lie behind so many crises. It's worth revisiting the startling data mentioned earlier from the Institute for Crisis Management in Denver, Colorado which shows that more than half of all corporate crises are caused by management—either management action or inaction.

I have already introduced a number of formal processes for identifying issues and potential crises, as well as many other tactical responsibilities of top executives in crisis proofing. These include:

- Act as crisis spokesperson.
- Appoint and lead the Crisis Management Team.
- Build and utilise networks.
- Establish a social media and public profile.
- Ensure blame-free upward communication of concerns.
- Empower senior managers to identify and act on crisis risks.
- Allocate funds for effective media and environmental monitoring.
- Promote cross-functional cooperation.
- Demand up-to-date manuals and documentation.
- Participate in regular exercises/training.

However, in this final chapter, I want to focus more on broader executive roles beyond day-to-day tactics, which promote a crisis mindset and a culture of preparedness and proactivity, and set the tone for effective crisis response.

CRISIS AND LEADERSHIP

I have mentioned earlier that arguing about definitions can be a dangerous quagmire, and that there is no real agreement between experts on, for example, what's a crisis, what's an issue and how you measure reputation. But those terms seem to be child's play compared to defining leadership, and I'm not even going to try.

Although academics and senior executives feel that they intuitively know what leadership is, it has different meanings for different people. One expert has reported that in the 50 years between 1940 and 1990 more than 65 theories were proposed to describe and classify leadership,[2] and the pace of new theories shows no sign of slowing. Which I guess means either: (a) we know a lot about it, or (b) we are still totally confused.

I have already referred to US Supreme Court Justice Potter Stewart who famously wrote (on the subject of pornography): 'I know it when I see it.' That surely must also apply to leadership, and leadership is never more on display than in a crisis. This is certainly reinforced by the real-life examples throughout this book where great crisis leadership has been demonstrated—and disastrous lack of leadership has been exposed.

There is no argument that top-level leadership is needed for crisis proofing to be successful, and it's not surprising that a crisis situation turns the spotlight very firmly onto the CEO and other senior executives. One of the leading authorities on crisis and reputation, Leslie Gaines-Ross, points out that CEOs are regarded by many stakeholders as the human face of any organisation: 'Just as CEOs receive most of the credit when things go right, they are also expected to accept the majority of the blame when things go wrong, particularly in times of crisis.'[3] She added that her research found when a crisis strikes, 'nearly 60 per cent of the responsibility is attributed to the CEO'.

One unfortunate result of this focus on the CEO is that much of the crisis literature concentrates on the role of the leader as spokesperson. But, as I have already shown, there is a lot more to executive crisis leadership than speaking on behalf of the organisation—albeit a crucial responsibility.

Yet if it's well understood that the leader's role is so much more, why isn't that broader leadership the norm?

Dominic Cockram, CEO of the British crisis consultancy Steelhenge, says that while each crisis situation is unique to the organisation involved, every crisis requires leadership, both internally and externally, in front of the public, the media and a plethora of other stakeholders. Cockram concludes that, as the human face of the organisation, it is not just personal reputation which is at risk but also that of the whole organisation:

> When a leader appears in control, confident and empathetic, they can win the trust of the public and safeguard the reputation both of themselves and their organisation, and move forward towards a resolution.[4]

LEADERSHIP IN CRISIS MANAGEMENT

A good leader provides the crisis management team with:
- *Focus*. A strong leader provides focus in a complex and fast-moving situation, identifying what really matters and allowing necessary actions to move more quickly.

- *Direction.* A leader provides direction and guidance to people when they most need it, moving them quickly towards achieving that all-important control of the situation.
- *Decision.* It is the role of the leader to make difficult decisions, almost always in the face of uncertainty and often with unhappy outcomes as the 'lesser of two evils'.
- *Support.* An effective leader gives support to those less strong than themselves, helping to manage emotions in very tense environments.
- *Humanity.* A good leader gives the organisation a human face, which the public needs to see in any crisis.
- *Drive.* Preventing procrastination and decision avoidance is a leader's role.
- *Clarity.* This is a great challenge, but if the leader can give clarity to an otherwise chaotic situation, then control will soon follow.
- *Accountability.* The ultimate accountability for the way the incident is managed lies with the leader; this is often a double edged sword that can—and frequently does—result in resignation.

Dominic Cockram. Reprinted with permission.

BARRIERS TO EXECUTIVE LEARNING

Earlier we met the indefatigable duo Thierry Pauchant and Ian Mitroff, who analysed interviews with over 350 executives and identified what they called a 'culture of faulty rationalisations' as to why organisations fail to put effective crisis processes in place.

To properly understand these perceived barriers I undertook my own research interviewing regional CEOs and top executives in the chemical and energy industry.[5] Their responses largely fell into six common areas:

1. *Denial and failure to prioritise.* Some of the interviewees called it the 'It can't happen to me syndrome' and emphasised that managers will generally 'find something better to do'.
2. *Lack of experience and full understanding of potential risks.* As one CEO told me: 'I think you underestimate the risk until you've been through one of these. You probably don't have a concept of how bad it can

be. So it's like anything else. If you don't think it's going to happen, and you think if it does it's no big deal, then you're not going to plan for it. Why would you?'
3. *Inadequate systems, processes and management discipline.* The value of systems and processes was another strong common theme among the executives I interviewed, which was not surprising as they were all local leaders of major multinational companies. However, rather less expected was the divide which emerged between: (a) respondents who appeared to implicitly rely—perhaps over-rely—on the effectiveness of systems and processes; and (b) those who felt that no amount of process would provide a sufficient safeguard without strong leadership and personal skills.
4. *Insufficient size and therefore available resources.* There was a unanimous view among respondents that, as with systems and processes, major multinationals have the advantage of size, resources and international exposure. By contrast, they felt smaller organisations probably regarded crisis management as too expensive and too hard to establish, plus they thought smaller organisations could believe they are less likely to be hit by a crisis.
5. *Unwillingness or lack of opportunity for executives to share crisis experience.* A somewhat less expected perception from the executive suite was that senior executives are reluctant to share crisis experiences with executives from other companies, or lack the opportunity to do so. The interviewees offered various possible reasons for this deficiency including embarrassment, legal constraints, competitive pressure and unwillingness to discuss areas where one's own organisation is weak and the effect that might have on reputation.
6. *Failures of leadership and upward communication.* We'll come to this final topic in detail shortly, but the executives interviewed had very strong opinions about deficiencies of culture. One CEO told me: 'If leadership from the very top of the organisation doesn't give adequate focus to crisis management, then why would you expect that layers of leadership further down the organisation would give it adequate focus?'

LEADERSHIP CRISIS ROLES

In addition to identifying barriers to crisis proofing, my CEO crisis study also used survey responses and interviews to understand what top executives involved in hands-on management believe are *their* roles in crisis preparedness and crisis prevention.[6]

Not surprisingly, the crisis roles identified by senior executives overlap with some of the identified barriers. But most importantly they reflect not the views of consultants and academics, but rather the raw perspective from experienced individuals with day-to-day crisis responsibility.

The leadership roles identified in the study—in the words of the executives themselves—can be categorised under eight headings:

- Encourage a proactive crisis culture.
- Establish and enforce standards and processes.
- Prioritise and set an example.
- Properly assess the full range of risks.
- Promote open upward communication.
- Build relationships before the crisis.
- Be ready to deal with the news media.
- Encourage a learning environment and share experience.

Given that some of these areas have been covered elsewhere, I will focus on three of the broad strategic leadership themes to emerge from this study with direct implications for senior executives.

PROACTIVE CRISIS CULTURE AND UPWARD COMMUNICATION

In some organisations, terms like 'open door policy' and 'open communication' are little more than clichés or management jargon with no real meaning at all. Who hasn't experienced the manager who *says* he or she has an open door policy, but it's well known throughout the organisation that no one dares cross the threshold with bad news. Yet the importance of upward communication in crisis prevention and crisis management cannot be overstated.

I like the pithy description by Kurt Stocker at Northwestern University, Chicago, who argued that for organisational leaders, getting information about a potential crisis—what could go wrong or may already be going wrong—is the first step:

> Keep in mind that top management, by definition, is the least informed group in the company when it comes to bad news. Nothing moves more slowly than bad news running up a hill, a very steep hill. In most internally generated crises, the knowledge and potential for a problem was well known in advance of the onset of the public crisis, and top management found out about it as it was going public.[7]

Pithy, yes, but also rather depressing. Moreover, this upward communication needs to go right to the top of the organisation, including to the Board of Directors. Following the 2005 fatal accident and fire at a BP Texas refinery near Houston, which killed 15 and injured 170, it was reported that 'only good news flowed upward' to then CEO John Browne.

The BP case is also instructive in respect of further upward communication, particularly the important role of the board in terms of crisis preparedness and prevention. At the end of an exhaustive investigation into the disaster, an inquiry led by former US Secretary of State James Baker delivered a devastating indictment of warnings and near misses ignored, excessive cost cutting, poor safety culture and, most importantly, deficient leadership right to the top of the company.

The inquiry found that while BP's Board of Directors had been monitoring process safety performance of BP's operations based on information presented by management, a 'substantial gulf' appeared to have existed between actual on-ground performance and the company's perception of that performance. Furthermore, the Baker Inquiry concluded that, although BP's executive and refining line management was responsible for ensuring the implementation of an integrated, comprehensive and effective process safety management system, the board had failed to ensure that management did so.[8]

The panel recommended that BP's Board of Directors and executive management must provide effective leadership on, and establish appropriate goals, for process safety, and more specifically that the board should monitor the implementation of the recommendations of the panel and the ongoing process safety performance of BP's US refineries.

This idea of a proactive crisis culture and shared responsibility right at the top of the organisation was well captured by Mark Nadler, writing about a board's role in corporate crises:

> There is an implicit assumption that crisis management is all about the CEO donning a Superman cape and single-handedly defending the corporation. That view was always simplistic and in today's world, it's irrelevant ... Empowered boards and smart CEOs are coming to realise that boards have such an important role to play, not just when a crisis erupts, but during the preparation and recovery stages as well.[9]

Sadly, such involvement seems to be far from the norm. A global survey of board members, published in 2016,[10] found that fewer than half of the non-executive directors questioned reported they had engaged with management to understand what was being done to support crisis preparedness, and only half the boards had undertaken specific discussion with management about crisis prevention.

RISK ASSESSMENT AND SIGNAL DETECTION

The second important theme from my research relates to the fact that not only must there be good upward communication, but the people at the top also need real skill in evaluating risk and identifying potential crises, which is a core leadership responsibility. It's not an easy judgement, as I have shown by numerous examples in previous chapters where organisations failed to see, or take heed, of red flags and warnings ... and paid a high price.

Here again I can draw on a smart description of this management role, in this case by Dutch academics Paul 't Hart and Arjen Boin:

> Leaders are routinely engulfed in oceans of information and advice. Moreover, they face ambiguous and contradictory signals. Warnings do not come with flashing lights; they are hidden in expert reports, advisory memos, or a colleague's casual remark. The warnings have to be distilled from a series of seemingly minor and insignificant indications.[11]

ENCOURAGEMENT AND PROMOTION OF A LEARNING ENVIRONMENT

It's often said that the lesson of history is that we don't learn the lessons of history, and my third important theme focuses on that challenge. Even worse than an organisation suffering a crisis is when an organisation suffers the same crisis all over again. I have already discussed examples including NASA's *Challenger* and *Columbia* space shuttle disasters; Firestone's tyre recalls in 1978 and 2000; the repeat crowd-crush disasters during the Hajj in Saudi Arabia; and the repeat food contamination crises at Japan's Snow Brands. As the Nobel Prize winning Irish playwright George Bernard Shaw wrote: 'Success does not consist in never making mistakes, but in never making the same one a second time.'

What, then, are the opportunities for learning to help prevent crises? How can organisations learn before the crisis occurs rather than in the heat of post-crisis emotion and acrimony?

It's all too easy to find reasons *not* to learn from a crisis, especially when—as so often happens—the crisis was precipitated by management error or systemic failure. This means questioning the actions and decisions of senior executives, and that's always going to be awkward. However, given that the core beliefs, values and assumptions of senior managers have long been considered important in incubating the potential for crises within organisation, leadership is inarguably where change needs to begin if the incubation cycle is to be broken and crisis proofing is to be effective.

As one of the respondents in my CEO crisis research commented:

> We find ourselves dealing with crises from time to time to varying extents. And there is always the case for learning from past events, learning from the incident and how it was managed. I think that's the key, that the process of learning is embedded in the culture of the organisation.

Or as I like to put it, there are no new crises, only new lessons to learn.

There's an old proverb that a burnt child dreads the fire, and the same applies in crisis proofing. Corporations or business sectors which have felt the heat of a crisis are generally more aware of the terrible impact of crises; they assign more resources to crisis preparedness and crisis prevention; and they tend to be more receptive to new ideas and concepts.

Similarly, individual top executives who have experienced first-hand the pain of a crisis often become champions of the need to do better. Take Andy Grove, co-founder and CEO of Intel, following his company's infamous Pentium chip recall, which is regarded as the first internet-generated corporate crisis.

Mr Grove—later *Time* magazine's Man of the Year—was so concerned about what his company had learned, and what other companies could learn, that he spoke and wrote extensively about the crisis, including his book *Only the Paranoid Survive*.

Not every CEO needs to write a book about it, but crises are more apt to be seen as sources of opportunity rather than threats when top executives adopt a learning orientation—when they use prior experience, or the experience of others, to develop and introduce new processes and behaviours. That can only happen when leadership is strong and focused.

An important tool for post-crisis learning is the 'after action report', sometimes called the 'lessons learned report'. This needs to focus on processes, not people. In other words, what went wrong, not who did wrong. But, regardless, it has to lead to action, and that needs wholehearted executive commitment to change. Unfortunately, in times of crisis, some executives strive solely towards restoring the status quo as soon as possible—known as normalisation—rather than looking for opportunities to change.

So, what is the role of executive leadership in the wake of a crisis? I believe it's to drive a learning orientation which will:

- facilitate an honest and objective formal review of past crises—inside and outside the organisation—linked directly to structural and organisational assessment and improvement
- encourage genuine 'no fault' reporting and review of near misses, also linked directly to assessment and improvement
- reward managers at all levels of the organisation for honestly identifying and implementing lessons learned
- and, most importantly, provide leadership by example of willingness to admit mistakes and make change.

CRISES AND PERSONAL COST

The impact of crises on organisations has been covered in earlier chapters, such as loss of markets, loss of reputation, loss of share value and potentially even the demise of the entire enterprise.

But crises also have the capacity to make or break individual leaders, and the personal cost when things go wrong should never be underestimated. I have given examples of where top executives have been forced to resign in the wake of a crisis, and examples where their own unwise statements or actions have actually triggered the crisis.

A study by international law firm Freshfields Bruckhaus Deringer examined 78 major reputation crises across 16 stock exchanges—including New York, London and Australia—and found not only a share price hit but also an increased departure rate among executives in companies which were less able to resolve a crisis.[12]

The departure rate of senior executives from companies which suffered a share price hit averaged almost 10 per cent within a year of the crisis breaking. This increased to 15 per cent among executives unable to steer their company's share price back to previous levels within six months, compared to just 4 per cent among those who did. Contrast this with an average boardroom attrition rate of just 8 per cent among the crisis-hit company's direct competitors listed on the same exchange but unaffected by a crisis of their own.

Crisis guru James Lukaszewski says crises today take a huge toll on leadership. Companies don't fire the PR or HR people, the lawyers or marketing people. It's the person who's running the organisation and on whose watch the crisis occurred who gets fired. And, he adds, they all get a big fat cheque too.[13]

Yet job security is by no means the limit to personal risk. In the first *Spider-Man* movie, Uncle Ben said 'With great power, comes great responsibility' (though of course it wasn't original).

Leaving aside the world of super-heroes, take the case of Stewart Parnell, former owner of the Peanut Corporation of America, who was sentenced in 2015 to 28 years in prison after peanut butter produced by his company caused an outbreak of salmonella poisoning which killed nine Americans and sickened hundreds more.[14] His brother Michael and the plant's former quality control manager, Mary Wilkerson, were also convicted and received lesser sentences.

Or the 2008 crisis when the Chinese dairy giant Sanlu was bankrupted after melamine-contaminated infant formula killed six babies and sickened perhaps another 300,000. CEO Tian Wenhua was sent to prison for life, other managers received shorter prison terms, and two contractors were executed for their role in the scandal.[15]

Or consider Lalit Kishore Chaudhary, Indian head of the Italian auto parts company Graziano Trasmissioni, who was beaten to death in his factory near Delhi after it was invaded and vandalised by more than 100 workers who were laid off after they had demanded a pay rise and allegedly ransacked the office. The crisis followed a prolonged industrial dispute about conditions at the company, which is owned by Oerlikon of Switzerland.[16]

I hardly need to say that such dramatic personal cost is not common, but it is a reminder that a great deal more than simply reputation may be at stake when crisis leadership fails.

RESPONSE VERSUS RESPONSIBILITY

There are special leadership qualities needed when a crisis actually strikes, and I have already discussed some of those. But crisis response is not a skill to be learned in the midst of the storm.

Some executives who operate well when the sun is shining are found to be sadly wanting when everything starts to go wrong. The Greek philosopher Epicurus put his finger on it more than 2000 years ago: 'Skilful pilots gain their reputation from storms and tempest.' In modern language, that means responding to a crisis is a test of the quality and character of the leader as much as it is a test of their skills and expertise.

For a total contrast in leadership response, consider when Hurricane Katrina hit southeast Louisiana in August 2005. Investigative reporter Gary Rivlin claims in a new book that Louisiana Governor Kathleen Blanco alone took the hurricane threat seriously and initiated effective action, while New Orleans Mayor Ray Nagin and President George W. Bush became characterised by well-documented inaction, misjudgement and failure of leadership.[17]

While knowing how to respond to a crisis is critical to success, the best crisis is the one which doesn't happen, and a focus which is primarily reactive can overshadow the equally important area of what can be done by executive leadership to reduce the chance of a crisis happening.

This is because crisis proofing is much more than just what to do when a crisis strikes. Sure, it's about minimising the amount of damage from any crisis which occurs and increasing your organisation's capacity to survive. But it's also about reducing the risks of a crisis occurring in the first place—making your organisation less vulnerable to a potential crisis.

There's no doubt that crisis prevention is the far more difficult element of crisis proofing and demands genuine commitment from management at the highest level. This book has described the awful impact of failing to do so, and has detailed what you need to do to crisis proof your organisation, which is a mixture of both the strategic and the tactical.

But before concluding, it's worth asking: 'What does a crisis-proof organisation look like? What are you realistically trying to achieve?'

INTRODUCING THE CRISIS-PROOF ORGANISATION

Like any worthwhile goal, crisis proofing should have an element of stretch, and recognise that every organisation has its own specific needs and capabilities. The characteristics of the crisis-proof organisation, which have been developed throughout this book, are drawn together here to remind you in summary why it's important and what needs to be done to save your company from disaster.

The crisis-proof organisation has:

- robust mechanisms to identify risk issues, potential crises and other red flags
- the capability to recognise and respond to crises at all levels, both operational and managerial
- an executive approach which acknowledges that crises are not simply events but also are part of an integrated management process
- open, blame-free upward communication
- effective media and environmental monitoring to ensure no surprises
- a learning environment to honestly evaluate past crises and make changes

- up-to-date and tested crisis plans and documentation
- a well-trained crisis management team which is exercised regularly
- senior executives who lead by example
- cross-functional cooperation to minimise silo thinking
- a strong social media presence and profile
- clear rules on who speaks for the organisation in a crisis
- planning which distinguishes between crisis preparedness, crisis prevention and crisis response
- effective tools for hearing concerns of clients, customers, employees and other stakeholders
- established plans to prepare for the most obvious industry- or company-specific crises
- a repeatable, formal method to prioritise issues
- firm links between issue management, crisis prevention and strategic planning
- a responsive legal team which understands crisis management and post-crisis risks.

This list may seem long, and it represents the outcome of both strategic and tactical activities, as well as both preventive and reactive measures. Yet none of these activities is fundamentally difficult. It's true that short-term, tactical matters are much easier to identify, quicker to implement and more readily delegated down the chain of command. But the role of top executives in crisis proofing demands a longer-term commitment.

Experience clearly shows that nothing damages an organisation faster and deeper than a crisis or an issue mismanaged, and the responsibility to prevent such damage lies squarely in the executive suite. All the top executive needs is to use the tools and processes described in this book, plus a true desire to change and to protect the organisation and its stakeholders.

CHAPTER KEY TAKEAWAY
The organisation can never become crisis proof or even crisis-resistant if top executives don't provide leadership.

REFERENCES

Preface

[1] Schannon, M. (2006). Risk, issue and crisis management: Ten observations on impediments to effectiveness and what can be done about them. *Journal of Promotion Management*, 12(3/4), 7–38.

Chapter 1

[1] Sweetman, B. (2000, May). Managing a crisis: Communicating quickly and accurately is vital when an airliner goes down, and planning is key. *Air Transport World*.

[2] Taylor, D. (2005, 13 December). Debunking the myth of Kryptonite locks and the blogosphere. *Intuitive Systems*.

[3] Kirkpatrick, D. (2005, 10 January). Why there's no escaping the blog. *Fortune*.

[4] Heath, R. L. (2002). Issues management: Its past, present and future. *Journal of Public Affairs*, 2(4), 209–214.

[5] Mitroff, I. I. (2000). The Tylenol crisis 1982. In *Managing Crises Before they Happen: What Every Executive and Manager Needs to Know About Crisis Management* (pp. 13–20). New York: AMACOM.

[6] Rennie, G. (2004). Nuclear energy to go: A self-contained portable reactor. *US Department of Energy Research News*.

Chapter 2

[1] Budd, J. F. (1998). The downside of crisis. *Public Relations Strategist*, 4(3), 36–37.

[2] Dezenhall, E. (2014). The eight most baseless crisis management clichés. *Glass Jaw: A Manifesto for Defending Fragile Reputations in an Age of Internet Scandal* (pp. 111–132). New York: Twelve.

[3] Grove's remark after the 1994 Pentium chip crisis was engraved onto keychains made from the faulty microprocessor chip and given to Intel employees.

[4] Coleman, L. (2004). The frequency and cost of corporate crises. *Journal of Contingencies and Crisis Management*, 12(1), 2–13.

[5] Penrose, J. M. (2000). The role of perception in crisis planning. *Public Relations Review*, 26(2), 155–171.

6. Bhattacharjee, N. (2015, 13 April). India's Satyam founder sentenced to seven years in jail in fraud case. *Reuters*.
7. Buckingham, L. & Kane, F. (2014, 22 August). Gerald Ratner's 'crap' comment haunts jewellery chain. *The Guardian*.
8. O'Connor, C. (2015, 2 February). Lululemon billionaire Chip Wilson quits board, moves into performance cashmere. *Forbes*.
9. McSherry, M. (2014, 18 December). American Apparel CEO Dov Charney fired: The fall of a merchant of sleaze. *The Guardian*.
10. Swaine, J. (2014, 4 April). Mozilla CEO Brendan Eich resigns in wake of backlash to Prop 8. *The Guardian*.
11. Wikely, R., Bell, J. & Lankston C. (2015, 19 August). Herve Leger executive 'axed' after claiming 'committed lesbians' and 'fat' women shouldn't wear the brand's iconic bandage dresses. *Daily Mail*.
12. Guglielmo, C., King, I. & Ricadela, A. (2010, 7 August). HP Chief Executive Hurd resigns after sexual-harassment probe. *Bloomberg*.
13. Fitzgerald, D. (2016, 29 April). Priceline CEO Darren Huston resigns over relationship with employee. *The Australian*. This article summarises a number of similar cases.
14. Gianakaris, N. (2015, 26 May). Sex, lies and their impact on a corporate reputation. *Drexel Newsblog*.

Chapter 3

1. Petroff, A. (2015, 2 October). Volkswagen scandal may cost up to $87 billion. *CNN Money*.
2. Selyukh, A. (2013, 24 April). 'White House explosions' Twitter hoax shakes US markets. *Sydney Morning Herald*.
3. Ibid.
4. Hall, L. (2014, 25 July). Hoax emailer Jonathan Moylan free after sentencing. *Sydney Morning Herald*.
5. Thielman, S. (2015, 15 July). Twitter's shares jump after fake story on company's $31bn takeover offer. *The Guardian*.
6. Fombrun, C. J. & Van Riel, C. B. M. (2004). *Fame and Fortune: How Successful Companies Build Winning Reputations*. Upper Saddle River: FT/Prentice Hall.
7. Knight, R. F. & Pretty, D. J. (1999). Corporate catastrophes, stock returns and trading volume. *Corporate Reputation Review*, 2(4), 363–378. This famous study was reported in 1999 and nothing has since been published to contradict it.

8   Chesters, L. (2015, 3 July). Shares in oil giant BP climb on news it has finally settled long-running US court case over Deepwater Horizon oil spill. *Daily Mail*. This article includes an annotated graph of the BP share price since the disaster.

9   Institute of Practitioners in Advertising (2006). The intangible revolution. *Ipa.co.uk*.

10 Ocean Tomo (2015, 5 March). Annual study of intangible asset market value from Ocean Tomo. www.oceantomo.com.

11 Weber Shandwick (2007). *Safeguarding reputation*. Issue 1. Weber Shandwick survey conducted with KRC Research. www.corporatereputation12steps.com.

12 Burson-Marsteller (2009, 5 November). New survey shows that only half of European firms have a crisis plan in place in spite of the significant financial and reputational benefits of crisis preparedness. www.oursocialmedia.com.

13 Pagliery, J. (2013, 5 March). Man behind 'Carry On' T-shirts says company is 'dead'. CNN Money.

14 Ebersole, J. G. (2005). Crisis management planning—What's happening where we work? www.evancarmichael.com.

15 Galbraith, J. (2015, 4 March). The five C's of communication trends: Interrelated elements coming to the fore. *IPRA Thought Leadership*.

16 Based on research in 2009 by Burson-Marsteller.

17 Deloitte, Touche Tohmatsu & Forbes Insights (2016). *A Crisis of Confidence*. This is based on a survey of 317 non-executive board members in EMEA, Asia-Pacific and the Americas.

18 Mitroff, I. I. & Pauchant, T. C. (1990). *We're So Big and Powerful Nothing Bad Can Happen to Us: An Investigation of America's Crisis Prone Corporations*. New York: Birch Lane Press. This ground-breaking research was first reported in 1990 and has since been updated.

19 Jaques, T. (2011). Barriers to effective crisis preparedness: CEOs assess the challenges. *Asia Pacific Public Relations Journal*, 12(1).

Chapter 4

1   Sundance board were flying on banned airline (2010, 23 June). *The Australian*.

2   Wall, M. (2015, 27 October). Six things firms should do to improve cybersecurity. *BBC News*.

3   Greenberg, A. (2014, 2 September). Plan ahead: Prepare for the inevitable data breach. *SC Magazine*.

4. Bazerman, M. H. & Watkins, M. D. (2004). *Predictable Surprises: The Disasters You Should Have Seen Coming, and How to Prevent Them*. Boston: Harvard Business School Publishing. Their conclusions about the 9/11 terrorist attacks were further explored in Bazerman, M.H. & M. Watkins M. D. (2005). Airline security, the failure of 9/11, and predictable surprises. *International Public Management Journal*, 8(3), 365–377.

5. National Commission on Terrorist Attacks Upon the United States (2004). *The 9/11 Commission Final Report. Executive Summary*.

6. Phelps, R. (2005, 21 September). *All hazards vs homeland security planning. Disaster resource guide*. www.ems-solutionsinc.com/pdfs/MeettheExperts.pdf.

7. Madhu Beriwal was CEO of the company that primarily managed the simulation. *Preparing for a Catastrophe: The Hurricane Pam Exercise* (2006, 24 June). Statement before the Senate Homeland Security and Governmental Affairs Committee.

8. Lipton, E. & Shane, S. (2005, 4 September). Homeland Security Chief defends federal response. *New York Times*.

9. Brown, A. (2002). Avoiding unwelcome surprises. *The Futurist*, 36(5), 21–23.

10. Select Bipartisan Committee (2006). *A Failure of Initiative: Final Report of the Select Bipartisan Committee to Investigate the Preparation for and Response to Hurricane Katrina*. Washington, DC: US Government Printing Office.

11. Pilkington, E. (2010, 24 July). Deepwater Horizon alarms were switched off 'to help workers sleep'. *The Guardian*.

12. Wack, P. (1985). Scenarios: Shooting the rapids. *Harvard Business Review*, November-December, 139–150. Wack was one of the first to develop the use of scenario planning in the private sector, at Royal Dutch Shell's London headquarters in the 1970s.

13. Mitroff, I. I. (2002). Crisis learning: The lessons of failure. *The Futurist*, 36(5), 19–21.

14. Roux-Dufort, C. (2007). A passion for imperfections: Revisiting crisis management. In C. M. Pearson, C. Roux-Dufort & J. A. Clair (eds), *International Handbook of Organizational Crisis Management* (pp. 221–252). Thousand Oaks: Sage.

15. Sheaffer, Z., Richardson, B. & Rosenblatt, Z. (1998). Early warning signals management: A lesson from the Barings crisis. *Journal of Contingencies and Crisis Management*, 6(1), 1–22.

16. Clark, N. (2008, 21 February). Société Générale posts record loss on trading scandal, subprime exposure. *International Herald Tribune*.

17 Stout, D. (2009, 3 September). Report details how Madoff's web ensnared SEC. *New York Times*.
18 Permanent Sub-Committee on Investigations, US Senate (2013). *JP Morgan Chase Whale Trades: A Case History of Derivative Risk and Abuses*.
19 Fitzpatrick, D., Patterson, S. & Zuckerman, G. (2013, 14 March). Senate slams bank on 'whale'. *The Wall Street Journal*.
20 Baker, J. A. (2007). *The Report of the BP US Refineries Independent Safety Review Panel*. Houston: British Petroleum Company.
21 Warnings of catastrophe: Pike report (2012, 5 November). *Daily Telegraph*.
22 Westcott, R. (2015, 1 December). AirAsia probe: Anatomy of an avoidable crash. *BBC Asia*.
23 González-Herrero, A. & Pratt, C. B. (1996). An integrated symmetrical model for crisis-communication management. *Journal of Public Relations Research*, 8(2), 79–105.
24 Mitroff, I. I., Harrington, K. L. & Gai, E. (1996). Thinking about the unthinkable. *Across the Board*, 33(8), 44–48.

Chapter 5

1 These concepts are based on the relationship between language and action and the way in which listeners and speakers reinforce one another's behaviour. Influential writers in this area include B. F. Skinner and Ullin Place.
2 Heath, R. L. (1997). *Strategic Issues Management: Organizations and Public Policy Challenges*. Thousand Oaks: Sage.
3 Smith, D. (1995). The dark side of excellence: Managing strategic failures. In J. Thompson (Ed.), *The CIMA Handbook of Strategic Management* (pp. 161–191). Oxford: Butterworth Heinemann. Smith reiterated this view 10 years later in Smith, D. (2005). Business (not) as usual: Crisis management, service recovery and the vulnerability of organisations. *Journal of Services Marketing*, 19(5), 309–320.
4 Chase, H. W. (1976). Objectives of CPI. *Corporate Public Issues and their Management*, 1(1), 1. Unlike most management developments, we know the exact place and date when issue management was born. The first recorded use of the term was when Howard Chase published the first issue of his new publication on 15 April 1976. The discipline really took off with the publication of his ground-breaking book in 1984: Chase, W. H. (1984). *Issue Management: Origins of the Future*. Stamford: Issue Action.
5 Jaques, T. (2007). Issue or problem? Managing the difference and averting crises. *Journal of Business Strategy*, 28(6), 25–28.

⁶ Pauchant, T. C. & Mitroff, I. I. (1992). *Transforming the Crisis-Prone Organisation: Preventing Individual, Organisational and Environmental Tragedies*. San Francisco: Jossey-Bass.

Chapter 6

1. Jaques, T. (2007). Issue management and crisis management: An integrated, non-linear, relational construct. *Public Relations Review*, 33(2), 147–157.
2. Grunwald, M. (2001, 28 October). A tower of courage: On September 11, Rick Rescorla died as he lived: Like a hero. *Washington Post*. Rescorla was also the subject of a 2005 television documentary film, *The Man who Predicted 9/11*.
3. Charan, R. & Useem, J. (2002, 27 May). Why companies fail. *Fortune*.
4. A series of settlements in late 2014 and early 2015 cost power distributor SP Ausnet well over A$650 million and Utility Services Corporation more than A$20 million. State of Victoria government agencies agreed to pay a further nearly A$150 million 'for inadequate warnings at the time of the fire and insufficient controlled burns'.
5. Roux-Dufort, C. (2000). Why organisations don't learn from crises: The perverse power of normalization. *Review of Business*, 21(3/4), 25.
6. Pinedo, M., Seshadri, S. & Zemel, E. (2000). *The Ford-Firestone Case*. New York: New York University School of Business.
7. Dugdale, A. (2010, 5 May). Tony Hayward; CEO BP, not Frodo. *Fast Company*.
8. Hopkins, A. (2009). *Failure to Learn: The BP Texas City Refinery Disaster*. Sydney: CCH Australia.
9. Heidrick & Struggles (2015). The CEO Report: Embracing the paradoxes of leadership and the power of doubt. *www.heidrick.com*.
10. Grove, A. S. (1996, 2 September). How we miscalculated: A minor flaw in its biggest chip awakened Intel to a new business reality. *Newsweek*, 60–62. Grove's admission was made two years after the product recall crisis, which cost Intel US$475 million.
11. Fink, S. (1986). *Crisis Management: Planning for the Inevitable*. New York: American Management Association.
12. Hart P. & Boin R. A. (2001). Between crisis and normalcy: The long shadow of post-crisis politics. In U. Rosenthal. R. A. Boin & L. K. Comfort (Eds.), *Managing Crises: Threats, Dilemmas and Opportunities*. Springfield: Charles C. Thomas.
13. Lynda Mapes citing Washington University Law Professor William Rogers in *Seattle Times* (2008, 26 June). Supreme court drastically cuts payouts for plaintiffs in Exxon Valdez spill.

Chapter 7

1. Details of the Shell issue identification process and examples of scenarios can be seen at http://www.shell.com/global/future-energy/scenarios.html.
2. BASF (2013). *Identification and Management of Sustainability Issues.* https://www.basf.com/en/company/sustainability/management-and-instruments/topics.html.
3. McGrath, G. B. (1998). *Issues Management: Anticipation and Influence.* San Francisco: IABC.
4. *Report of WPC80 independent inquiry for Fonterra Board.* (2013). Wellington: Fonterra. The independent inquiry into the Fonterra crisis was scathing about the company's lack of social media presence and monitoring in the key Chinese market.
5. Slovic, P. & Peters, E. (2006). Risk perception and affect. *Current Directions in Psychological Science*, 15(6), 280–285.
6. Burton, B. (2007). *Inside Spin: The Dark Underbelly of the PR Industry.* Sydney: Allen and Unwin. Reports that after legal action was launched in the Australian Federal Court, shopping mall giant Westfield admitted it had been behind a supposed community group, and went even further, confessing it had been involved in 11 other 'grass-roots' campaigns against rival retail developments.

Chapter 8

1. Ewing, R. P. (1997). Issue management: Managing trends through the issue lifecycle. In C. L. Caywood (Ed.), *The Handbook of Strategic Public Relations and Integrated Communications* (pp. 173–187). New York: McGraw-Hill.
2. Coombs, W. T. & Holladay, S. J. (2007). *It's Not Just PR: Public Relations in Society.* Malden: Blackwell.
3. Catania, T. F. (2002). Whirlpool integrates issue management for strategic gain. *Corporate Public Issues and their Management*, 24(1), 1–7. Catania was speaking at an Issue Management Council conference in 2002.
4. Jaques, T. (2000). *Don't Just Stand There: The Do-It Plan for Effective Issue Management.* Melbourne: Issue Outcomes. The Do-It Plan model has subsequently appeared in other publications.
5. Holladay, S. J. & Coombs, W. T. (2013). Successful prevention may not be enough: A case study of how managing a threat triggers a threat. *Public Relations Review*, 39(5), 451–458.

6. Boutilier, R. (2011). *A Stakeholder Approach to Issues Management*. New York: Business Expert Press.
7. Swann, P. (2008). Shark fin soup: Hong Kong Disneyland seeks cultural and environmental balance. *Cases in Public Relations Management* (pp. 295–298). New York: McGraw-Hill.
8. Jaques, T. (2014). *Issue and Crisis Management: Exploring Issues, Crises, Risk and Reputation*. Melbourne: Oxford University Press. This contains a fully worked hypothetical example of how a plan could be developed to respond to a specific issue.
9. Goodwin, D. (2000). Issues management: The art of keeping the elephants away. *Corporate Public Affairs*, 10(1), 5–8.
10. Heath, R. L. (1997). *Strategic Issues Management: Organizations and Public Policy Challenges*. Thousand Oaks: Sage.
11. Jaques, T. (2009). Integrating issue management and strategic planning: Unfulfilled promise or future opportunity? *International Journal of Strategic Communication*, 3(1), 19–33.
12. Regester, M. & Larkin, J. (2005). *Risk Issues and Crisis Management: A Case Book of Best Practice* (3rd edn). London: Kogan Page.
13. McGrath, G. B. (1998). *Issues Management: Anticipation and Influence*. San Francisco: IABC.

Chapter 9

1. *Report of WPC80 Independent Inquiry for Fonterra Board* (2013, October). Wellington: Fonterra. As well as assessing the Fonterra incident, it contains a very useful section on crisis management 'best practice', which includes my own relational model from Chapter 6.
2. *The WPC80 Incident: Causes and Responses* (2014, November). Wellington: NZ Government Inquiry into the Whey Protein Concentrate Contamination Incident. This official report had a strong additional focus on the government's own shortcomings in responding to the Fonterra botulism crisis.
3. Mitroff, I. I., Pauchant, T. C., Finney, M. & Pearson, C. (1989). Do (some) organizations cause their own crisis? The cultural profiles of crisis-prone vs crisis-prepared organizations. *Organization and Environment*, 3(4), 269–283.
4. Tony Hayward says BP was 'not prepared' for the Gulf oil spill. (2010, 9 November). *BBC News*. Hayward's startling admission was made in his first major interview following his resignation as CEO of BP.
5. Rawlinson, K. (2015, 9 January). Sony boss: 'No playbook' for dealing with hack attack. *BBC News*.

6   Stocker, K. P. (1997). A strategic approach to crisis management. In C. L. Caywood (Ed.), *The Handbook of Strategic Public Relations and Integrated Communication* (pp. 189–203). New York: McGraw Hill.

7   Grove, A. S. (1995). *Only the Paranoid Survive: How to Survive the Crisis Points that Challenge Every Company and Career.* New York: Currency-Doubleday.

Chapter 10

1   Hileman, D. (2015). *You Need More than a Continuity Plan to Prepare for Crisis.* Institute for Crisis Management.

2   Levick, R. S. & Slack, C. (2010). *The Communicators: Leadership in the Age of Crisis.* Washington, DC: Watershed Press. Pitt was SEC Chair in 2001–03 and is now CEO of a Washington-based strategic consulting company.

3   Canadian Investor Relations Institute (2011, 12 April). Few companies are prepared to manage a crisis. *Business Wire.*

4   Burton, R. (2014, 17 November). 10 benefits to exercising. *Preparedex.*

Chapter 11

1   Letter From GM CEO: 'Deeply regret' need to recall 1.6 million cars (2014, 4 March). *Wall Street Journal.*

2   Scanlon, J. (1975). *Communication in Canadian Society.* Toronto: B. D. Singer.

3   Reed, S. (2012, 1 September). Tony Hayward gets his life back. *New York Times.*

4   Lustrin, M. & Janis, L. (2013, 14 November). Is Lululemon chairman's apology the worst ever? *ABC News.*

5   Lac-Megantic oil train disaster inquiry finds string of safety failings (2014, 20 August). *The Guardian.*

6   Holmes, P. (1992, 5 October). Ashland: The anti-Exxon. *The Holmes Report.*

7   Ibid.

8   Small, W. J. (1991). Exxon Valdez: How to spend billions and still get a black eye. *Public Relations Review,* 17(1), 9–25.

9   Some experts have argued that Rawl was right to remain at headquarters but wrong to stay silent.

10 Holusha, J. (1989, 21 April). Exxon's public relations problems. *New York Times.*

11 Reilly, W. K. (1999, 24 March). The lessons we've learned in years since Exxon Valdez. *San Francisco Chronicle.*

12 Virtually no change in Harris poll Confidence Index for last year. (2010, 9 March). *Business Wire.*

13. Pinkham, D. (2011, 27 November). Public opinion of business may surprise you. *Public Affairs Council Blog*.
14. Weber Shandwick (2015). The CEO reputation premium: Gaining advantage in the engagement era. *www.webershandwick.com.au*. The study surveyed 1700 executives in companies of US$500 million or more revenue, across 19 countries.

Chapter 12

1. These academic approaches include post-crisis discourse, post-crisis discourse of renewal and image restoration theory.
2. Chesters, L. (2015, 3 July). BP shares soar on US spill deal. *Daily Mail*.
3. Gilbert, D. & Scheck, J. (2014, 4 September). BP is found grossly negligent in Deepwater Horizon disaster. *Wall Street Journal*.
4. Hart, P. & Boin, R. A. (2001). Between crisis and normalcy: The long shadow of post-crisis politics. In U. Rosenthal, R. A. Boin & L. K. Comfort (Eds.), *Managing Crises: Threats, Dilemmas and Opportunities* (pp. 28–46). Springfield: Charles C. Thomas.
5. Phelps, N. L. (1986). Setting up a crisis recovery plan. *Journal of Business Strategy*, 6(4), 5–10. Phelps was a very early writer who addressed the concept of crisis recovery planning as part of broader business strategy.
6. Darling, J. R. (1994). Crisis management in international business: Keys to effective decision making. *Leadership and Organization Development Journal*, 15(8), 3–8.
7. Heath, R. L. (2004). After the dance is over: Post-crisis responses. In D. P. Millar & R. L. Heath (Eds.), *Responding to Crisis: A Rhetorical Approach to Crisis Communication* (pp. 247–249). Mahwah: Lawrence Erlbaum.
8. Copping, J. (2013, 23 June). Family hope pardon for shamed Admiral Byng will finally arrive. *The Telegraph*.
9. Morrison, E. W. & Milliken, F. J. (2000). Organisational silence: A barrier to change and development in a pluralistic world. *Academy of Management Review*, 25(4), 706–725.
10. Elliott, D., Smith, D. & McGuinness, M. (2000). Exploring the failure to learn: Crises and barriers to learning. *Review of Business*, 21(3), 17–24.
11. Based on data from the Institute for Crisis Management, introduced in earlier chapters.
12. Geier, B. (2014, 28 December). GM's Mary Barra: Crisis manager of the year. *Fortune*.

[13] Tyler, L. (1997). Liability means never being able to say you're sorry: Corporate guilt, legal constraints, and defensiveness in corporate communications. *Management Communication Quarterly*, 11(1), 51–73.

[14] Smith, D. & Sipika, C. (1993). Back from the brink: Post-crisis management. *Long Range Planning*, 26(1), 28–38.

[15] Syed, M. (2015). *Black Box Thinking: The Surprise Truth About Success*. London: John Murray.

[16] Mason, R. O. (2004). Lessons in organizational ethics from the Columbia disaster: Can a culture be lethal? *Organizational Dynamics*, 33(2), 128–142.

[17] Gibson, D. C. (2000). Firestone's failed recalls, 1978 and 2000: A public relations explanation. *Public Relations Quarterly*, 45(4), 10–13.

[18] Factbox: Disasters at annual Muslim haj pilgrimage (2015, 25 September). *Reuters*.

[19] Wrigley, B. J., Ota, S. & Kikuchi, A. (2006). Lightning strikes twice: Lessons learned from two food poisoning incidents in Japan. *Public Relations Review*, 32(4), 349–357.

[20] Elliott, D. & Smith, D. (1993). Football stadia disasters in the UK: Learning from tragedy. *Industrial and Environmental Crisis Quarterly*, 7(3), 205–229.

[21] A fresh inquest into the deaths was ordered in 2015 after disclosure of a series of worrying facts about the case, and in April 2016 it was found that the 96 who died had been unlawfully killed.

Chapter 13

[1] West, G. E. & Larue, B. (2005). Determinants of anti-GM food activism. *Journal of Public Affairs*, 5(3/4), 236–250.

[2] Bakir, V. (2006). Policy agenda setting and risk communication: Greenpeace, Shell and issues of trust. *Harvard International Journal of Press/Politics*, 11(3), 67–88. The Shell crisis has been extensively analysed in the literature. Mr Fay's assessment was made in the BBC TV documentary *The Battle for Brent Spar*, broadcast on 3 September 1995.

[3] Herkstroter, C. (1996). Dealing with contradictory expectations: Dilemmas facing multinationals. *Vital Speeches of the Day*, 63(4), 100–104. Mr Herkstroter was speaking at a major conference in the Netherlands on 11 October 1996.

[4] Carlton, J. & Yoder, S. K. (1994, December 21). Humble pie: Intel to replace its Pentium chips. *The Wall Street Journal*.

[5] Vidal, J. (1999, October 7). We forgot to listen, says Monsanto. *The Guardian*.

6. Larkin, J. (2003). *Strategic Reputation Risk Management*. Basingstoke: Palgrave Macmillan.
7. Otani, A. (2015, 6 February). America's most loved and most hated companies. *Bloomberg*.
8. Machlup, F. (1962). *Knowledge Production and Distribution in the United States*. Princeton: Princeton University Press.
9. Arbesman, S. (2012). *The Half-Life of Facts: Why Everything We Know has an Expiration Date*. New York: Current (Penguin).
10. Oliver, J. E. & Wood, T. (2014). Medical conspiracy theories and health behaviors in the United States. *JAMA Internal Medicine*, 174(5), 817–818.
11. Procter & Gamble awarded $19.25 million in Satanism lawsuit (2007, 20 March). *Fox News*.
12. Jury, L. (2011, 23 October). Nike to trash trainers that offended Islam. *The Independent*.
13. Coca-Cola's official response to the Arabic logo rumour appears on their website, alongside many other myths about the company; see http://www.coca-colacompany.com/contact-us/coca-cola-rumors-facts. It links to a formal rebuttal by the Grand Mufti of Al-Alzhar.
14. How firms should fight rumours (2011, 10 February). *The Economist*.
15. Richtel, M. & Barrionuevo, A. (2005, 22 April). CSI: Wendy's restaurants. *New York Times*. As part of Wendy's response, the company's PR executive gave this lengthy profile interview.

Chapter 14

1. Fitzpatrick, K. R. (1996). Public relations and the law: A survey of practitioners. *Public Relations Review*, 22(1), 1–8.
2. For information on litigation PR and its role in crisis management see, for example, Beke, T. (2013). *Litigation Communication: Crisis and Reputation Management in the Legal Process*. London: Springer; Roschwalb, S. A. & Stack, R. A. (Eds.) (1995). *Litigation Public Relations: Courting Public Opinion*. Littleton: Rothman; and Gorney, C. E. (1995). The new rules of litigation public relations. *Public Relations Strategist*, 1(1), 23–29.
3. For information on law firm PR see, for example, Levick, R. (2001, February). Ten myths of law firm PR. *Professional Marketing*; and O'Brien, K. (2014, 17 April). The future of law firm PR: The good, bad and ugly, *Law360*.

4   Cooper, D. A. (1992). CEO must weigh legal and public relations approach. *Public Relations Journal*, 48(1), 39–40.

5   Magid, C. (1995, November). Balancing legal and reputational issues in crisis. *Reputation Management*, 79–80.

6   Levick, R. S. & Slack, C. (2010). *The Communicators: Leadership in the Age of Crisis*. Washington DC: Watershed Press.

7   Corrado, F. M. (1991). Environment crisis management: Attorneys and communications professionals working together. *Environmental Law Reporter*, 21(3), 1–4.

8   Flood, A. (2010, 7 July). Mt Dew mouse would have been 'jelly like', Pepsi argues. *Legal Newsline*.

9   Cohen, A. (2009, 31 May). The Lord Justice hath ruled: Pringles are potato chips. *New York Times*.

10 Cited in Kuszewski, J. (2010, 6 July). McLibel: Reputation damage writ large. *Ethical Corporation*.

11 The two defendants later appealed to the European Court of Human Rights arguing that they were virtually penniless and refusal to provide legal aid had meant they were denied a fair trial. In 2005, the court found in their favour and ordered the British government to pay £57,000 damages and costs.

12 Kuszewski, ibid.

13 Litigation Communications survey report (2016). *Green Target*, http://greentarget.com.

14 Levick & Slack, ibid.

15 Small, W. J. (1991). Exxon Valdez: How to spend billions and still get a black eye. *Public Relations Review*, 17(1), 9–25.

16 Jaques, T. (2009). Learning from past crises—Do iconic cases help or hinder? *Public Relations Journal*, 3(1).

17 Brooks, D. (1987, 19 February). Johnson and Johnson attorney says role of business lawyers expands during crises. *New Jersey Law Journal*.

18 Ross, J. (1993). Crisis management: Four lessons learned. In J. Fay (Ed.), *Encyclopaedia of Security Management* (pp. 207–211). Newton: Butterworth Heinemann. Mr Ross' comments were reported from an address to the American Petroleum Institute in Dallas, Texas in September 1990.

19 Wile, R. (2014, 8 June). Walmart confirms one of its trucks was involved in the Tracy Morgan accident. *Business Insider*.

Chapter 15

1. Hickson, G. B., Clayton, E. W., Githens, P. B. & Sloan, F. A. (1992). Factors that prompted families to file medical malpractice claims following perinatal injuries. *JAMA* 267, 1359–1361.
2. Vincent, C., Young, M. & Phillips, A. (1994). Why people sue doctors: A study of patients and families taking legal action. *Lancet*, 343, 1609–1612.
3. Sack, K. (2008, 18 May). Doctors start to say 'I'm sorry' before 'See you in court'. *New York Times*.
4. Cohen, J. R. (1999). Advising clients to apologize. *Southern California Law Review*, 72, 1009–1069.
5. Patel, A. & Reinsch, L. (2003). Companies *can* apologise: Corporate apologies and legal liability. *Business Communication Quarterly*, 66(1), 9–25.
6. Ibid.
7. Behar, R. (1990, 26 March). Exxon strikes back. *Time*, 135, 62–62.
8. Sontag, D. (1997, 29 June). Too busy apologizing to be sorry. *New York Times*.
9. Tolchin, M. (1992, 11 December). Packwood offers apology without saying for what. *New York Times*.
10. Abercrombie & Fitch CEO Mike Jeffries finally says sorry over comments (2013, 23 May). *News.com*.
11. Vasek, L. (2012, 23 October). Abbott apologises to PM for remark. *The Australian*.
12. Dumas, D. (2015, 24 July). Labor lobbyist Hawker Britton makes embarrassing email error. *Sydney Morning Herald*.
13. Vanovac, N. (2012, 19 December). Jones comments incited riots: Trad. *Sydney Morning Herald*.
14. Agnes, M. (2012, 29 May). Does saying you're sorry in a social media crisis put you at legal risk? *Melissa Agnes Blog*. http://melissaagnes.com.
15. Memmot, M. (2013, 14 May). It's true: 'Mistakes were made' is the king of non-apologies. *National Public Radio*. http://www.npr.org/sections/thetwo-way/2013/05/14/183924858/its-true-mistakes-were-made-is-the-king-of-non-apologies
16. Patel, A. & Reinsch, L. (2003). Companies *can* apologise: Corporate apologies and legal liability. *Business Communication Quarterly*, 66(1), 9–25.
17. Anderson, E. (2012, 5 June). Courageous leaders don't make excuses, they apologise. *Forbes*.
18. Cohen, ibid.

Chapter 16

1. Veil, Shari R., Petrun, Elizabeth L. & Roberts, Holly A. (2012). Issue management gone awry: When not to respond to an online reputation threat. *Corporate Reputation Review*, 15(4), 319–332.
2. Many companies still not leveraging social media as a crisis management resource. (2013). *PwC Business Continuity Survey*.
3. PGA of America president ousted over tweet (2014, 25 October). *USA Today*.
4. Roberts, D. (2014, 2 September). Centerplate CEO Des Hague out after internet backlash, *Fortune*.
5. Gorman, R. (2014, 5 May). 'No excuses, zero tolerance': PayPal exec fired after bizarre late-night Twitter rant against colleagues he had known for less than two months. *Daily Mail*.
6. Dillon, N. (2015, 28 April). AT&T fires exec for sending racist texts and images, faces $100m employee discrimination suit. *New York Daily News*.
7. Brinded, L. (2015, 1 April). Royal Bank of Scotland boss out weeks after these Snapchat pictures were put on Instagram by his daughter. *Business Insider*, UK.
8. Nielsen (2012). *State of the Media: Social Media Report 2012*. http://blog.nielsen.com.
9. DeGoede, C. (2013, 18 December). 14 Tips for building your social media crisis communications plan. *Fresh Ideas*. These useful distinctions follow Dallas Lawrence, Vice President for Corporate Affairs at Mattel, at a PR conference in Washington DC in late 2013.
10. Frazier, E. (2010, 20 May). Facebook post costs waitress her job. *Charlotte Observer*.
11. Dietrich, G. (2012, 13 January). How FedEx turned a disaster into a PR win. *PR Daily*.
12. Geeknet (2010, 21 June). Geeknet apologises to National Port Board for unicorn meat confusion. *www.thinkgeek.com*.
13. Skidmore, S. (2010, 22 June). Pork Board squeals over unicorn meat. *NBC News*.
14. Roberts, H. (2012, 24 January). #McFail! McDonalds' Twitter promotion backfires as users hijack #McDstories hashtag to share fast food horror stories. *Daily Mail*.
15. Tracy, T., O'Connor, T. & Gregorian, D. (2014, April 23). #myNYPD Twitter campaign backfires, promotes photos of police brutality instead of positive encounters with public. *New York Daily News*.
16. Ross, M. (2015, 10 November). #Yourtaxis: Social media campaign by Victorian Taxi Association backfires as Melbourne users share horror stories. *ABC News*.

17   The Dave Carroll protest song video can be seen at http://www.youtube.com/watch?v=5YGc4zOqozo.

18   Ayres, C. (2009, 22 July). Revenge is best served cold, on Youtube: How a broken guitar became a smash hit. *The Times*.

19   Sawhney, R. (2009, 28 July). Broken guitar has United playing the blues to the tune of $180 million. *Fast Company*.

20   Carroll, D. (2012). *United Breaks Guitars: The power of one voice in the age of social media*. Carlsbad: Hay House.

21   Hamilton, G. (2012, 9 April). Quebec juice maker pays opponents legal fees after a soap ruling gets Twitter in a lather. *National Post*.

22   Adams, S. (2013, 1 February). Don't fire an employee and leave them in charge of the corporate Twitter account. *Forbes*.

23   Crawford, A. P. (1999). When those nasty rumours start breeding on the web: You've got to move fast. *Public Relations Quarterly*, 44(4), 43–45.

24   Crush, P. (2006, 29 November). Fire fighting in the digital age. Crisis conference report. *PR Week*, 24–26.

25   Pownall, C. (2015). *Managing Online Reputation: How to Protect Your Company on Social Media*. Basingstoke: Palgrave Macmillan.

26   Kelly, R. & Critchlow, A. (2010, 28 December). Qantas copes with aftermath of A380 crisis. *Wall Street Journal*.

27   International Air Transport Association (2012). Dealing with the news media after an aviation accident: Best practices in the age of social media. *www.iata.org*.

28   Cohn, R. (2014, 13 March). How social media is elevating airline crisis communication. *Socialfresh*.

29   Sillito, D. (2009, 16 January). Twitter's iconic image of US Airways plane. *BBC America*.

30   Weigel, D. (2015, 15 November). One man's hard lesson after the Eiffel Tower's darkness was mistaken for a moving tribute. *Washington Post*.

31   Continuity Insights (2014, 14 March). Crisis communications 2014: Social media & notification systems. *Continuity.com*.

Chapter 17

1   Perry, D. C., Taylor, M. & Doerfel, M. L. (2003). Internet-based communication in crisis management. *Management Communication Quarterly*, 17(2), 206–232.

2   Taylor, M. & Perry, D. C. (2005). Diffusion of traditional and new media tactics in crisis communication. *Public Relations Review*, 31(2), 209–217.

3. Graham, M. W., Avery E. J. & Park, S. (2015). The role of social media in local government crisis communications. *Public Relations Review*, 41(3), 386–394.
4. Flandez, R. (2009, 20 April). Domino's response offers lessons in crisis management. *Wall Street Journal*.
5. Clifford, S. (2009, 15 April). Video prank at Domino's taints brand. *New York Times*.
6. The Patrick Doyle YouTube video can be seen at https://www.youtube.com/watch?v=dem6eA7-A2I.
7. O'Brien, T. (2012). *When Social Media Crises Hit* (white paper). timobrien@timobrienpr.com.
8. Walter, E. (2013, 12 November). 10 tips for reputation and crisis management in the digital world. *Forbes*.
9. Bindley, K. (2013, 26 April). Boston Police Twitter: How cop team tweets led city from terror to joy. *Huffington Post*.
10. Millar, D. P. & Smith L. (2011). *Crisis Management and Communication* (3rd edn). San Francisco: IABC.
11. Swissair was once so profitable it was known as the Flying Bank. Three years after the crash, in 2001, it collapsed under the weight of debt and was declared bankrupt.
12. Is Malaysia Airlines Doing Enough? (2014, 10 March). *Bizcom in the News*.
13. Andriole, S. J., Schiavone, V. J., von Hoyer, E., Langsfeld, M. D., & Harrington, M. R. (2013). Avoiding #Fail: Mitigating risk, managing threats and protecting the corporation in the age of social media. *listenlogic.com*.
14. Research undertaken by SIFA Strategy in partnership with Deloitte LLP. Reputation: Time to be viewed as capital (2016). *sifastrategy.com*.
15. Mutzabaugh, B. (2014, 14 April). US Airways apologizes for lewd photo sent via Twitter. *USA Today*.
16. Agnes, M. (2012, 4 October). KitchenAid: An excellent example of successful crisis management. *Melissa Agnes Blog*, melissaagnes.com.
17. The Fortune 500 CEOs most active on social media are all newcomers (2015). *CEO.com*.
18. Weber Shandwick (2015). *The CEO Reputation Premium: Gaining Advantage in the Engagement Era*.
19. CEO, social media & leadership survey (2012). *Brandfog*.
20. Nolan, L. (2015). The impact of executive personal branding on non-profit perception and communications. *Public Relations Review*, 41(2), 288–292.

21. Gibson, K. (2016, 26 January). Oprah loses 26 pounds, Weight Watchers gains 20 percent. *CBS Moneywatch*. http://www.cbsnews.com/news/oprah-loses-26-pounds-weight-watchers-gains-20-percent/
22. Energy broker EnergyWatch counts cost of CEO's offensive Facebook rant. (2012, 6 April), *The Australian*.
23. Tate, R. (2011, 5 April). 20,000 Customers stampede away from GoDaddy over elephant hunting. *gawker.com*.
24. Walsh, B. (2011, 4 April). GoDaddy CEO on shooting an elephant: I'm not sorry. *Time*.
25. Business Continuity Institute (2016, 27 January). Boards of directors lack understanding of the cyber risk. www.thebci.org.
26. Fail! Qantas red-faced after Twitter campaign backfires (2011, 22 November). *News.com*.

Chapter 18

1. Ansell, C., Boin, A. & Keller, A. (2010). Managing transboundary crises: Identifying the building blocks of an effective response system. *Journal of Contingencies and Crisis Management*, 18(4), 195–207.
2. The concept of disaster versus crisis is spelled out in the definitions table in Chapter 5.
3. Yardley, J. (2013, 30 December). Clothing brands sidestep blame for safety lapses. *New York Times*.
4. McKenzie, N. & Baker, R. (2016, 21 February). Surf clothing label Rip Curl using 'slave labour' to manufacture clothes in North Korea. *The Age*.
5. Houston, P., Thelen, B., Turner, M. & Miller, J. (2012). Supply management at a crossroads: Lessons for success in turbulent times. *Booz and Co*.
6. For an overview of the Kilwa massacre and other incidents involving foreign mining companies in Africa, see Fitzgibbon, W., Hamilton, M. & Schilis-Gallego, C. (2015, 11 July). Danger underground. *Sydney Morning Herald*.
7. Adapted from Nigh, D. & Cochran, P. L. (1991). Crisis management in the multinational firm. *Proceedings of the International Association for Business and Society, Sundance, Utah* (pp. 214–227).
8. Kiselyova M. & Sichkar, O. (2014, 25 July). Russia takes aim at McDonald's burgers as U.S. ties worsen. *Reuters*.
9. Spar, D. L. & La Mure, L. T. (2003). The power of activism: Assessing the impact of NGOs on global business. *California Management Review*, 45(3), 78–101.
10. Decision to close factory results in anti-Nokia backlash in Germany (2008, 20 January). *m-GovWorld*.

11. Bonds latest brand to head offshore (2009, 25 February). *Sydney Morning Herald*.
12. Jaques, T. (2015). Cadbury and pig DNA: When issue management intersects with religion. *Corporate Communications: An International Journal*, 20(4), 468–482.

Chapter 19

1. Kurzbard, G. & Siomkos, G. J. (1992). Crafting a damage control plan: Lessons from Perrier. *Journal of Business Strategy*, 13(2), 39–43.
2. Diermeier, D. (2011). *Reputation Rules: Strategies for Building Your Company's Most Valuable Asset*. New York: McGraw Hill.
3. Zaun, T. & Dvorak, P. (2000, 5 September). The recall rolls on: Firestone's Japan parent appears anxiety-free despite US recall. *The Wall Street Journal*.
4. Booth, R. & McCurry, J. (2008, 30 May). They are not being nice to the Dalai Lama, who is a very good friend of mine. *The Guardian*.
5. Herkstroter, C. (1996). Dealing with contradictory expectations: Dilemmas facing multinationals. *Vital Speeches of the Day*, 63(4), 100–104.
6. Faulds, E. & Morrison, F. (1998). A new way of doing business. *Focus*. Shell UK in-house magazine included in the company's online *Brent Spar Dossier* (pp. 17–20).
7. Nielsen, A. G. (2008). We had to set things straight. *Communication Director*, 1, 60–63.
8. Coombs, W. T. (2014). Carrefour, China and the Olympic torch relay. In *Applied Crisis Communication and Crisis Management: Cases and Exercises* (pp. 111–118). Thousand Oaks: Sage.
9. Thomas, M. T. (2007). The Alang Ship-Breaking Yard. *Asian Case Research Journal*, 11(2), 327–346.
10. Hope, C. (2013, 18 July). Major GM food company Monsanto 'pulls out of Europe'. *The Telegraph*.
11. Taylor, M. (2000). Cultural variance as a challenge to global public relations: A case study of the Coca-Cola scare in Europe. *Public Relations Review*, 26(3), 277–293.
12. Tai, S. H. C. (2008). Beauty and the Beast: The brand crisis of SK-II cosmetics in China. *Asian Case Research Journal*, 12(1), 57–71.

Chapter 20

1. Hopkins explores the concept of mindful leadership in his definitive analysis of the 2005 Texas City disaster: Hopkins, A. (2009). *Failure to Learn: The BP Texas City Refinery Disaster*. Sydney: CCH Australia.

REFERENCES

2. Waters, R. D. (2013). The role of stewardship in leadership: Applying the contingency theory of leadership to relationship cultivation practices of public relations practitioners. *Journal of Communication Management*, 17(4), 324–340.
3. Gaines-Ross, L. (2008). *Corporate Reputation: 12 Steps to Safeguarding and Recovering Reputation*. Hoboken: John Wiley.
4. Cockram, D. (2013, February 15). Why is leadership so important in a crisis? *Business2Business* blogsite, www.business2community.com.
5. Jaques, T. (2011). Barriers to effective crisis preparedness: CEOs assess the challenges. *Asia Pacific Public Relations Journal*, 12(1).
6. Jaques, T. (2012). Crisis leadership: A view from the executive suite. *Journal of Public Affairs*, 12(4), 366–372; Jaques, T. (2013). The leadership role in crisis prevention. In A. DuBrin (Ed.), *The Handbook of Research on Crisis Leadership in Organizations* (pp. 270–289). New York: Edward Elgar.
7. Stocker, K. P. (1997). A strategic approach to crisis management. In C. L. Caywood (Ed.), *The Handbook of Strategic Public Relations and Integrated Communication* (pp. 189–203). New York: McGraw Hill.
8. Baker, J. A. (2007). *The Report of the BP US Refineries Independent Safety Review Panel*. Houston: British Petroleum Company.
9. Nadler, M. B. (2006). The board's role in corporate crises. In D. A. Nadler, B. A. Behan & M. B. Nadler (Eds.), *Building Better Boards: A Blueprint for Effective Governance* (pp. 192–211). San Francisco: Jossey Bass.
10. Deloitte, Touche Tohmatsu & Forbes Insights (2016). *A Crisis of Confidence: Survey of 317 Non-Executive Board Members in EMEA, Asia-Pacific and the Americas*.
11. Boin, A. & 't Hart, P. (2003). Public leadership in times of crisis: Mission impossible? *Public Administration Review*, 63(5), 544–553.
12. Freshfields Bruckhaus Deringer (2012). Rogue employees and company misconduct spook markets most. *www.freshfields.com*.
13. Lukaszewski, J. (2015, 8 April). Inside the mind of a crisis strategist. *www.communitelligence.com*.
14. Dennis, B. (2015, 21 September). Executive who shipped tainted peanuts gets 28 years; 9 died of salmonella. *Washington Post*.
15. Veil, S. R. & Yang, A. (2013). Sanlu milk contamination crisis. In S. May (Ed.), *Case Studies in Organizational Communication: Ethical Perspectives and Practices* (2nd edn, pp. 111–118). Thousand Oaks: Sage.
16. Lamont, J. (2009, 28 March). Murder of an Indian chief executive. *Financial Times*.
17. Rivlin, G. (2015). *Katrina: After the Flood*. New York: Simon and Schuster.

INDEX

Abbott, Tony 165
Abercrombie & Fitch 165
ad hoc management 87
Agarwal, Rocky 171
Agnes, Melissa 166
air accident investigation model 133–4
AirAsia 32
alliances, use of 69
American Apparel 12
American Trader oil spill 159
Anderson, Warren 117
Anvil 200
apologies
  effective apologies 163–4, 167
  effects of 163
  legal advice regarding 161–2, 169
  legal liability and 162, 167–8
  non-apologies 164–7
  and reputation 167–9
  safe apologies 169
Apple 16
Arla 210
Arthur Andersen 1, 11
Ashland oil spill 114, 160
Asiana 180
astro-turfing 69
Australian Wheat Board (AWB) 15

Baia Mare disaster 197–8
Barings Bank 30
Barra, Mary 111, 131
BASF 64
Bausch + Lomb 207
Bazerman, Max 26–7
Belasco, David 77
Bernays, Edward 34
Bhopal chemical leak 117, 201
Black, Conrad 11
Black Saturday bushfires 53–4, 234*n6:4*
Black Swan events 28–9
blame for crises, allocation of 127–8
Blanco, Kathleen 226
Blatter, Sepp 55
Bohr, Niels 27
Boin, Ajen 125, 222
Bok, Derek 74
Boston Marathon bombing 185–6
BP
  American Trader oil spill 159
  Deepwater Horizon oil rig disaster 18, 29, 45, 96, 104, 112, 117, 123
  Texas City refinery disaster 31, 57, 221
Brent Spar case 138–9, 209–10
Budd, John 9
Burkhardt, Edward 112
Bush, George W. 116–17, 226
business continuity 37, 59, 124
business continuity and recovery plans 99
Byng, John 127–8

Cadbury 204–5
Cameron, David 117, 166
Carrefour 210–11

Carroll, Dave 161, 175
CEOs
   barriers to learning 218–19
   cost of bad behaviour 11–12
   credibility gap 118–19
   as crisis spokespersons 115–16, 118
   leadership crisis roles 220–4
   making balanced judgements 155
   person costs of crises 225–6
   personal online presence 190–3
   presence at scene of crisis 116–18
   role in social media effectiveness 187–95
Challenger space shuttle 132
challenges, definition 36
Charney, Dov 11–12
Chase, Howard 76–7, 293n5:4
Chernobyl disaster 198
Christian Dior 208–9
citizen journalism 180–1
Clemenceau aircraft carrier 211
Coca-Cola 144, 212–13, 240n13:13
Cockram, Dominic 217
Cohen, Jonathan 168–9
Columbia space shuttle 132
command post exercises 107
communication
   24/7 communication 201
   corporate communication credibility gap 118–19, 145
   issue communication 36
   upward communication 220–2
   use of data and facts 145–6
   see also crisis communication
confirmation bias 137
conflict zones, doing business in 200
corporate blogs 186
corporate crises, causes 215
corporate responsibility 5
Couderc, Patrick 12
crash management 46
creeping crises 58

crises
   categories 94–5
   causes of corporate crises 215
   cost of mismanagement 15–22
   definition 37, 43
   distinguished from issues 43–6
   duration 45
   impact on organisations 48
   as inevitable 23, 24–5
   as opportunities 8–10
   personal cost 225–6
   as predictable 25–8
   red flags and warnings 28–32
   self-inflicted 10–12
   as threats 8–9
   undervaluing impact of 93–5
'crisis after the crisis' 125–6
crisis communication 37
   balancing reputation and legal liability 159–60
   CEOs presence at scene of crisis 116–18
   CEOs as spokespersons 115–16, 118
   credibility gap 118–19
   and crisis proofing 111
   dos and don'ts 119–20
   flow of information 155–7
   impact of bad communication 112–13
   key initial steps 120–1
   spokesperson's role 113–14
   stalling 158–9
crisis communication plans 99
crisis incident management 55–8
crisis management
   choices 44
   costs considerations 45
   definition 37, 43–6
   leadership and 216–18
   objective 46
   as oxymoron 110–11

planning vs the plan   92–3
positioning within organisation   46–8
relational model   49–60
relationship to issue management   38
urgency   44
see also international crisis management
Crisis Management Teams (CMTs)   51, 98
 activating   101–2
 chairperson   101
 contact lists   104
 core team   100
 crisis training   105–9, 194
 location   102–3
 pre-approved information   104–5
 roles and responsibilities   103–4
 selection   99–101
 supplementary teams   100
crisis planning
 lawyer's role   150–1
 need for   19–22
 planning processes   52
 planning vs the plan   92–3
crisis plans
 business continuity and recovery plans   99
 crisis communication plans   99
 form and content   98–9
 operational crisis plans   99
 planning vs the plan   92–3
crisis preparedness   3, 5, 20, 29
 activities   50–3
 failure at Fonterra   91–3
crisis prevention   3, 29
crisis-proof organisations, characteristics   227–8
crisis proofing
 executive responsibilities   216
 as goal   2–3
 importance of   1–2
 as leadership goal   1–2, 5, 6

objectives   25
what is possible   4–5, 6, 7
crisis recognition   55–8
crisis resolution, illusory nature   125–6
crisis response
 central challenge   111
 leadership and   226–7
crisis training   51–2, 105–9
'crisis training fatigue'   107
crisis-management infrastructure   51
cross-border crises   206–9
cross-border crisis impact, recognising   209–11
Cullinan, Rory   171
cultural differences, recognising   211–14
cyber risk   193
cyber security   25, 96, 193

dark websites   105, 185–7
Darling, John   125–6
data
 information sufficiency   145–6
 misapplication   137–40
 problems relying on   141–5
Deepwater Horizon oil rig disaster   18, 29, 45, 96, 104, 112, 117, 123
Dimon, Jamie   31
disaster management   37, 197
disaster response   197
disasters, definition   37
Do-it Plan   77–89
Domino's Pizza   173, 183–4
Dupont   62
duration, issues vs crises   45

e-crises   194
Ebbers, Bernie   10
Eich, Brendan   12
emergencies, definition   36
emergency responses   36, 54
employee conduct crises   94

Enron 1, 5, 11, 53
environmental crises 94
ethics, and legal advice 154–5
evaluation and modification
   barriers to 130–3
   issue management process 85–7
   post-crisis management and 60, 130–3
Ewing, Ray 76
executive learning, barriers to 218–19
executives, person cost of crises 225–6
Exxon 59, 117, 131, 158, 163–4
Exxon Valdez disaster 45, 59, 117, 123, 131, 157–8, 163

facts
   information sufficiency and 145–6
   nature of 140–3
   non-facts 141–2
false allegations, responding to 143–5, 176–7, 181
false reports, impact on market value 16–17
Faulds, Eric 210
FedEx 173
FIFA 1, 55
Firestone 56, 132, 208
Fisher, Ted 171
Fonterra 64–5, 90–3, 96, 127
Ford–Firestone crisis 56, 208
Fowler, Andrew 19
full-scale exercises 106

Gaines-Ross, Leslie 217
General Motors 111, 131
Global Financial Crisis (GFC) 13, 56, 117
goals, unclear goals 87
GoDaddy 192–3
Goodwin, David 85
Graziano Trasmissioni 226
Greenpeace 138, 153, 209, 211
Grove, Andy 9, 139, 224

Hague, Des 171
Hajj pilgrimage stampedes 133
'half-life of knowledge' 141
Hall, John 114
Hawker Britton 165
Hayward, Tony 96, 112, 117
Heath, Robert 88, 126
Herkstroter, Cor 139, 209
Herve Leger 12
Hewlett Packard 12
Hillsborough Stadium disaster 132–3, 239n12:21
HMV 176
hoaxes 16, 17, 143
Hollinger Inc. 11
Hopkins, Andrew 215
Hurd, Mark 12
Hurricane Katrina 27–8, 58, 116, 127, 226

IATA, social media best practice guide 178–80
identification of issues 62–4
information sufficiency 145–6
intangible assets 18–19
Intel Pentium chip crisis 57, 58, 139, 140, 224, 229n2:1
international crisis management
   cross-border crises 206–9
   meanings 196
   multinational organisational crises 198–9
   organisational crises across borders 199–200
   recognising cross-border crisis impact 209–11
   recognising cultural differences 211–14
   transboundary crises 197–8
Isman, Bruce 2
issue communication, definition 36
issue definition

PROBLEM + IMPACT formula 79–80
  two-way stakeholder input 80–1
issue information/status sheets 75–6
issue management 38–43
  choices 44
  costs considerations 45
  definition 36, 38–42
  development of discipline 293n5:4
  objective 46
  positioning within organisation 46–8
  role 54
  vs issues management 39
issue management process
  barriers to success 86–7
  Do-it Plan 77–8
  evaluation 85–6
  intended outcomes 83–4
  issue definition 79–81
  overarching objective 81–2
  processes and models 76–7
  strategic planning 87–9
  tactics 84–5
  values for effectiveness 77
issue prioritisation 70–4
issue scanning 62–4
issues
  characteristics 40
  distinguished from crises 43–6
  distinguished from problems 40–2
  duration 45
  identification 62–4
  impact on organisations 45–6
  linking to risk 66–8
  sources 64–6
  see also post-crisis issues

Jeffries, Mike 165
Johnson & Johnson 158
Johnson, Ashley 173
Jones, Alan 165–6
JP Morgan Chase 31

Kennedy, John F. 93
Kilwa massacre 200
Kozlowski, Dennis 10

labour relations crises 94
language
  definitions of key terms 35–8
  importance of terminology 34–6
  positioning and 46–8
Lassonde Industries 175–6
law-firm PR 148
leadership
  crisis management and 216–18
  and crisis proofing 1–2, 5, 6
  mindful leadership 57, 215
learning environment 223–4
legal advice
  on apologies 161–3, 169
  failures of 151–4
  on flow of information 155–7
  importance 149, 157
  role in crisis planning 150–1
  and statutory obligations of executives and boards 157–8
  for strategy development 149–50
  vs ethical response 154–5
  vs PR advice 147–8, 152
legal crises 94
legal PR 148
legal response syndrome 86–7
litigation PR/journalism 148
Lockerbie disaster 12
London Greenpeace 153
'London Whale' trading scandal 31
Lowe's 184, 185
Lululemon 11, 112
Lynton, Michael 96

McDonald's 32, 152–4, 174, 202
McLibel case 152–3
Madoff, Bernie 11, 30–1
Malaysian Airlines 16, 187

management conduct crises 94
management tools, application 39–40
market value
  false reports and 16–17
  relationship with crises 16–18
Marshall, George 83
mindful leadership 57, 215
mindful organisations 215
Mitroff, Ian 21, 29–30, 218
modification of plans, processes and operations *see* evaluation and modification
Monsanto 139–40, 211
Montreal, Maine & Atlantic Railway 112
Morgan Stanley 52–3
Mountain Dew mouse case 151
Moylan, Jonathan 17
Mozilla 12
multinational organisational crises 198–9
multinationals
  crisis proofing 205
  different national environments 203–4
  foreignness outside home country 201–2
  geographic diversity 202–3
  long distances and multiple time zones 201
  national employee differences 204
  nature of 201
  operational portability 203

Nadler, Mark 222
Nagin, Ray 226
NASA 132
Nasser, Jacques 56
'natural' crises 95–7
natural disasters 95
New York Police Department 174
Nike 143–4
9/11 terrorist attacks 26–7, 52–3
Nixon, Richard 166
Nokia 203

operational continuity 124
operational crises 94
operational crisis plans 99
optimism, bias towards 56
organisational media presence 188–9
'organizational silence' 129
outcomes, intended vs desired 83–4

Pacific Brands 203
Pan American Airways (Pan Am) 14
Parnell, Michael 225–6
Parnell, Stewart 225
Parsons, Bob 192–3
Pauchant, Thierry 21, 218
Peanut Corporation of America 225–6
Pepsi 151
perception, vs reality 68
Perrier 14–15, 207
Phelps, Norman 125, 130
Pike River mine disaster 31, 53
Pitt, Harvey 102
planning *see* crisis planning; crisis plans
Polis, Ben 192
positioning, language and 46–8
post-crisis issues
  impact of 59–60, 125–8
  responding to 129–30
post-crisis learning
  barriers to 130–3
  post-crisis reviews 133–4
post-crisis management 58–60
  clusters of activity 123
  evaluation and modification 130–3
  neglect of 122
  post-crisis issue identification and management 59–60, 125–8
  recovery/business resumption 124
  responding to post-crisis issues 129–30
  reviewing and learning 133–4
post-crisis phase, defining 122–3
prediction of crises 25–8
Pringles 152

proactive crisis culture 221–2
proactive mode 110
PROBLEM + IMPACT issue
    definition 79–80
problems, distinguished from
    issues 40–2
Procter & Gamble 143, 152,
    176, 213
product crises 94
products, 'proofing' of 4–5, 6
public relations counsel
    on flow of information 155–7
    vs legal counsel 147–8, 152
Putin, Vladimir 117

Qantas 178, 180

Raju, Ramalinga 11
Ratner, Gerald 11
Rawl, Lawrence 117, 164
reactive mode 86, 110
recognition of crises 55–8
recovery/business resumption 124
red flags 28–32, 53–4, 222
relational model of crisis
    management 49–50
    crisis incident management 55–8
    crisis preparedness 50–3
    crisis prevention 53–4
    post-crisis management 58–60
reputation
    apologies and 167–9
    impact of crises 18–19
    social media and 177, 184–5, 190
Richards, David 166
Rip Curl 200
risk
    as analysis 66
    as feelings 66, 67–8
    vs resources 68–9
risk analysis, categories of 67
risk assessment 222
risk management 54

risks, arising from issues and
    crises 66–8
Ross, John 159–60
Roux-Dufort, Christophe 30, 55
rumours 143, 181

Sandman, Peter 137
Sanlu 15, 226
Satyam 11
scorched earth legal strategy 59, 157
self-inflicted crises 10–12
Shapiro, Bob 140
shareholders' interests 157–8
Shell 62, 138, 140, 209–10
'shiny thing syndrome' 33
Simon, Bill 160
simulation exercises 51–2, 106, 107–8
SK-II cosmetics 213
Slator, Aaron 171
Smith, Kevin 183
Snow Brand 133
social concerns 95
social media
    as accelerant of crises 175–6
    calamities 171–2
    CEO role 187–95
    controlling one's own
        messaging 185–7
    as crisis management resource 170,
        182–3
    as extinguisher of crisis 176–7
    impact on crisis management 172
    as instigator of crises 173–4
    managing interaction 183–4
    monitoring and responding 177–81,
        187–8
    official spokespersons 189–90
    organisational presence 188–9
    reputation risk and 190
    tips for reputation and crisis
        management 184–5
social media strategy 194–5
Société Générale 30, 53

Sony 177
Sony Entertainment 96
Southwest Airlines 183
stakeholders
  failing to listen to 138–40
  and issue definition 80–1
  protecting interests 158
Stocker, Kurt 220–1
Stone, Sharon 208–9
strategic crisis management 46
strategic planning, and issue management 87–9
strategy development, legal advice and 149–50
Sundance Resources 24–5
Swartz, Mark 10
Sweetman, Bill 2
Swissair 186–7
system activation 58

't Hart, Paul 125, 222
table-top simulations 106
tactical crisis response 46
tactics, issue management process 84–5
Taleb, Nassim Nicholas 28–9
technological crises 94
terminology
  defining key terms 35–8
  importance of 34–6
ThinkGeek 174
Titanic 2
Toyota 15–16, 214
training exercises 51–2, 106–8

transboundary crises 197–8
tsunami effect 12–13
Twitter 17
Tyco 10
Tylenol case 158

Union Carbide 117, 201
United Airlines 161–2, 175, 190
upward communication 220–2
urgency, issues vs crises 44
US Airways 180, 190
US Federal Emergency Management Agency (FEMA) 27
US Securities and Exchange Commission 30–1

ValuJet 14
Victorian Taxi Association 174
Volkswagen 1, 16

Walmart 160
war-room exercises 107
warnings of impending crisis 28–32, 53–4, 222
Watkins, Michael 26–7
Weibo 64–5
Weichat 64–5
Wendy's hoax 144
Westfield 235*n*7:6
wilful blindness 57
Wilkerson, Mary 226
Wilson, Chip 11, 112
Winfrey, Oprah 192
WorldCom 1, 10, 11